The ECONOMICS *of* FULL EMPLOYMENT

Six Studies in Applied Economics
prepared at
THE OXFORD UNIVERSITY
INSTITUTE OF STATISTICS

REPRINTS OF ECONOMIC CLASSICS

AUGUSTUS M. KELLEY · PUBLISHERS
NEW YORK · 1967

First Edition 1944

(Oxford: Basil Blackwell, 1944)

Reprinted 1967 by

Augustus M. Kelley · Publishers

By Arrangement with Basil Blackwell

Library of Congress Catalogue Card Number

« 67 - 16340 »

PRINTED IN THE UNITED STATES OF AMERICA

by SENTRY PRESS, NEW YORK, N. Y. 10019

FOREWORD

THERE is fairly wide agreement now among economists that as long as business activity is determined by decisions of business alone the economic system will remain liable to periodic fluctuations. In order to avoid instability the State must assume the responsibility for controlling the volume of employment. This is recognized in the recent White Paper on Employment Policy (Cmd. 6527) which was issued when this book was in the Press. The immediate and main objective of the policy proposed in the White Paper is the avoidance of mass unemployment by taking counter-measures at the onset of depression. The studies in this book go beyond this aim. They are not concerned merely with mitigating economic fluctuations, but with the permanent maintenance of a state of full employment, i.e. such a state in which everybody who wants work can find it at established rates of pay.

Full employment is, however, a formal concept. Unemployment counts at certain dates will always show a certain number of unemployed persons: persons changing over from one job to another, and a small number of people who are difficult to place at short notice or who are waiting to be re-trained for a different occupation. There may also be seasonal unemployment in particular trades or for the economy as a whole. The statistical minimum of this frictional and seasonal unemployment cannot be determined a priori. It will depend on the efficiency of the organization of the labour market, the adaptability of managements and labour to changing circumstances, the changeability of demand, and the smoothing and regulating policies of the State. These mutable institutional factors will determine whether the minimum of 'visible' or 'statistical' unemployment will be nearer, say, 5 per cent or 2 per cent. When we speak in this book of full employment, we have in mind an economy which carries no more than this minimum of 'involuntary' unemployed in transition from one job to another already waiting for them.

Full employment, thus defined, takes no account of its economic and social content. There is an infinite number of ways by which full employment can be reached and maintained, and to each one corresponds a different distribution of incomes, a different standard of welfare and a different structure of industry and foreign trade. Digging holes in the ground and filling them up again will, as Lord Keynes has

put it, produce full employment, and so will the pyramiding of armaments or of industrial equipment. By embarking upon such wasteful
employment schemes a country's standard of welfare may, indeed, be
raised above that which would otherwise prevail in conditions of
depression. But by choosing useful public works, by subsidizing mass
consumption, or by redistributing incomes, employment can be pushed
to the same level and, at the same time, the standard of living of the
community as a whole be raised higher than by digging useless holes.
The social and economic content of full employment cannot be determined by the economist. The economist must indicate, however, the
choices before the community and the price which may have to be
paid for them.

What road the community is going to take must be a matter of
social and political preference, but a rational choice implies that it should
know the alternatives. Not all the possible alternatives have been
elaborated here. Full employment by way of cumulative inflation or
by greater luxury spending, and similar types of full employment
leading to greater inequality, have been neglected in this book, though
some reference is made to such forms of full employment in the
discussion of the German experiment at the end of the book.

The result of the analysis is neither a blue-print of full employment
in any particular country nor a reconstruction scheme, but an outline
of the strategic factors in a policy of permanent full employment in
industrial countries. For under-developed poor countries with surplus
populations and a general shortage of social and private capital, different, and, in many respects, more formidable, problems arise. If a fairly
rapid rate of industrialization is desired, a higher degree of direct
controls and of other methods, not unlike those employed in a war
economy, will probably be needed. For similar reasons the transition
from war to peace, the reconstruction period, cannot be treated as a test
case of full employment policies. Pent-up demand of many war years,
shortages of equipment, and arrears of repairs would tend to produce
over-employment if left uncontrolled. It is widely agreed, at least in
Great Britain, that economic controls can only be relaxed gradually
as the shortages disappear. It is when the re-equipment and restocking
drive is over and the stream of·supplies admits the decontrolling of
major sectors of the economy, that the problem treated in this volume
will re-emerge: how to maintain consumption and investment permanently at a level which guarantees full employment. These long-
run problems are, however, of immediate importance. The policy
of the transition from war to peace determines the setting in which a

policy of full employment will begin to operate. There cannot be a
successful 'transition' unless we keep in mind the end we hope to
achieve.

Each of the six studies of the book deals with a particular aspect of
the problem. Together they form a whole in the double sense that the
setting and the arguments of the various studies claim to be consistent
with one another, though doubtless minor points of difference remain,
and that they attempt to show the working of the system as a whole
and to elaborate all the major principles which govern its operation.

The division of labour between the contributors can be seen from
the table of contents. A certain amount of overlapping was unavoidable, and seemed even desirable for elucidating the impact of the
new general theory of employment on the various branches of economics and economic policy.

Broadly speaking, the first study traces the historical setting of the
problem of unemployment; the second study gives a systematic
account of the theory of full employment and the main approaches
towards achieving this end. Particular aspects of this general theory are
elaborated in the following parts. The third study takes up the problem
of the stability and flexibility of a fully employed economy and
discusses the question of wage pressure and prices, of the elasticity
factors in the supply of labour, of spatial and occupational mobility
and the location of industry. The fourth part is devoted to a study of
the principles of public finance. It contrasts with the classical canons
of finance those which follow from the modern (Keynesian) economics
and analyses the scope and limits of various financial methods as
instruments of a full employment policy. In all these parts it is tacitly
assumed that the relation of a fully employed economy with the outside
world can be regulated satisfactorily. The fifth part makes this problem
its main subject and shows on what conditions free multilateral trade
can be made consistent with full employment in any member country
of the international system, or failing this, what other methods are
available to adjust the foreign balances of full employment countries
in a world where other economic units are subject to cyclical fluctuations. In order to test the value of our theoretical conclusions by a
critical interpretation of a historical case, the last study relates these
principles to the only practical experiment of a full employment policy
so far made in a capitalist society in peace-time—albeit in preparation
for war. Germany in the middle 'thirties presented the case of a deficit
country without foreign assets pursuing a policy of internal expansion
(while conditions in the rest of the world were unstable), and pushing

economic activity to the limit of full employment during the period under consideration and ultimately beyond it. The social content of German economic policy and the aggressive aims it served can at no point be ignored. But the main emphasis of this essay is upon the technical problems of economic control in full employment. We have attempted to distinguish between those methods which may be attributed to the 'logic of the situation' and those which were due to the social and political bias of the system. Even the negative lessons to be drawn from this case may be of value.

The book purports to be a manual in the sense that it does not appeal exclusively to the expert economist. Rigorous technical treatment of the problems has therefore been excluded from the text. However, since the subject matter is new and complex, the argument remains difficult in parts. It seemed preferable to us to admit complications rather than to err on the side of over-simplification.

The six studies of this book have been written by research workers of the Oxford University Institute of Statistics who for some years have co-operated in research on war economic problems. Although the book is in this sense the product of close teamwork and intensive discussion among all the contributors, the responsibility for each separate study rests with the individual contributor, who is not committed to every particular of the book.

The Institute of Statistics appears as the author because it would have been clumsy to give the names of six authors on the title page. The Institute, as a research institution, has no opinions and is not committed in any way by the views and arguments expressed by its research workers.

We should like to thank Miss Gisborne and Miss Weil for their energy and patience in typing numerous drafts, and Miss Shrimpton for preparing the diagrams.

F. A. B.

OXFORD, *July* 1944.

CONTENTS

THE ECONOMICS OF FULL EMPLOYMENT

PART I

THE CAUSES OF UNEMPLOYMENT
by F. A. Burchardt

FEW people will be prepared to deny that mass unemployment is a social evil. This consensus of opinion does not, however, provide a platform for common action. This for two reasons: because opinions about the causes of unemployment differ, and because—even if there were an agreed diagnosis—the treatment of the disease may be a matter of choice: the surgeon advocating the use of the knife, the specialist a new drug, and the general practitioner a tonic and cold compresses. Such a divergence of views may be rare in the medical field where expert opinion alone counts and can be tested by experiment. In social affairs it is the rule. The 'social organism' does not lend itself readily to experiment and group opinion, rather than expert opinion, determines diagnosis and therapy. In the case of unemployment the situation is even more complicated, because the experts—the economists—disagree about the causes and have only recently—one might say as the result of the severe unemployment of the nineteen thirties—found a satisfactory explanation. These modern views are still struggling for recognition in expert circles and it will take some time before a re-interpretation of economic facts filters down into the opinion of policy-forming groups.

Broadly speaking—and neglecting hybrid types which are naturally very common in a period of transition—three explanations of the phenomenon of unemployment are offered:—

(a) The first and oldest one regards unemployment as a penalty for deviating from *laisser-faire* in the sense of free competition and free trade. We may call it the '*laisser-faire* competition theory.'

(b) The second explanation regards unemployment as due to the complex of causes generating the trade cycle and emphasizes that ups and downs of business activity are natural, ineradicable, and if fairly moderate, wholesome. For our purpose it will suffice to sketch in broad outline the contribution of trade cycle analysis to the factual study of unemployment, to the formulation of new problems, and to the armoury of remedial policies against cyclical unemployment. Under the heading 'Natural wave theories' we consider that type of trade cycle study, running parallel to the development of the classical system, which regards fluctuations of business activity as only partly controllable. The line of division chosen is thus an arbitrary one, based upon the attitude of theorists to trade cycle policy. From the theoretical point of view some of the 'natural wave theories' shade over into the modern type of theory which regards a full control of the trade cycle and the maintenance of full employment as at least a theoretical proposition.

(*c*) The third explanation attributes unemployment to a lack of effective demand, to a deficiency of outlay on consumption and/or investment. Elements of this 'demand deficiency' theory can be traced right back in the nineteenth century but as a 'general theory' it was first developed by Lord Keynes in the 'thirties.

All three explanations occur in a number of variants and to each theory is related, though not uniquely, a typical remedy or cure for the disease of unemployment. A study of the three main theories will help to clarify some of the fundamental concepts which play a part in the academic and non-academic discussion of the employment problem.

I. THE *LAISSER-FAIRE* COMPETITION THEORY

According to this theory unemployment is due, either to Government interference with the free play of market forces, or, more generally, to monopolistic practices. If only the Government would not meddle with economic affairs by social legislation, subsidies, duties, etc., and would leave the field to private initiative and to free bargaining in the market a high level of employment would automatically be secured. This *laisser-faire* argument is sometimes extended by lumping together State restrictions of free competition with restrictive practices of private monopolies. Monopolistic organizations in industry and in the labour market have, it is argued, the same effect as State interference, namely to restrict output and employment opportunities. If we could do away with monopolies and replace them by a really competitive system, or control them in such a way as to make them behave like competitive units, unemployment would tend to disappear; the interest of the individual would coincide again with that of society as a whole.

These popular and rudimentary versions of the theory of unemployment are, in their pure form, not very widely held in this country. They are, however, vigorously propagated in the United States by economists, business men, and politicians, and they are still in this country, though in a less rigid form, fundamental ingredients of the public's attitude to unemployment.

Reduced to theoretical terms the argument runs as follows: unemployment exists because wages are too high; this unduly high level is maintained by monopolistic trade union practices (and indirectly by the dole system which guarantees a minimum standard). If these restrictions were removed competition would force wages down to the level where it becomes profitable to entrepreneurs to employ more labour.

The theory derives support in business circles from a plausible but erroneous generalization; as an explanation of the real world it depends upon the validity of certain assumptions.

The Classical Theory of Wages and Employment

Let us begin with a case which is somewhat unrealistic but theoretically simple: a simultaneous all round reduction in wages. And let us assume that wages are fully used for consumption.[1] Employers may react upon the reduction of wages in two ways: (a) they may either act as if perfect competition existed, or (b) they may lower prices immediately in the hope of selling more.

(a) When wages are reduced on the day X, employers will have in hand the revenue from sales made on the previous day (X—1) at prices of the previous day. They find now that they will have to pay out less for wages than previously and that the balance—equal to the difference between the old and the new wage bill—will be in their hands. Thus in the first round part of the wage bill will accrue to employers as increased profits. If these profits induce entrepreneurs to increase immediately their investment or to raise their consumption, total employment will increase. There will be first a rise in employment in the industries producing investment goods or goods for capitalist consumption. The money wage bill will therefore fall in a smaller proportion than money wage rates. On the other hand labour costs in the wage goods industries will be lower in the same proportion as wage rates. The fact that the wage bill changes less[2] than wage rates while money wage costs in the wage goods sector are lowered proportionately to

[1] We disregard for the moment the effect of wage changes on foreign trade, and the existence of fixed income receivers.

[2] In a system with an elastic supply of credit the money wage bill may even rise if a sufficiently great number of additional workers is employed in the non-wage goods industries.

wage rates will make it profitable to expand the output of wage goods. The wage bill in real terms will therefore increase. Real wage rates will, however, fall because the expansion proceeds—in the short run and under conditions of free competition—along upward sloping marginal cost curves. If the additional profits arising out of the general expansion of output induce firms to maintain (or to increase) their increased outlay on investment goods, or on goods of capitalist consumption, employment will be maintained at the higher level (or be increased).

In the longer run new equipment will come into operation. Assuming long-period constant costs for the industry and for the firms, and no change in technical efficiency, the ratio of capital to labour employed will be restored to its old level. Output of wage goods will now be greater in strict proportion to the increase in employment in the wage goods industries. Prices will therefore fall proportionately to money wage rates and long run equilibrium is reached.

Thus, where employers use profits accruing from wage reductions for raising their own consumption or for additions to the capital stock, an all round reduction of wages increases employment. The crucial point in this theory is the assumption that employers react on the initial increase in profits immediately with increased outlay on capital goods or on their own consumption. If they hesitate to do so immediately, employment will not be increased.[1] Employment and hence output will remain unchanged in the first round as there is no reason to curtail it merely because of the reduction in wage costs. If manufacturers wish to sell their current output (and are unwilling to increase inventories) prices will inevitably fall proportionately to money wages. This wipes out prospective extra profits and thus justifies *ex post* the original hesitation of employers to increase their outlay in response to a given wage reduction.[2]

The validity of the classical employment theory depends, then, entirely on the assumption that employers respond to wage reductions immediately with decisions to increase their outlay.

(*b*) Now take the second case, that employers will respond to wage

---

[1] See M. Kalecki, *Essays in Economic Fluctuations*, pp. 78–80.

[2] If some prices and incomes in the community are fixed (rent, debenture interest, etc.) the price fall implies a redistribution of the given real income away from wage and profit earners towards fixed income receivers. If the latter do not wish to consume the whole of their increased real income the shift from wages to fixed income will lead to a fall in employment. The shift from profits to rent income may, on the other hand, lead to increased consumption and hence to a rise in employment. As before we shall, however, disregard the modifying influence of price rigidities in our analysis and assume that the economy contains only wage and profit earners.

cuts with price reductions in the hope that lower prices will bring higher sales. Employers may adopt this attitude when they are working under conditions of imperfect competition. There is evidence that under these conditions employers tend to determine prices by adding to prime cost a certain percentage for gross profits. This is a well-known practice in retailing where the retail price is fixed by adding a percentage (say 50 per cent) to the wholesale price. If manufacturers in general are in the habit of basing prices on prime cost plus percentage profit ('marking up') a rise (fall) in wage rates will automatically lead to a corresponding rise (fall) in price. Unless the degree of monopoly changes, real wages and real profits will, therefore, remain constant. There may still be an incentive to increase investment if entrepreneurs act as if any price reduction will attract more custom and neglect the effect that a general wage reduction might have on the demand for their products. They anticipate a rise in demand and, without waiting for it to materialize, begin immediately to order additional capital equipment. Incomes earned by the newly employed factors will then be capable of buying the additional goods produced and entrepreneurial expectations of higher sales will not be disappointed.

How much employment will increase in response to a given wage reduction will in this case depend upon entrepreneurs' estimates of the prospective increase in sales. If few employers expect higher sales, or if most of them are not certain what increase to expect, the employment effect may be small and *vice versa*. Or to put it the other way round, any practicable reduction in wage rates may be insufficient to raise profit expectations appreciably. As in the case of perfect competition the stimulus of wage reductions may or may not work in the case of imperfect competition. If entrepreneurs feel inclined to wait and see whether demand rises in response to the price reduction instead of anticipating the rise by immediately giving investment orders, events will justify their hesitation: neither sales nor employment will rise. The inclination to 'wait' may, in fact, be stronger when wages and price are reduced simultaneously. In conditions of imperfect competition the connection between wage reductions and revision of entrepreneurial expectations may, thus, be somewhat looser than in the original classical case of perfect competition. This raises the problem whether there are not other methods, apart from the manipulation of wages, which can be used to alter entrepreneurial expectations; a problem which is treated more systematically by the modern theory of effective demand.

The Neo-Classical Theory

Two attempts to salvage at least part of the classical theory of employment have been made: the one argues that wage reductions accompanied by price reductions tend to reduce interest rates, the second that they will improve the country's foreign trade position by stimulating exports.

When lower money wages are not associated with a simultaneous increase in employment, the fall in the volume of transactions (in money terms) leaves the public with more cash relative to the reduced turnover. Given the desire for holding cash (rather than other assets) entrepreneurs will try to redress the increase in liquidity by buying short- and long-term assets. This will tend to lower the general level of interest rates. It is clear that the same effect could have been produced, with given money wage rates, by increasing entrepreneurial liquidity through the supply of additional cash by the Central Bank. Similarly, a general reduction of money wages (efficiency rewards to factors) is to all intents and purposes equivalent to a depreciation of the currency.

Lower short-term rates of interest may, however, not reduce long-term rates appreciably and thus not provide a noticeable stimulus to investment, while in the short run, profit expectations may be adversely affected by the painful process of the downward adjustment of wages and prices. How far a reduction of the efficiency rewards to factors will improve the external balance will depend upon various demand and supply elasticities and other elements, as we shall see later.[1] These indirect repercussions of wage cuts cannot, therefore, be relied upon to push employment to full capacity level.

The result of this analysis of the classical theory of employment may be put as follows: (1) The assumption that competitive wage reductions will increase employment presupposes that entrepreneurs will always and immediately react on a temporary increase in actual profits with increased outlay. This is an unrealistic assumption because expected profits rather than actual ones determine investment decisions. Moreover, to plan for increased output, and still more for increased investment, takes time; and in any case employers are likely to be inclined to take a wait-and-see attitude when wages are lowered. A time lag between the wage reduction and the offsetting expansion of entrepreneurial spending will, however, leave real wages and profits unchanged and thus confirm the entrepreneurs' original hesitation. A down-

[1] See Part V.

ward bidding of prices, coupled with uncertainties about future wages and prices, may actually affect entrepreneurial expectations adversely and lead to a contraction of output and employment. Moreover, profit expectations are influenced by numerous other factors apart from changes in costs. When mass unemployment exists and entrepreneurs experience a period of falling demand and falling prices, a cut in wage rates is not likely to produce an upward revision of profit expectations. The classical precept of wage cuts is—paradoxically enough—likely to be ineffective in bringing about an increase of employment when trade is slack and unemployment high and rising, whereas it might speed up the re-employment of workers in times of improving trade prospects and rising employment, when wage reductions are neither needed nor practicable.

For all these reasons it is unlikely that a general or generalized reduction in money wages will increase employment by raising profit expectations and hence investment. The indirect effects of wage reductions *via* the rate of interest and changes in the foreign balance are somewhat uncertain and can in any case be obtained more easily and directly by an appropriate monetary policy. The classical conception of a unique wage level which would bring about equilibrium at full employment loses its force when lower money wages do not lead to lower real wages and investment decisions are not automatically increased in response to a reduction in money wages.

The Social Background of the Classical Theory

The matter could be left to rest there as far as the theoretical argument is concerned. But it may be useful to enquire why economists in the past century and business men until to-day adhere persistently to the belief that there is always a wage level which provides employment for the whole labour force and that wage reductions can cure or reduce general unemployment. By tracing their opinions we may discover why the old theory dies so hard and finds so many defenders among employers. Three different strands of thought appear to give support to the argument that wage reductions promote employment. (*a*) To the individual business man a reduction in his firm's or industry's wages means lower costs which enable him to sell more at lower prices. In times of falling employment it seems, therefore, reasonable to him to press for lower wages. If his workers, as is likely, buy only a negligible fraction of his own output, and if wages of other firms and industries are kept constant (or lowered less), he will gain a differential advantage, increase his profits and in many cases extend his output. Steeped in the ideology that by following intelligently his own interests he is promoting the interest of the community as a whole, he concludes that what is right and profitable to the individual business must be so for the business community. It is precisely this generalization which is wrong. Only because wages in other firms and industries are not reduced (or at least not proportionately), only if he marches a step ahead in the battle for wage reductions, will his own policy be successful and profitable. If other firms and industries follow his example and—maybe—outpace him, wage and price reductions become generalized and initial differential advantages are partly or wholly lost. Moreover, in this painful process of downward adjustments of wages and prices even those entrepreneurs who gain at the expense of others will hesitate to embark upon new investment and thus effective demand is not increased.

A policy of wage reductions appeals to business men, although it is based on the fallacy that what is profitable for the individual is profitable and advantageous for the community, because it is part and parcel of the competitive game of securing differential advantages. That such advantages are gained at the expense of other industries or groups, and therefore represent a beggar-my-neighbour policy against their fellow employers, might not dissuade employers in a depressed industry from using this method, particularly as the repercussions of their action on the rest of the community are beyond their horizon and not easily traced back to actions of an individual industry.[1] Spurred by slack trade the beggar-my-neighbour game of wage reductions becomes tempting, and since the worsening of competitive behaviour cannot easily be distinguished from genuine competition every player plays it with a good conscience. Only if employers realize that there are different ways out of the depression, ways which secure better markets, not at the expense of other employers, but by expanding total market demand, will they become inclined to resist the temptations of competitive wage reductions which on balance do not make employers better off than before and are, indeed, likely to make them and the community worse off owing to their damping effect on investment.

(b) The second mainstay of the business world's conviction of the remedial nature of wage reductions is derived from the nineteenth century theory and practice of international trade and exchange. In a system of fixed exchange rates, such as the gold standard, a disequilibrium in a country's foreign balance, appearing, for instance, in the form

---

[1] Attempts to keep prices rigid by monopolistic practices have a similar effect; they tend to make employment and output fluctuate more in the economy as a whole.

of a loss of gold, will, according to one version of the classical theory, be remedied by a fall in wages and prices unaccompanied by a fall in real income and employment. This would be true if a crude quantity theory of money were accepted, or if money wage rates were infinitely flexible and the Central Bank had control not only over monetary policy but also over money wage rates. Disturbances of the international balance could then be restored by uniform alterations of money wage rates and prices without any restriction of employment and output. Such alterations of money wage rates and prices would be equivalent to variations in the value of the currency.

In actual practice the Central Bank has, however, direct control only over monetary policy. If it wishes to ward off a loss of gold it will allow (or induce) interest rates to rise. Higher interest rates may, or may not, attract foreign capital and thus stop the outflow of gold; their effect on internal activity will be to discourage investment. A reduction in the rate of investment will, however, generate a general fall in employment and income. The decline in income will by itself tend to reduce imports and to stimulate exports. If money wage rates were absolutely rigid balance could only be restored by variations in income and employment and the associated changes in costs and prices. In reality wages are not completely inflexible. Under the pressure of unemployment wage rates will be lowered, though not uniformly, and prices are likely to follow suit. Balance will then be restored partly by a fall in employment, and partly by a fall in money rewards to factors which is itself induced by greater unemployment. This so-called process of deflation is the ultimate mechanism of adjustment in a system of fixed exchange rates, especially where the international flow of capital is not highly elastic with regard to differences in interest rates between national economies. When the risk element in international lending is small and fairly stable, long-term capital will flow readily according to interest differentials and to that extent relieve deflationary pressure. Rapidly changing risks, leading to substantial movements of short-term funds and to unwillingness of lending on long term will, on the other hand, intensify the degree of deflation necessary to restore balance. More will be said about this in the fifth study of this book.

It is, however, important to consider some of the implications of deflation as a method of adjusting the foreign balance of a country. If pressure on money wage rates improves a country's balance, it becomes possible for home producers to gain advantages at the expense of foreign producers, and thus to shift the incidence of unemployment on to other countries. These other countries who find their exports declining and their imports rising will react on the resulting unemployment by putting pressure on their own wages. If, however, wage cuts in country A are followed or outpaced by wage cuts in country B the former does not obtain a net advantage. Similarly wage and price reductions may not produce an improvement in the balance of trade if demand and supply elasticities are unfavourable. As in the internal struggle for competitive wage reductions the effects of the beggar-my-neighbour policy upon the world as a whole are hidden from the business man's view. Faced with shrinking markets he strives to retain or increase his share in total sales by lowering money costs. He may even claim that in such circumstances wage reductions are in the 'national interest' as they stimulate exports and hamper imports and thus tend to assist home employment. Once such a coincidence between apparent 'business interests' and 'national interests' is thought to demand a lowering of wages it is likely to get strong support.

A system of fixed exchange rates presupposes variable employment and/or flexible wages and prices. When wages are moderately sticky variations in employment must be fairly large to restore equilibrium. But deflation in one country is likely to produce deflation in other countries and, by spreading unemployment, to make the process of adjustment more painful for all countries. It was because countries were not willing to pay the price of great internal instability for the sake of maintaining the stability of foreign exchange rates that the gold standard broke down in the nineteen-thirties.

To the extent that flexible exchange rates or foreign trade controls provide the possibility of regulating the foreign balance, internal contraction and hence pressure on money wages is obviated. Any level of internal employment can be maintained if the external adjustment is manipulated by appropriate currency and trade policies. Under this system there can be no general reason for lowering money wage rates to maintain or restore the external balance, nor is such pressure likely to be successful if employment is not falling. If, therefore, the real world moves towards a system of managed currencies and trade balances—as it did in the 'thirties—the foreign trade argument for wage reductions loses its force; if the world returns to the system of fixed exchange rates, as it prevailed in the late 'twenties, adjustment by internal contraction or deflation is likely to be accompanied again by pressure on money wages.

(c) The hold which the 'competitive theory of employment' has over the minds of business men does not depend, however, upon such roundabout deductions of economic theory. Its roots go far deeper.

It is the idea that business left to itself will, through the interplay of anonymous market forces, produce a natural equilibrium which represents the greatest welfare for the community as a whole. What had been to the eighteenth century a shockingly revolutionary theory, namely that the interplay of independent individuals, each striving after his own personal advantage, would result not only not in chaos but in the greatest welfare for all, became the accepted ideology of the nineteenth century. It postulated, in principle, that economic life should be free from State interference because it was regulated ideally by the competitive play of business units. This belief in the beneficial nature of the automatism of the market process received many blows and was constantly modified with changing circumstances but remained the *credo* of business men in all capitalist countries. It made business men masters in their own house and subject only to the unwritten laws of competitive economics.

If it is now felt that a public agency should regulate the level of employment and the external balance, because experience has shown that *laisser-faire* does not produce under all circumstances—internal and external—a steady and high level of employment, the very substance of nineteenth-century belief in a free and unmanaged economy seems to be attacked.

If the State assumes new and positive functions in the economic field, if not mere competition between businesses but deliberate guidance and management of economic forces are required to secure stability and maximum utilization of resources, then it is argued, freedom, initiative, security from arbitrariness and even rights of private property will be in danger. If the anonymity of market forces is replaced by conscious public decisions the individual will be at the mercy of the complex machinery of the modern State, represented by bureaucrats and politicians following their own ends. This deep-rooted distrust of the State using or misusing regulative powers in the economic field, thus harming or favouring sectional groups; the fear of granting economic power to a public authority with codes of conduct different from those of private business; the fear that this power may slip into the hands of groups who will use it for what are called political purposes; such considerations produce the strong and passionate support for the admittedly grossly imperfect autonomous system of competitive economy, while traditional economic theories about wages, investment and foreign trade serve mainly as rationalizations. The attraction of a self-regulated economic system, even if it does not work well, outweighs in the minds of many people the attraction of a more perfect system in which public political decisions in economic matters are an essential ingredient.

II. 'NATURAL WAVE' THEORIES

For more than a hundred and fifty years the economic growth of industrial countries has proceeded by fits of booms followed by slumps. The ups and downs of employment and income occurred at sufficiently regular intervals and had so many features in common that a general explanation of the periodic fluctuations seemed justified. Throughout the nineteenth century and up to the present time many theories were advanced to explain these cycles of business activity which did not fit at all into the picture of the economic process drawn by classical economists. On the basis of their theoretical system one should expect a steady advance, disturbed perhaps by random fluctuations, but not a regular cyclical pattern.

Special theories, outside the general body of classical assumptions, were therefore developed and, whatever the explanatory value of individual theories, this was a great step forward in the search for the causes of unemployment. Whereas the classical system reduced the problem of unemployment ultimately to wage rigidity and frictions, the trade cycle theories found a number of new factors which purported to explain at least the periodic fluctuations in employment. Broadly speaking they departed in two directions from the classical system. Some assumed that the data varied periodically, and hence that exogenous factors, shocks from outside the system, produced the ups and downs. Others tried to demonstrate the possibility of a self-generating (endogenous) cycle by giving up the classical assumption of synchronized processes and introducing instead time sequences as a variable. In this case the formal problem was to find the appropriate economic variables and time lags which would describe the pattern of a self-perpetuating cycle. Examples of the first (exogenous) type are theories which explain the cycle by regular variations in harvests, by waves of entrepreneurial optimism and pessimism, by periodic shocks administered to the system by errors in banking policy, by periodic shocks of inventions and so forth.

The second type is represented, for instance, by theories which emphasize the tendency of an expansion to produce disproportional developments in the sense that some sectors of the economy over- or under-spend, and that this lopsided development becomes stronger as the expansion proceeds. There comes a point where these disproportions break the expansion and turn it into a contraction which then corrects sectional maladjustments and lays the basis for a new advance. Almost all these theories make use of time-lag factors (wages lagging behind prices, market rates of interest lagging behind the 'natural' rate, the period of production generating excessive price increases or over-ordering, etc.) to explain the growing disproportion in the system; but often they use the time-lag factor without seeing its intrinsic importance and combine it with elements of the exogenous theories. A systematic development of time-lag theories is of comparatively recent date and outside the scope of this survey. The same applies, for obvious reasons, to trade cycle theories developed on the basis of the 'Effective Demand Theory'; the latter and the employment policies associated with it will be discussed in the following section.

It is impossible within the framework of this book to analyse in detail the two main types of theories mentioned above, or to test their empirical validity. It must suffice to indicate some general results which trade cycle analysis has contributed to the discussion of the problems of unemployment.

The Nature of Periodic Unemployment

All trade cycle theories try to explain the recurrence of mass un-employment at regular intervals and all agree that periodic unemploy-ment is not due—or at least not primarily due—to mere frictions or the rigidity of money wages, which was the classical explanation of un-employment.

Even if it is assumed that no unemployment exists at the top of the boom, it is evident that, taking good and bad trade periods together, average unemployment of a non-frictional type exists on a mass scale. However, not many theories demonstrate or attempt to demonstrate that the expansion of the economy in the upward phase of the cycle must always be carried to the point where all the unemployed are absorbed. If, however, there is no general or automatic force which drives activity up to the limit of full employment, then it is possible to have general unemployment over a number of cycles. This poses the question of an economy with permanent unemployment.

When data became available and methods were developed to meas-ure cyclical phenomena it became possible to determine quantitatively various types of unemployment, cyclical and seasonal and the rest, which was often further subdivided into frictional and general, or into frictional and structural unemployment. The latter was explained in classical terms to be due to heavy and persistent frictions (immobility) owing to the decline of localized industries. As will be argued in Parts II and III, this explanation is more than doubtful. Moreover, under-employment at boom levels has been observed in many other countries where the specific British factors of declining local industries were not present.

The notion that the cycle will reproduce itself has been interpreted differently in different theories. The pattern of the cycle was partly conceived as something unavoidable, imposed by natural, uncontrollable conditions, which could not and should not be interfered with. When one thinks of harvest fluctuations, or changing psychological moods, or time-lags, it seems plausible to conclude that the resulting business cycle is beyond human control and that there is nothing to do but submit to it. This view is reinforced (especially in periods when *laisser-faire* is an accepted ideological principle) by the belief that any interference with the laws of the economic mechanism would make things worse and not better. The idea that the self-regulating forces of supply and demand produce a sort of 'natural order' was taken over by some trade cycle theories and transformed into a dynamic automatism, produced by similar anonymous and inescapable forces. These dynamic factors, it was stated, do not bring about the harmony and steadiness described in the classical system; but cyclical instability, it was argued, is the price we have to pay for progress and expansion. Some theories went further and tried to show not only that depressions followed inevitably upon expansions, but that depressions had a positive and wholesome function. Adherents to this view—and there are many among economists, administrators and business men—point out that depressions are necessary to eliminate the excesses of the boom, to correct maladjustments, to wipe out the inefficient producers who would otherwise be kept in existence and constitute a drag on progress, as a corrective against the rapid growth of financial titles, stock exchange booms and over-capitalization which could obviously not go on for ever. In fact, if slumps did not come about automatically, they would have to be invented.

A third group of theorists takes the line that the conditions which reproduce the cycle are largely outside social control, and that some fluctuations are therefore inevitable. They believe, however, that the amplitude of these fluctuations can be influenced to some extent by deliberate public action. Many variants of this view exist; some suggest that an appropriate adjustment of interest rates by the Central Bank could mitigate the violence of the trade cycle; others that anti-cyclical variations in public investment would damp down the cyclical amplitude. In both cases the basic idea is to alter the distribution of a given aggregate volume of employment over time. By directing, for instance, that part of investment which is already under public control in such a way that, of a given volume of public works to be undertaken in any case, more are produced in bad times and less in good times, inverse variations of private investment can be partly offset. Instead of having, say, 1 million unemployed at the top of the boom and 3 million at the bottom of the slump, anti-cyclical public works programmes would reduce slump unemployment to, say, $2\frac{1}{2}$ million and increase boom unemployment to, say, $1\frac{1}{2}$ million.

We shall see later that there is no need to restrict a public works policy to a mere redistribution over time of a given amount of public works and that the planned total of works can (if it is desired, as for instance in war-time) be increased until all cyclical and non-cyclical unemployment is eliminated. This implies, however, a departure from the concept of a natural cycle which cannot or should not be completely abolished. To the extent that an increase of total public works over the trade cycle is advocated, trade cycle policy aiming at smoothing the violence of the movements shades over into the Demand Deficiency Theory which we shall discuss in the next section. Before we can do this we must, however, examine the above interpretations of the trade cycle as a 'natural wave.'

The Control of Cyclical Fluctuations

Does it follow that business cycles are inevitable and incurable if uncontrollable data fluctuate cyclically? Is it necessary or even desirable to pay the price of depressions to reap the fruits of progress? What are the merits and demerits of attempts to smooth the cycle? These are some of the questions which require an answer, not only for the sake of theoretical clarity but above all because they are the stock in trade of contemporary writing and speeches, both here and in U.S.A.

It can easily be shown that the argument that the cycle is beyond human control, because it is impossible to alter or influence certain variations in data (e.g. harvest fluctuations, assuming that they generate the cycle), is erroneous. Certainly we cannot control the weather and hence cannot control the size of agricultural output. But we can eliminate the effects of variations in crops on the social system. The Old Testament knew already that the remedy against the succession of seven fat and seven lean years was the accumulation of stocks in good years and their dispersion in lean years. In modern language, buffer stocks are a form of social control of the natural cycle in agriculture.

Moreover, it is by no means true that the fall in prices of agricultural products creates a general fall in industrial output; its main effect is to redistribute real incomes between agricultural producers and urban consumers. Similar considerations apply to psychological factors (such as changing expectations of entrepreneurs) or disproportions and time factors which cannot be influenced directly. Here again, their operational effects can be changed by appropriate measures: pessimistic expectations for instance by subsidies to private investment, and over-optimism by global controls such as raising interest rates, or by specific direct controls such as licensing of investment, and so forth. Self-generating cycles are therefore not like tidal waves to whose force we must submit blindly, but social phenomena which can be managed and controlled by social action.

The theory of the corrective functions of depressions needs only a few comments. First of all, it must be asked whether it would not be less wasteful to carry on 'inefficient' producers for some time rather than to let the whole economy slide into a depression. The process of, elimination of inefficiency will occur gradually when employment is maintained, it will be concentrated into a short space of time when employment is allowed to fall. There can be little doubt that the waste involved in mass unemployment of plant and labour is greater than any gain in efficiency resulting from the more rapid elimination of the 'marginal producer.'

Those who are concerned about maladjustments and advocate *laisser-faire* as a corrective forget too often that the whole classical theory, with its *laisser-faire* implications, proceeds upon the assumption of gradual and small changes. Sudden and major changes, such as are created by wars, trade restrictions, or major depressions, are not within the orbit of classical analysis and require, even according to classical prescriptions, a positive public policy transforming the sudden change into a gradual process. This may imply subsidies or stock-piling for a transition period, accompanied by measures of rationalization and possibly contraction, based on the long-period prospects of the industry. Vis-à-vis major maladjustment the battle cry of *laisser-faire* is equally futile and as theoretically unjustifiable as the counter-claim of un-conditional protection of the maladjusted position. A planned and gradual correction of the excess or the deficiency broadly in the direction indicated by the classical theory, is clearly the most rational solution, both from the point of view of theory and policy. This is generally recognized in dealing with major maladjustments produced by a war in the immediate reconstruction period. Nobody suggests that it should be left to the free play of the market to eliminate the excess capacities, say in the engineering industries or in the non-ferrous metal industry, but many suggest that major maladjustments occurring subsequently or in peace should be eliminated by a process of competition. Such a policy is impracticable and leads usually to mere protection without a positive policy of reorganization and transfer.

Secondly, it is by no means certain that a depression will put the technically least efficient producers out of business; it may well eliminate —and particularly so under monopolistic conditions—the financially weakest unit. The main argument is, however, that any depression overdoes the job by removing not only excesses of the boom and marginal inefficiencies, but by creating new excesses in the opposite direction: prices fall 'too much,' firms with sound prospects in the longer run get into difficulties as a result of the depression and efficient plant and equipment are forced into idleness. In other words, even if one assumes for the sake of argument that an expansion creates excesses which must be corrected, a cumulative depression, the depth of which cannot be foreseen, is the most clumsy and wasteful instrument to put matters right. If it should prove necessary to have special correctives against disproportions or to penalize inefficiency, it is clearly preferable to use other, more discriminating methods.

Finally there is the question of trade cycle policy. This will be taken here in the narrow sense of merely mitigating business fluctuations and not in the wider sense in which it may mean the maintenance of a steady or increasing rate of output at full employment level. The implied ironing out of fluctuations attempts to distribute the incidence of a given amount of unemployment more equally over the various phases of the cycle. Until about a decade ago opinions differed about the best methods of achieving this end. Since then it has become fairly generally agreed that public works, timed in an anti-cyclical sense, can usefully contribute towards damping cyclical fluctuations. The underlying assumption is simple: we have variations in private investment which generate cumulative upward and downward processes of the economic system as a whole. This cyclical behaviour of private investment is the root of the trouble and must be taken as a datum in our society. Hitherto the ups and downs of private investment have been (more often than not) reinforced by simultaneous and parallel fluctuations in public works. But public investment is not—or at least not primarily —undertaken for profit, and so need not follow this pattern. Since this sector is in any case under public control and not primarily determined by profit considerations it can be manipulated so as to offset—as far as possible—variations in private investment. Ideally, public works should be at a minimum when private investment is booming, at a maximum when private investment is at a low ebb. In other words, ideally speaking, public works should lag behind private investment by half a cycle. It will be observed that greater stability of the system as a whole is thus achieved by creating artificially an instability (of public works) to compensate the basic instability (of private investment). Such a procedure can be criticized on various grounds.

Once it is realized that public works need not follow in the wake of private investment and can—within certain limits—be timed independently, it seems equally undesirable to have them fluctuate parallel with, or opposite to, the cycle of private investment. Taken as such, it would clearly be preferable to have a steady rate of public works. Only if it can be shown that there are no ways of regulating private investment, and only if the latter is regarded as of paramount importance and public investment as a stop-gap with little or no priority of its own, is the policy of subordinating and de-stabilizing public works to the whims of private investment justified.

Part only of public investment can be adjusted anticyclically. Some public works are bound up with the flow of private investment and consumption (e.g. streets, sewerage, etc., with private house building; telephones for private users, etc.); some are of a long-term nature (such as forestry programmes) or otherwise impossible to postpone (e.g. armaments or current repairs of existing assets).

The remainder of 'timeable' public works is (in the western democracies) largely determined and undertaken by local authorities which for various administrative and financial reasons cannot easily postpone or antedate works demanded and approved by local interests. It will need the overhauling of the relations of central to local government and a strengthening of the powers of direction of the central authority to make works of local authorities reliable instruments of trade cycle planning.

Even if the vested interests of local governments were successfully overcome, the volume of timeable public works is (or at least was in the past) so small in comparison with the amplitude of fluctuations in private investment that its smoothing effect would not be appreciable and perhaps not worth the political price of radical interference with local self-government.

If these arguments against trade cycle policy in the narrow (traditional) sense be accepted, the way out would seem to be either to envisage a considerably greater volume of timeable public works than that to which we have been accustomed in the past (the New Deal may be regarded as an experiment and lesson in this direction), or to reconsider the possibilities of steadying the apparent villain of the piece: private investment. Such considerations are clearly outside the framework of the 'natural wave theories' and so is the question which we have so far pushed into the background, namely that of the causes and cures for general unemployment. To these problems, which are analysed systematically in the Keynesian theory of effective demand, we turn in the following section.

III. THE DEMAND DEFICIENCY THEORY

The starting-point of this theory of unemployment is the simple and commonsense statement that unemployment exists because demand for goods and services is insufficient to make use of all the real resources available. If demand were greater more factors would be employed and if, as in war-time, demand is exceedingly high in relation to available resources, factors will tend to be over-employed. This statement might seem to be acceptable to almost any school of economic thought. The crucial point at which opinions divide is, however, in explaining the conditions under which demand is deficient to employ all the existing real resources. The classical theory held, as we saw, the view that, given sufficient mobility of factors and flexibility of prices and wages, demand could never fail (in the longer run) to be adequate to employ all the factors seeking employment. Deficiency of demand could only come about as a result of artificial market imperfections and rigidities. Trade cycle theories (of the type discussed above) attempted to show the possibility of periodic fluctuations in total demand, but by concentrating on the mechanism of the cycle very often failed to explain the basic factors which make for a deficiency of demand in the long run, and the problem of idle reserves of labour at the top of the boom.

This fundamental problem of the general factors which determine the level of demand and employment was reconsidered in the 'thirties[1] and systematically developed by Lord Keynes and a number of other economists. The gist of this theory must be briefly recounted as it forms the background of the studies in this book.

THE ELEMENTS OF THE THEORY

Assume as a starting-point a state of affairs where all the factors of production are employed and where the community spends the whole

[1] J. M. Keynes, *General Theory of Employment, Interest and Money*; J. Robinson, *Essays in the Theory of Employment*, and by the same author, *Introduction to the Theory of Employment*.

of its net income. How can this state of full employment be disturbed and how can demand become insufficient to employ all the factors of production?

A mere shift of demand from one product to another obviously does not reduce total effective demand, and cannot, given some mobility of factors, lead to more than temporary frictional unemployment. Deficiency of demand does arise, however, when some members of the community wish to reduce their expenditure on consumption while other members are unwilling to spend more than their income on goods and services of some kind or another. If less is spent on consumption by one sector of the community and this is not made up by more 'spending of others' or by 'spending on something else' total demand for goods and services will decline, factors of production will become unemployed and the income of the community will fall.

We call people's desire to spend less than their income on consumers' goods their 'desire to save'; we describe the uses to which resources released by saving may be put, provisionally, as 'offsets to savings' or 'offsetting spending.' The term 'offsetting spending' may cover a variety of uses: either the savers themselves may wish to spend on other than consumption goods, i.e. newly produced investment goods (such as plant and equipment, houses, etc.), or other private persons or public agencies may wish to spend the saver's unused purchasing power on investment goods (such as mentioned above) or on consumption goods (e.g. the State on soldiers' food or dole payments, the private person through instalment purchases). We shall discuss the significance of the various kinds of 'offsets' later, and for convenience retain the very formal concept of 'offsetting spending' for the initial stages of our analysis.

The fundamental theorem of the Demand Deficiency Theory may now be put thus: If people desire to save out of a given income more than the community wishes to absorb in offsetting spending, total demand, income and employment will decline below that level; or still more briefly: if planned savings[1] exceed offsetting spending, employment will fall. If at the lower level of employment people still wish to save more than the community uses for offsetting spending, there will be a further decline of employment, until what people wish to save out of a given income is equal to what the community decides to use for offsetting spending at that level of income. Whatever the state of employment, an excess of intended savings over offsetting

---

[1] By 'planned savings' or 'desired savings' we shall understand throughout 'savings out of a given income.'

spending generates a decline in employment. This holds true for stationary and growing economies, for static and dynamic models, and provides in this sense the nucleus of a general theory of unemployment. While the classical theory attempted to demonstrate the law of the conservation of purchasing power, we see now a chance of explaining a deficiency of purchasing power.

Moreover, it is easily seen that if the above relation between 'intended savings' and 'offsets' is reversed, the result will be an increase in demand and employment. If people wish to save less out of their given income than the community uses for offsetting spending, or more shortly, if offsetting spending exceeds planned savings, aggregate demand and employment will rise. If this excess occurs in an economy with idle reserves of men and equipment, some or all of these factors will be re-employed and output will rise. If the economy is already working at full employment capacity an excess of offsets over planned savings will lead to over-employment, i.e. in the limiting case where all possibilities of voluntary overtime working are exhausted, to a rise in demand unaccompanied by an increase in the volume of employment and output. In this case more factors would be employed if they were available. If they are not forthcoming, demand for output rises but output cannot rise, with the result that the excess of offsets over desired savings produces nothing but a rise in prices. Over-employment in the limiting case of complete inelasticity of supply is, therefore, equivalent to pure inflation.

By how much a given increment in offsetting spending (or a reduction in planned saving) will raise employment or income is determined by the community's marginal propensity to save. An increment of extra spending will raise employment and income primarily in those industries which directly or indirectly produce to satisfy this extra demand. Income earned in these industries will, however, be partly or wholly spent on consumption goods and thus will generate secondary incomes and employment. If the community chose to consume the whole of the extra income, employment and income would rise indefinitely as a result of the given increment in the rate of offsetting spending or consumption.[1] If the community wishes to save part of the new income, the secondary effects of the primary spending will be *pro tanto* reduced. As part of the income is saved at each stage or round through which the income stream passes, the amount available for spending on consumption becomes smaller and smaller at each round.

[1] Or to put it differently, when the marginal propensity to save is zero, a *single act* of offsetting spending will produce an equal and lasting increase in the level of income and employment and income.

There is thus a series of decreasing increments of demand, summing up to a finite multiple of the increment in offsetting spending. The multiplier, measuring the ratio of the increases in total to primary employment and income, can easily be determined as the reciprocal of the propensity to save. The greater (smaller) the marginal propensity to save the smaller (greater) will be the secondary or multiplier effect of a given increment in primary spending. That this must be so follows from the general theorem, given above, that employment and income will rise as a result of an increment in offsetting spending until what people wish to save out of the extra income is equal to this increment.

It should be noted, however, that at any given moment and for any period of time actual savings are necessarily equal to actual offsets. Since actual savings are nothing but claims against such offsets, they can be neither greater nor smaller than the latter.[1] The finance of off-setting spending looks after itself in the double sense that any act of offsetting spending is *ipso facto* an act of saving and that any rate of offsetting spending will generate incomes until the rate of intended savings (what people wish to save out of their extra income) is sufficient to finance the rate of offsetting spending *in perpetuo*.

A decrement in offsetting spending, or an increase in the propensity to save unaccompanied by a corresponding increase in offsetting spending, will set the multiplier working in a downward direction and reduce incomes by a multiple of the original fall, until people wish to save out of the lower income not more than is needed for the lower rate of off-setting spending or consumption. The desire to save more than other people wish to offset leads to a fall in income which wipes out the savings planned by these groups of people by the dissaving of others.

At any given level of employment actual savings will thus be equal to actual offsets and, unless decisions with regard to saving or offsetting spending change, employment and output will continue at this level. If we now introduce a change and assume that there is additional offsetting spending, employment and output will be higher and this will generate further increases in employment and income until what people wish to save out of the extra income is equal to the additional offsetting spending. This new position must, however, not be interpreted as a final or equilibrium position. For the increase in output from a lower to a higher level may in turn affect the rate of offsetting spending which people plan as the situation changes. About this inter-

[1] See Part II, p. 41.

action of offsets, savings and income in the process of time more will be
said later.

THE DETERMINANTS OF SAVING AND INVESTMENT

We have so far discussed these determinants in a purely formal
manner, taking hypothetical relations of savings and offsets to demonstrate the mechanism. We must now push a step further and ask
what factors determine the propensity to save, what is the meaning
of the formal term 'offsets to savings,' and what factors regulate
decisions to absorb the community's intended savings.

Decisions to save, made by private individuals or firms and institutions, are governed partly by individual or social habits and tastes.
Of two comparable families with the same income the one may save
a certain proportion of its income, the other may not save at all or run
into debt. If we look, however, at social groups or income groups
where individual differences in thriftiness are averaged, we can test
three hypotheses: (a) that the same absolute amount is saved at different
income levels; (b) that the same proportion is saved at each income
level; and (c) that the proportion saved increases as we move to higher
income groups. Observation shows that, after allowance for corporate
savings, hypothesis (c) is the realistic one, at least for industrial countries
like Great Britain and the U.S.A. It follows that the more unequal the
distribution of incomes the higher will be, *ceteris paribus*, the community's saving out of a given income. The tendency to save a greater
proportion out of a higher income applies also to changes in the community's total income. The higher the level of employment and hence
of aggregate real income (given the distribution of incomes) the
greater the proportion the community wishes to save. If rising (falling)
aggregate incomes are associated with shifts in the distribution of
incomes towards (away from) profits, as is frequently the case, the rise
(fall) of the proportion saved will be correspondingly increased. This
shows that savings are not only an increasing function of the level of
real income, but that they change in a higher proportion than income.[1]

What about offsets to savings? Who undertakes offsetting spending
and for what purpose? The individual saver may abstain from consumption in order to spend on goods which are normally not paid for
out of current income, e.g. to build a house; or a firm may plough

---

[1] Statistics of savings at different income levels are scanty. See however: *National Resources
Committee*, 'Consumers' Expenditures in the United States,' Washington, 1939; M. Ezekiel,
'Savings, Consumption and Investment,' *American Economic Review*, March, June, 1942; Marvin
Hoffenberg, 'Estimates of National Output, Distributed Income, Consumers' Spending, Saving
and Capital Formation,' *The Review of Economic Statistics*, 1943; Colin Clark, *National Income and
Outlay*, London, 1937; Charles Madge, 'War-Time Pattern of Saving and Spending,' Occa-
sional Paper IV, *National Institute of Economic and Social Research*, 1943.

back profits to equip a factory. Other individuals or agencies may be willing to offset other people's savings by acquiring additional capital goods or by spending in excess of their income. If we generalize the concept of borrowing so as to include borrowing of savings from one-self, we can say that savings are offset by borrowing for expenditure on capital goods or consumption goods, or briefly, by loan expenditure on goods and services. Given the propensity to save, income and employment will be higher the higher the amounts spent out of loans.

What determines the rate of loan expenditure? In answering this question we must distinguish between loan expenditure made by private individuals and agencies and by public authorities. The con-siderations determining private loan expenditure differ in important respects from those which apply to loan expenditure by the State. Let us assume then, as a first approximation, that public authorities do not borrow on balance and that all offsets to savings must come from private loan expenditure. When private decisions with regard to savings and offsetting loan expenditure are the only factors determining the level of employment, we have evidently the relevant case where we can test whether the balance of these two sets of decisions will always be such as to produce sufficient demand to absorb the available labour supply.

Private borrowing may be used for spending more than one's income on immediate consumption or for purchasing additional capital goods, for addition to the capital stock of the economy. Private borrowing for consumption purposes is not entirely alien to the capitalist system (*vide* for instance, the hire-purchase system, or parents borrowing for the education of their children, or unemployed persons getting into debt with retailers), but it is limited in scope by the unwillingness of the saver and would-be lender to lend without 'security,' that is, without the possibility of laying his hands on a tangible, saleable asset, and by the unwillingness or inability of the would-be borrower to reserve part of his present and future income for servicing and amortizing the loan.

This leaves as the main outlet for private loan expenditure additions to the capital stock, i.e. net investment. The main issue thus hinges on the question of private investment and the factors determining the willingness to invest.

It is obvious that there are many factors which an entrepreneur weighs up in his mind when he considers whether to invest and how much to invest. Economic theory attempts to select the dominant considerations and to describe their interactions, but full agreement has not yet been achieved in this subject. The following paragraphs list a number of inducements and deterrents, the balance of which may be regarded as determining the investment plans of entrepreneurs.[1]

1. *Expected Marginal Profits*

In deciding how much to invest an entrepreneur will in the first instance estimate the prospective yield of various amounts of invest-ment in particular lines of production. If his firm is working under conditions of perfect competition, so that his own output decisions do not affect the prospective price of the product, the scale of his invest-ment plan will be unlimited as long as he expects constant or increasing returns from any increment of investment he is contemplating. If he believes that by extending the scale of his operations unit costs will rise while the effect of his increased output on prices can be neglected (ex-pected dis-economies of large scale), or if he operates under conditions of imperfect competition and must therefore assume that the price of his product will fall as he extends output, the expected profit from additional doses of investment (the expected marginal profit) must evidently decline. As market imperfections are present in almost all fields of economic activity we shall proceed under the assumption that expected marginal profits will decline as the size of the investment contemplated by firms increases.

2. *The Long-Term Rate of Interest*

How far will entrepreneurs or firms push investment along the schedule of marginal expected profits? The obvious answer is: they will increase their investment plans as long as it pays them; in other words, as long as they can earn at least as much by investing in bricks and mortar as they could earn by putting funds to alternative uses. The next best alternative open to them is long-term lending, i.e. buying securities. They will, therefore, compare the yield on long-term securities with the expected profits associated with investment plans of different magnitude, and will push their investment plans certainly not beyond the point where the marginal prospective rate of profit is equal to the current rate of interest on long-term securities. They are, in fact, likely to stop short of this point because they will be influenced in their decisions by various risk factors, for which allowance must be made. But let us disregard these elements of risk for a moment and

[1] The theory of inducements to invest has generally been much oversimplified by most writers. The account given here is based on the *Studies in Economic Dynamics* of Mr. M. Kalecki who has broken much new ground in this field. We present here only an outline; for a more rigorous treatment the reader is referred to Mr. Kalecki's book.

let us inquire first, how the rate of interest, which sets at least an upper limit to entrepreneurial investment planning, is determined.

Interest is the price paid or the reward received for lending. It is paid in order to induce people to part with assets which are immediately usable for purchasing goods and services of any description. Such liquid assets which can be converted without risk, trouble or loss of time into other goods are cash and bank deposits, in short, money. The rate of interest is therefore the price which equates the public's desire to hold assets in the form of money (i.e. their unwillingness to lend money) with the quantity of money available; it balances, in other words, the demand for holding money with the supply of money. What proportion of their wealth people wish to hold in the form of money rather than in other assets is determined by tastes and preferences, which differ from one individual to another and vary according to circumstances. The supply of money is regulated by the Central Bank (an agency outside the market nexus with the status of a public authority) in conjunction with the private banks of the system. Given the desires or 'tastes' of the public for holding money at various prices for lending, the Central Bank will by increasing the supply of money lower the level of interest rates and by decreasing the supply of money raise the level of interest rates. And similarly, if liquidity preferences of the public are changing owing to variations in the volume of transactions or in the state of confidence, the Central Bank (in co-operation with the private banks) can, by satisfying them through changes in the supply of money, keep interest rates at a desired level.

It should be noted, however, that banking policy affects, in the first instance, the various short-term rates of interest, whereas it is the long-term rate which is, as we saw, relevant to investment decisions. The margin between short- and long-term rates varies not only in the short run but also in the longer run. Prospective short-term rates (apart from actual ones) in relation to actual and expected long-term rates, the proportion of long- and short-term assets held, the inconveniences and costs of holding different types of assets and similar factors (such as rates of taxation) are taken into account by people in allocating their funds between long- and short-term assets.[1] The relationship between short and long rates of interest is influenced by these different factors, which on balance keep the long-term rate steadier than the short-term rate and the former always above the latter. The higher the level of the long-term rate of interest thus determined, the

[1] For a discussion of these factors see M. Kalecki, *Studies in Economic Dynamics*, Essay No. 2, 'The Short-Term and the Long-Term Rate of Interest.'

less far—other things being equal—will firms push investment along a given schedule of marginal prospective profits.

3. *Borrower's Risk*

But interest rates are—as already mentioned—not the only factor which limits investment plans at any given moment. Business men will also take into account the effect of investment schemes of different sizes on their 'financial status'; for bigger schemes mean bigger commitments. A small increase they may be able to finance out of their own capital and reserves. Larger increases they must meet by incurring debts. The more a firm borrows, however, the greater will be the risk to the earning power of its own capital and the greater therefore the deterrent to increase its investment plans. Business men seem to regard a certain ratio of total capital to 'own capital' (share capital plus reserves) as desirable or safe and to require an increasing premium to deviate more and more from what they regard as an appropriate ratio. The growing reluctance of entrepreneurs to incur debts out of proportion to the firm's own capital for financing bigger and bigger investment schemes means that the marginal risk is rising as investment plans increase ('borrower's risk').

4. *Lender's Risk*

Even if entrepreneurs were not constrained by such financial risks to limit their investment plans, they would find that the capital market or potential lenders impose the limit. In order to avoid the risk of growing indebtedness firms may attempt to raise their own capital by issuing shares. However, as the size of share issues for any particular firm increases, the selling price of new shares must (assuming conditions of imperfect competition in the capital market) be lowered. This will make the scaling up of investment schemes progressively more expensive to the firm and thus set a limit to its attempts at increasing its dividend capital. The amount which a firm can borrow for increasing its fixed capital in the form of debentures and preference shares is similarly restricted by the growing unwillingness of potential lenders to put more eggs into one basket. The increasing risk premium demanded by the capital market or the lender as the size of the bond or share issue placed on the market by an individual firm at a given time increases, we may call the 'lender's risk.'

The four factors influencing entrepreneurial investment decisions which we have discussed so far, can be combined in one schedule. The figure below shows the relation of the four factors. If investment plans are OM, the expected marginal profit is MP and the marginal borrower's risk is PB. The rate of interest is MR and the lender's

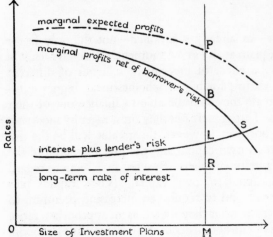

risk RL. In deciding about the size of the investment an entrepreneur will compare the expected profits net of borrower's risk, i.e. $MP - PB = MB$, with the rate of interest plus the lender's risk premium, i.e. $MR + RL = ML$. As long as MB is greater than ML it will pay the entrepreneur to increase his investment plans. Expected net profits will be maximized if they are at any given moment adjusted in such a way that the expected marginal rate of profit minus the marginal rate of borrower's risk is equal to the rate of interest plus the appropriate lender's risk, i.e. at the point S in the diagram.

5. *The Process of Re-investment*

Assuming that the schedules of expected profits and rates of interest remain unchanged and that the investment decisions indicated by the position of the four determinants have been taken, does it follow that all investment decisions are then exhausted and that investment activity will come to an end? Obviously not. Some forces must operate which induce entrepreneurs to go on investing. This incentive is provided by the depreciation allowances and profits accruing to entrepreneurs out of current sales. These savings become currently available and by re-investing them partly or wholly, entrepreneurs do not increase their indebtedness and do not, therefore, incur increasing risk. The inflow of funds available to firms for investment purposes will, during any given short period, tend to lower the marginal risk (borrower's risk) and not involve a lender's risk and thus provide the incentive for new investment decisions. Firms will tend to re-invest their own gross savings partly or wholly at any given level of demand or income; though they will have—other things being equal—no incentive to plan investment which implies either an increasing borrower's or lender's risk. The inflow of savings into firms thus explains the continuation of investment when other demand and supply factors are not changing and establishes a relation between the rate of investment and the level of income.

6. *The State of Demand*

Let us now consider how changes of economic data affect the investment plans of entrepreneurs. It is evident that while such changes take place the rate of investment decisions will be altered. If, for instance, the rate of profit increases during a period, the rate of investment decisions will be higher. At first sight it seems that this impact effect will wear out when the rate of profit ceases to rise. It will have, however, some more lasting effects due to the partial re-investment of savings earned by firms or entrepreneurs owing to the temporarily higher rate of investment. We shall first consider the 'impact effect' of various changes and introduce the 'lasting effect' later.

The impact effect will in all cases work by altering profit expectations. Business men seem to be agreed that what they call the 'state of demand' or 'expected changes in demand' are by far the most important factors in their investment decisions. The dependence of the latter on changes of demand is usually formulated as the 'acceleration principle' which makes the rate of investment decisions a function of the rate of change of demand. If, for instance, demand rises at a steady rate investment decisions will be made at a constant rate; if the expansion of demand slows down the rate of investment decisions will decline; and if there is an absolute fall in demand investment will be 'negative,' there will be disinvestment. In the strict form the acceleration principle does not describe accurately the observed facts.[1] It could be modified by taking into account the degree of utilization of equipment. When unused capacities are small and employment is at a high level, small variations in the rate of change of demand may produce a higher rate of investment decisions than the same variations in demand induce when there are large unused capacities and employment is correspondingly low. In this case the influence of the acceleration principle would be retarded at low levels of employment and reinforced at high levels.

In our model the impact effect of changes in demand would be expressed in upward and downward shifts of the marginal profit schedule, the rate of shift indicating changes in the level of investment decisions in response to changes in demand.

[1] See Tinbergen, 'Critical Remarks about some Business Cycle Theories,' *Econometrica*, April 1942; and M. Ezekiel, 'Savings, Consumption, and Investment,' *American Economic Review*, March, June 1942.

7. The State of Supply

In analogy to the 'state of demand' one could also speak of the influence of the 'state of supply' on investment decisions. Two factors may be listed on the supply side. Firstly, innovations in technique or organization increase the expected profitability of a given dose of investment and thus make for bigger investment decisions than would otherwise have been taken. Secondly, variations in the volume of equipment in excess of changes in demand alter profits and hence profit expectations. If the volume of equipment rises while the national income remains constant, profits per unit of equipment will evidently fall, because the additional equipment competes with the old equipment for the same market. Similarly, if the volume of equipment rises more quickly (slowly) than demand, profit rates will tend to fall (rise). The operation of these two factors can also be represented by shifts in the marginal profit schedule.

8. Psychological Factors

Finally, we must include in the list of factors influencing the rate of investment decisions, changes in the long-term rate of interest and changes in risk rates (due, say, to optimism or pessimism). It is obvious that lowering (raising) of risk schedules and of interest rates will increase (decrease) investment plans.

Now let us return to the distinction between the 'impact effect' and the 'lasting effect.' A change of any of the above factors increases or decreases the rate of investment decisions. The additional investment actually undertaken creates, however, additional savings which will partly accrue to entrepreneurs and tend to reduce their degree of indebtedness. Entrepreneurs will respond to this tendency of a falling marginal risk by re-investing these additional savings partly or fully. Re-investment implies, however, that the level of investment (and hence of income) will remain higher after, say, a rise in demand or a reduction of the rate of interest, than it was before. An upward shift of the marginal profit schedule causes thus not only a temporarily higher rate of investment during the transition from a lower to a higher level of expected profits but also a certain more lasting increase. How long the effect will last will depend on the degree to which savings are reinvested. As savings are a function of income the connection between the *rate* of investment and the *level* of income becomes apparent again.

DEMAND DEFICIENCY AND EMPLOYMENT POLICY

Private Investment and the Level of Employment

Our list of the inducements and deterrents to invest may be incomplete and the interaction of the dominant factors may be more complex than we presented them. But even the brief survey given above seems to make it plausible that it is at least not self-evident that numerous independent units, each weighing up many uncertain factors relevant to their investment planning and finally deciding the size of their investment plans, should always tend to reach decisions which in the aggregate are just sufficient to provide that primary employment which generates full employment.

Moreover, investment decisions, made by one section of the community, are governed by the complex considerations of profitability outlined above; decisions to save, made by another section of the community, are determined by quite different factors such as saving habits and the distribution and level of incomes. There are no *a priori* reasons to assume that these two sets of decisions will always balance so as to maintain an existing level of employment and even less that they will balance at or near the full employment level. This is true even if we interpret the relationships in terms of static theory and abstract from time sequences. In this interpretation an inequality between the wish to save and the wish to invest generates changes in total demand and employment. When investment decisions exceed (fall short of) what people wish to save out of their present income, employment and income will rise (fall) until equality between the rate of investment decisions and the rate of planned savings out of higher (lower) incomes is established. The market decisions of savers and investors may thus lead to a temporary or lasting deficiency of demand and corresponding under-employment or by chance to full employment. In this interpretation full employment becomes one of many equilibrium positions at which the system may come to rest and loses its distinction of the equilibrium position *par excellence* to which the system automatically moves.

But such a static interpretation is highly unrealistic, because it neglects the interdependence of economic events in the process of time. As we saw in the description of the factors which influence investment activity, changes in data will alter entrepreneurial profit expectations and hence lead to a revision of investment plans. These revised decisions will tend to produce further changes in data, which in turn will influence profit expectations. Thus to-day's data, which are the result of yesterday's decisions, will evoke new reactions and thus determine to-morrow's data. This chain of time-linked actions and reactions gives a realistic picture of the economic process. If, however, any given change will start further changes it becomes possible that the system will never come to rest at any particular level, or that it develops, under certain conditions, periodic fluctuations. The cyclical variations which we observe are then explained by the complex interaction and time sequence of investment decisions governed by a multitude of past, present and expected events, which (as explained previously) form the basis of enterpreneurial profit expectations, and of saving or consumption decisions depending mainly on changes in the level and distribution of income. Whether such variations will be less or more violent and whether they will occur around a high or low level of employment, depends again upon the quantitative and time relationship between the propensity to save and the inducements to invest. When average incomes are fairly high, as in industrial countries, and the income distribution is fairly unequal, the tendency to save at moderately high levels of employment may tend to outstrip private investment decisions based on the 'state of demand' and thus prevent the market economy from ever reaching anything like full employment. The market forces as such do not, therefore, tend to push employment to full capacity level; they tend even less to maintain it there. The link which would permanently keep planned savings low enough and investment decisions high enough to prevent total demand from being deficient in giving employment to all labour seeking work is missing in capitalist societies. The recognition that the free play of the market, that business left to itself, cannot be relied upon to produce and to maintain full utilization of the available labour represents a revolution in economic thought and has very far-reaching implications indeed.

For if the balance of decisions of the numerous free and independent economic units playing upon the market is more likely than not to produce unemployment, the very justification for *laisser-faire* and liberalism in the economic field, namely that—taken all in all—this would produce the greatest welfare for all and the most rational use of resources, goes by the board. The liberal concept of the relation of State and industry becomes obsolete, not because social considerations demand some State action to protect or assist this or that social group against the result of the market forces (such concessions do not invalidate the principle); its very essence becomes obsolete if its claim that free play and abstinence from State interference produce optimum utilization of resources is disproved, and cannot serve any more as a criterion of policy.

To provide the missing link between desire to save and offsetting spending which makes the economy utilize the available labour fully, becomes, in principle, simple once we include the revenue and expenditure policy of the public authorities which we have so far disregarded in our considerations.

Government Finance and the Level of Employment

State finance differs from private finance both on the income side and on the expenditure side. The State derives its income not from offering goods or services for sale but by imposing taxation on the members of the community; the planned size of State revenue is determined by the needs of the community as interpreted by the government of the day. The State (meaning here the local as well as the central public authorities) may, like any other economic agency, decide to save, to spend less than the revenue (the case of a budget surplus) or to spend just the revenue (to balance the budget) or to spend in excess of the revenue by borrowing (to run a budget deficit). The effects of the three policies are, given the structure of taxation, the same as similar behaviour of firms or private individuals. A budget surplus will— *ceteris paribus*—depress income and employment; a balanced budget will neither add to nor detract from total demand; and a budget deficit, like private loan expenditure, will tend to raise the level of employment. It is obvious that these budgetary policies can be used to counterbalance variations of employment in the private sector; a tendency to over-employment could be met by aiming at a budget surplus; underemployment could be met by deficit spending.

The State possesses, however, another tool for forging employment policy: alterations in the structure of taxation with the aim of influencing the community's desire to save or to invest. By lifting taxes off the lower income groups with a high propensity to consume, and shifting taxes on to the high income groups (inclusive of undistributed profits) with a high propensity to save, the community's propensity to consume is increased; effective demand and employment are stimulated, provided the extra taxes on high incomes are designed in such a way as not to reduce the inducement to invest. Ideally speaking, taxation could be so adjusted that the private sector of the community wishes to save out of its net income (i.e. incomes after taxation) just the amount required to make the additions to the capital stock needed for the increase in the population and in technical progress in a fully employed economy. Provided these investments are undertaken by the private sector (and that may not come about automatically in all circumstances), such redistributive taxation will secure full employment without resort to deficit finance. It is obvious that an inflationary situation can also be brought under control by an appropriate modification of the tax system. Public finance provides thus two types of employment regulators which may be used singly or together: (a) deficit and surplus finance, and (b) redistributive taxation.

A variety of policies is thus open to the State, and tools are available which are powerful enough to control the level of demand and the utilization of the labour force. If full employment is to be secured, the State must take on the positive economic function of regulating the level of demand by appropriate financial policies and/or by other measures. The regulation of the economic process by market forces, incapable of maintaining steady full employment, must be supplemented by conscious and deliberate regulation of public authorities. Such deliberate public decisions in economic matters are often regarded as arbitrary, and contrasted with the 'natural,' 'non-arbitrary' results of the free interplay of economic units. This distinction can only be maintained as long as the laws of supply and demand, producing, say, unemployment or a distribution of goods according to ability to pay, is regarded as non-arbitrary. From a formal point of view the market acts as arbitrarily as a public agency; the former s anonymity hides individual responsibility for failures in the working of the system, the latter puts the issues before the public and places the responsibility squarely on the policy-making institutions and persons. In a way this is not new. State finance and expenditure have always been determined by public decisions. What is likely to be new, are the guiding principles and contents of such decisions and the need to supplement or to replace in some cases global (indirect) controls by specific (direct) controls.

The aim of State finance undergoes a fundamental change when it is directed towards securing full employment. The guiding principle in the past of balancing revenue and expenditure, thus (as might be thought) neither adding to nor taking away from total market demand, will be replaced by the criterion of maintaining full employment by adjusting saving and offsetting spending through fiscal methods of taxation and borrowing, or, failing that, by direct controls. Any deficiency of demand resulting from market decisions can be remedied either by increasing the propensity to consume and decreasing the propensity to save by taxing the savers (high income groups), or by increasing offsetting spending, that is by deficit spending. By spending in excess of revenue total demand is increased and, as argued above, by a multiple of the loan expenditure. This is true whether deficit spending is used for stimulating consumption or for expenditure on public investment.

These principles of State finance for full employment are a startling and paradoxical reversal of the principles of sound business and personal finance. To live beyond one's means or to borrow for consumption is likely to ruin the individual: why should the same behaviour which is unwise from a private point of view be beneficial and wholesome when the State is following it? The State can act differently from private business because it acts as the agent of the community as a whole and what it spends accrues to the community (disregarding leakages abroad); no single individual nor a monopoly can act like this because only part of the extra expenditure flows back as income to the individual business.[1] Secondly, the State need not pay attention to 'profitability' or to business codes of capital and revenue. As the Central Bank 'conditions' the state of liquidity, so State finance 'conditions' profitability by raising or maintaining effective demand. It does so by stimulating consumer goods demand and output directly (and hence capital goods industries indirectly), or by public works or assistance to private investment, thus fostering capital goods output directly and consumer goods demand and production indirectly. How deficit spending is divided between public works and assistance to private consumption may be decided by social preferences; a programme of 'butter instead of guns' produces full employment as well as a policy of 'guns and butter' or of 'guns instead of butter.' There will be cases (see below) where part of the deficit spending can usefully be diverted to increase industrial efficiency or to expand productive capacity, but over and above this the community is free to choose the direction of spending according to tastes and preferences. Moreover, the size of the deficit necessary to produce full employment is determined only when other things, such as the distribution of incomes, the system of taxation, etc., are taken as given. There again the community has the choice of altering by an appropriate public policy the distribution of incomes through taxation or by other means, thus reducing or eliminating the need for State borrowing.

Once it is realized that full employment can be maintained by different policies, the choice between which and the combination of which is largely a matter of social and political preference, it becomes

[1] It is true that only part of the deficit spending will flow back into the exchequer by way of increased tax revenue; but the remainder accrues to the business community and thus cannot be said to be lost or wasted.

obvious that attempts to delegate all or part of these decisions to
technical, functional bodies or institutions implicitly restrict the
choice of ends and means and underestimate the socio-political
importance of the interdependent public decisions to be taken to maintain full employment. How much and what kind of taxation the
community is to have and hence how much deficit spending will be
needed, and how the deficit shall be divided between stimulating consumption, public works, and other uses, and how with this internal
policy the country's external economic relations shall be adjusted—
this set of interdependent decisions is not made easier, but is prejudiced,
by counselling a 'capital budget' for deficit spending and a 'national
investment board' for planning and partly executing spending on
capital goods and so forth. Devolution and departmental specialization are inevitable in planning and execution, but it is important that
no agencies be set up which tend to narrow the choice or to obscure
the interdependence of the fiscal and regulative decisions taken to
maintain full employment.

Direct and Indirect Controls

This is important also because in maintaining full employment
specific and direct controls may in certain conditions be more useful
than global indirect controls, as is argued in the following studies.
Instead of lowering interest rates it may be preferable to subsidize
specific investments, or for the State to undertake investment in the
private sector; instead of global devaluation as a means of restoring
external balance it may be preferable to use import restrictions and
export premia for specific goods; it may be useful to apply price and
quality control to some group goods and to leave others uncontrolled,
or to subsidize goods in certain uses or for certain income groups and
not in others. These specific controls raise in a more acute form the
question of the arbitrariness of public decisions. It is frequently asserted
that global, indirect controls such as taxation, tariffs, devaluation, etc.,
act indiscriminately while specific controls are discriminatory inside
and/or outside the national economy and lend themselves more easily
to abuse. Take the case of import quotas *versus* tariffs, and assume
that imports of certain luxuries are to be limited because full employment has caused a shortage of foreign exchange. Tariffs would restrict
the quantity imported (the restrictive effect depending mainly upon
the elasticities of home demand and foreign supply) and would allow
domestic sales to be left to the usual market channels where they would
go to the highest bidder. Quotas may or may not discriminate against

various suppliers, as compared with tariffs having the same restrictive effect; but quotas set precise quantitative limits, possibly an upper and a lower limit, irrespective of supply elasticities abroad. The quota amount may be disposed of through market channels to the highest bidder as in the case of tariffs, or may be 'allocated' by specific controls to particular firms and/or to particular users (hospitals, children, etc.). Both the import quota and its internal allocation may be described as discriminatory, if the results of global controls such as tariffs and price bidding are taken by definition as non-discriminatory. But in our illustration it could obviously be argued that tariffs and the market discriminate against 'necessities' and a case could be made out against market discrimination according to capacity to pay and for discrimination by specific control. The same applies to a temporary shortage of an imported raw material, say cotton or timber, which the market would resolve by raising prices and allocating according to the highest price offer. In a full employment economy the responsible authorities may permit the sectional price rise and the accompanying speculative disturbances; they may, however, prefer to avoid price increases in the interest of price and wage stability and allocate according to other priorities, offering substitutes for 'socially less important' uses. To permit or not to permit price bidding as a means of allocating bottleneck supplies implies a public decision and there are no *a priori* reasons why market discriminations against those least able to pay should be regarded as a more objective criterion than discriminations consciously chosen by the community against certain uses or users.

The argument for global controls is not that their results are more objective or better, but that they are administratively handier, that they give more freedom to the individual in finding his own adjustment, that they are less open to administrative abuse. For this reason the studies in this book give preference to global (financial) methods of regulating full employment wherever this gives reasonably good results, and add specific controls as an alternative only where they offer particular advantages over the indirect methods.

This attitude is in conformity with the general assumption underlying this book of a market economy based on private ownership of the means of production with the profit motive as a driving force and competition of a more or less monopolistic character, which suffers from periodic and general under-employment. The problem we put ourselves was to investigate the conditions which must be fulfilled to make such a system run smoothly at a full employment level, on the assumption that the essentials of the capitalist system were to be preserved as far as possible and 'direct controls' kept to a minimum.

These assumptions must not be interpreted as apologetic or prophetic ones. They do not imply that capitalism with full employment represents the best of all worlds. Socialism may be a superior system but that is not the subject of our study, which merely shows under what conditions and by what policies capitalism can be made to work without unemployment. Nor should it be concluded that, because it has been shown how a capitalist economy can be maintained at full employment, any given country's economy will in the end be organized along these lines.

PART II

THREE WAYS TO FULL EMPLOYMENT

by M. Kalecki

THE purpose of this paper is to discuss the methods of achieving and maintaining full employment in a capitalist society. We shall consider throughout a closed economic system. This does not mean that we neglect the problems of foreign trade in the discussion of full employment, which present perhaps the greatest *practical* difficulties. They will be dealt with in a separate study. Here, however, we abstract from them in order to make clear the fundamental *theoretical* problems of full employment. Similarly we abstract from the question of mobility of labour, which again is examined in a special article. For the present it may be assumed that working time is variable within certain limits, which provides a sufficient elasticity in labour supply in the short period, while in the longer period one may rely on re-training of labour to restore equilibrium when the structure of demand changes.

First and foremost we shall deal in this article with the generation of effective demand adequate to secure and maintain full employment. Secondly we shall have to consider the problem of private investment in such a system in the short period and in the long run.

As the title indicates, we shall distinguish three ways to achieve and maintain full employment:

1. By Government spending on public investment (e.g. schools, hospitals, highways, etc.), or on subsidies to mass consumption (family allowances, reduction of indirect taxation, subsidies to keep down the prices of necessities)—provided that this spending is financed by borrowing. We shall call this method shortly Deficit Spending.

2. By stimulating private investment (through a reduction in the rate of interest, lowering of income tax or other measures assisting private investment).

3. By redistribution of income from higher to lower income classes.

We shall argue that the second method, i.e. stimulating private investment, is not satisfactory, but that both the first method and the third method provide adequate means to maintain full employment.

39

I. DEFICIT SPENDING

Deficit Spending generates effective demand in the following way. The Government undertakes public investment which does not compete with private enterprise (e.g. it builds schools, highways, hospitals and so on), or it subsidizes mass consumption (by paying family allowances, reducing indirect taxation or paying subsidies to keep down prices of necessities). This expenditure is financed by borrowing, and therefore does not involve curtailing private investment (provided the rate of interest is kept constant) or non-subsidized consumption and thus creates an additional effective demand.

It should be noted that the rise in incomes causes after some time an increase in the tax revenue so that the final Budget deficit is lower than the increase in Government expenditure.

The fundamental questions related to creating employment by deficit spending have been widely discussed in recent years. Nevertheless it seems useful to restate the main points of the discussion. These points are: (1) Where does the money come from? (2) Will such a policy not inevitably raise the rate of interest and thus affect adversely private investment? (3) If the rate of interest does not increase, will deficit spending not create inflation? (4) If the Budget deficit is a permanent feature: how can the burden of the increasing National Debt be tackled?

FUNDAMENTAL PROBLEMS

Where does the money come from?

Although it has been repeatedly stated in recent discussions that the Budget deficit always finances itself—that is to say, its rise always causes such an increase in incomes and changes in their distribution that there accrue just enough savings to finance it—the matter is still frequently misunderstood. We shall therefore demonstrate this fundamental theorem in the Budget deficit theory by means of a diagram. The left hand column on the diagram represents the national expenditure, i.e. the sum of Government expenditure, private expenditure on investment for replacement and expansion of capital (all purchases of new fixed capital *plus* changes in working capital and stocks), and expenditure on personal consumption. It is easy to see that in a closed economy in a given period this expenditure must be equal to the sum of wages, salaries, profits[1] (gross of depreciation) and indirect taxation. For the price of any object bought will be fully accounted for by these four items. Therefore the column on the right representing the sum of

[1] Inclusive of rent and interest.

these four items for the economy as a whole is equal to the column on the left representing the national expenditure. The right hand column is divided according to the use which is made of incomes. There is first taxation, both indirect and direct, paid by firms and individuals; next there is personal consumption; and the residual is saving gross of depreciation. For, if from the aggregate gross income plus indirect taxation we deduct all taxation and personal consumption, the remainder is saving gross of depreciation. The shaded area in the left hand column represents the excess of Government expenditure over taxation, i.e. the Budget deficit, and it follows directly from the consideration of the diagram that Budget deficit plus gross private

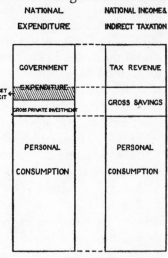

investment equals gross savings.[1] If we deduct from both sides of this equation depreciation, we see that the relation holds good if we substitute net savings for gross savings and net investment for gross investment. In other words, net savings are always equal to Budget deficit plus net investment: whatever is the general economic situation, whatever the level of prices, wages or the rate of interest, any level of private investment and Budget deficit will always produce an equal amount of saving to finance these two items. Thus the question how it is possible to increase Government expenditure if the expenditure on private investment and personal consumption is cut, is answered by the fact that there will always be such an increase in incomes as to create an increase in savings equal to the increase in the Budget deficit.

The Rate of Interest

Is it, however, not wrong to assume that private investment will remain unimpaired when the Budget deficit increases? Will not the rise in the Budget deficit force up the rate of interest so much that investment will be reduced by just as much as the Budget deficit is increased, thus offsetting the stimulating effect of Government expendi-

---

[1] We have tacitly abstracted in the above argument from transfers, i.e. Government expenditure on doles, pensions, interest on the National Debt, etc. But the argument holds good if we include transfers both in the national expenditure (as a part of Government expenditure) and in the national income (alongside wages, salaries, and profits).

ture on employment? The answer is that the rate of interest may be maintained at a stable level however large the Budget deficit, given a proper banking policy. The rate of interest will tend to rise if the public do not absorb the Government securities, by the sale of which the deficit is financed, but prefer to invest their savings in bank deposits. And if the banks, lacking a sufficient cash basis (notes and accounts in the Central Bank), do not expand their deposits and buy Government securities instead of the public, then indeed the rate of interest must rise sufficiently to induce the public to invest their savings in Government securities. If, however, the Central Bank expands the cash basis of the private banks to enable them to expand sufficiently their deposits, while maintaining the prescribed cash ratio, no tendency for a rise in the rate of interest will appear.

We have considered so far the rate of interest in general. The actual position is a little more complicated because we must distinguish between the rate on short-term and long-term assets. Even if the banks expand their deposits sufficiently to satisfy the demand of the public at a given level of the short-term rate of interest, they may absorb short-term assets while the Government is issuing long-term bonds. The long-term rate would then rise in relation to the short-term rate to such an extent that the public is prepared to absorb the bonds issued currently by the Government. This, however, may be dealt with easily by an appropriate issue policy of the Government. A good example is provided by the policy of the British Government during this war. The Government has long- and medium-term bonds, bearing $2\frac{1}{2}$ to 3 per cent interest, on tap. The public buy out of their savings as many of these bonds as they choose and the rest of the deficit is covered by an increase in floating debt, i.e. by the issue of short-term securities. In this way both the long-term and the short-term rate of interest are kept constant (the constancy of the latter is, of course, based on the policy of the Bank of England). The same method of keeping interest rates constant can be followed in peace-time. There is nothing peculiar in the war-time situation which makes this method easier than where a Budget deficit is used for financing public investment or subsidizing mass consumption. We may thus conclude that, provided the Central Bank expands the cash basis of the private banks according to the demand for bank deposits, and that the Government issues long- and medium-term bonds on tap, both the short-term and the long-term rates of interest may be stabilized whatever the rate of the Budget deficit.

The Danger of Inflation

If the rate of interest is kept constant, will not the increasing Budget deficit cause inflation, i.e. a vicious spiral of prices and wages? The reply is that inflation will result only if effective demand increases so much that a general scarcity of labour or equipment (or both) arises. Up to a point the short-period supply curves are horizontal or mildly rising for most commodities. But, when effective demand increases significantly beyond this point, the steeply upward sloping parts of the short-period supply curves become relevant. As a result there is a general increase in prices out of proportion with average prime costs, and in this way the vicious spiral of prices and wages is started. In order to avoid inflation the Government must, therefore, be careful not to push their deficit spending beyond the mark indicated by full utilization of labour and equipment.

It is thus evident that a prerequisite of full employment is a proper relation between existing equipment and available labour. The volume of equipment must be adequate to employ the available labour and still allow for reserve capacities. If the maximum capacity of equipment is inadequate to absorb the available labour, as will be the case in backward countries, the immediate achievement of full employment is clearly hopeless. If the reserve capacities are non-existent or insufficient the attempt to secure full employment in the short run may easily lead to inflationary tendencies in large sections of the economy because the structure of equipment does not necessarily match the structure of demand. And even if the structure of equipment *is* matched with that of full employment demand in the initial position the deficiency of reserves will cause trouble when shifts in demand occur subsequently.

In an economy where plant is scarce it is thus necessary to have a period of industrialization or reconstruction during which the existing equipment is expanded at a rather high rate. In this period it may be necessary to have controls not unlike those used in war-time. Only after the process of capital expansion has proceeded sufficiently far is a policy of full employment of the kind described above possible.

Another phenomenon may still arise in full employment which, although it is not inflation in the above sense, resulting from the disproportion between demand for and supply of consumption goods, may cause a continuous increase in prices. In a state of full employment the bargaining power of trade unions will be very strongly enhanced. Thus there may be a spontaneous tendency for money wage rates to increase which leads to a rise in prices and the cost of living; this in turn leads to a secondary rise in wages and so on.

In so far as the rise in wage rates is equal to the increase in productivity of labour the problem of the 'vicious spiral' does not arise, because wage costs per unit of output will remain stable and thus there will be no reason for a rise in prices. If, however, wage rates increase more than the productivity of labour, arrangements must be made to prevent prices running away. If no such steps are taken the workers as a whole do not benefit; for the increase in money wage rates will be offset by the consequent rise in prices. In addition, a quick upward movement of prices will be a disturbing feature in an economy of full employment. How money wages can be raised without causing a rise in prices is outlined in the section on 'Redistribution of Income' (pp. 55-7). For the present it is sufficient to mention that a rise in real wage rates, greater than an accompanying rise in productivity, in an economy of full employment must involve a curtailment of investment or consumption of non-wage earners. For otherwise the aggregate demand would exceed the aggregate supply and thus either prices *would* finally rise, or if prices are controlled, shortages and haphazard distribution would ensue.

The Burden of the Debt

If full employment is maintained by deficit spending, the National Debt will expand continuously, and the 'burden' of interest upon it will tend to rise. Will not this increasing 'burden' set a limit to deficit spending as a means to full employment? It may be well to begin by clearing up two popular misconceptions concerning the 'burden' of the Debt.

In the first place interest on an increasing National Debt (as indeed on all the Debt) cannot be a burden to society as a whole because in essence it constitutes an internal transfer. Secondly, in an expanding economy this transfer need not necessarily rise out of proportion with the tax revenue at existing rate of taxes. The standard rate of income tax necessary to finance the increasing amount of interest on the National Debt need not rise if the rate of expansion of the national income is sufficiently high, as a result of the increase in working population and technical progress. However, even if we abstract from this factor, it is fairly easy to devise a system of taxation to service the Debt which will not involve any disturbances in output and employment.

Imagine, for instance, that the interest on the National Debt is financed by an annual capital tax, levied on firms and person (shares and debentures being excluded from the valuation of wealth to avoid a double taxation of the capital of firms). The current income after payment of capital tax of some capitalists will be lower, and of some higher, than if the interest on the National Debt had not increased. But their aggregate income will remain unaltered, and their aggregate consumption will not be likely to change significantly. Further, the profitability of investment is not affected by a capital tax because it is paid on any type of wealth. Whether an amount is held in cash or Government securities or is invested in building a factory, the same capital tax is paid on it, and thus the comparative advantage is unchanged. And if investment is financed by borrowing its profitability is clearly not affected by a capital tax, because borrowing does not mean an increase in wealth of the investing entrepreneur. Thus neither capitalists' consumption nor the profitability of investment is affected by the rise in the National Debt, if interest on it is financed by an annual capital tax.

We shall now consider the order of magnitude of such a tax. If we imagine that the tax is imposed to finance the interest on the National Debt incurred after a certain fixed date (the interest on the 'old debt' being already accounted for in the Budget), the relevant average interest on the National Debt may be assumed to be in Great Britain about 2 per cent. This is approximately the present average cost of (short-term and long-term) borrowing and there is no reason to assume that it would increase in future.[1] The rate of the annual capital tax will thus be substantially lower than 2 per cent, because the tax to finance the interest on the 'extra debt' will be collected from all types of privately owned capital, of which the 'extra debt' constitutes only one item. If, for instance, this 'extra debt' were to rise to one half of all privately owned assets the annual capital tax would amount to 1 per cent.[2]

As an alternative to a capital tax, it is possible to devise a modified income tax, the influence of which upon the national economy as a whole would be more or less equivalent to that of a capital tax. Income

[1] The Government can continue to have on tap long-term and medium-term issues and finance the rest by floating debt (cf. p. 42). It is true that the cost of borrowing will increase if sales of long- and medium-term issues rise in proportion to the Budget deficit, but then nothing prevents the Government from reducing the rate of interest on these issues.
[2] The above argument still requires some elucidation. It seems reasonable to deduct the capital tax from income before income tax is paid. For instance, if an asset yields 4 per cent and the capital tax is 1 per cent, the income of 3 and not 4 per cent would be subject to income tax. This causes, of course, a certain reduction in the average yield of income tax, but this is offset by the income tax yielded by the interest on the National Debt. If the National Debt increases, the national income being constant, and the interest on National Debt is financed by a capital tax, the aggregate yield of income tax is unchanged. It is true that it is being reduced by the increasing amount of capital tax, but it is being *pro tanto* raised by the increasing interest on National Debt.

tax, as opposed to a capital tax, reduces the net rate of profit, thus weakening the inducement to invest. The following modification may remove this adverse effect. Imagine that income tax is charged on gross income, i.e. before deduction of wear and tear. On the other hand all investment in fixed capital, whether for the sake of replacement or expansion, is deducted from the taxable amount. (If it exceeds the taxable income the excess is carried over for deduction in subsequent years.) It is easy to show that such a tax does not affect the rate of profit expected on new investment. Indeed, suppose that an entrepreneur expects for each £100 invested in fixed capital a gross profit of £10 per annum. One shilling in the £ of income tax reduces this expected profit to £9½ per annum. But by investing £100 the entrepreneur gets a £5 reduction in his current income tax and thus the cost of investment is reduced to £95. Consequently the expected gross rate of profit is the same 10 per cent per annum as if the tax were not in existence.

DEFICIT SPENDING AND INVESTMENT

How Much Private Investment?

Having considered the possible objections to achieving lasting full employment by deficit spending, we shall now examine in more detail the functioning of such a system. Its principle is that the Government increases expenditure on public investment and subsidies to mass consumption, without changing the tax rates, up to a point where the effective demand created directly and indirectly by this spending (through the rising incomes) establishes full employment. Given that the Government keeps employment at this level, what will happen to private investment? Firstly, will private investment remain subject to cyclical changes? Secondly, what should be the 'equilibrium' level of private investment?

It is evident that the development of private investment under a regime of full employment will be steady. Violent cyclical fluctuations of investment under *laisser-faire* are due to violent fluctuations in profits.[1] In full employment, however, output and profits will show only long-term changes resulting from the increase in population[2] and

---

[1] The causation is actually double-sided: a fall in investment causes a fall in effective demand and profits and this in turn leads to a new decline in investment.

[2] Throughout this paper we refer, for convenience only, to an *increase* in working population. In the event of a decrease occurring the various conclusions arrived at should be modified accordingly.

increasing productivity of labour.[1] There may, of course, be accidental fluctuations in the rate of private investment, for instance as a result of discontinuous technical progress. Such accidental fluctuations can best be neutralized by an appropriate timing of public investment.

The question of the 'equilibrium' *level* of private investment at which we should aim in the regime of full employment requires some preliminary remarks about the concept of the degree of utilization of equipment, by which we mean the ratio of actual output to the maximum capacity of equipment. The degree of utilization must be neither too small nor too great. If it is too small there will be unused capacities which mean waste of productive resources; in the other case the reserves of equipment will be too small to provide sufficient elasticity for adjustments.

Let us imagine now that we start from a position where the degree of utilization of equipment is at what we consider a desirable level. It follows that in the next period we want this degree of utilization to be maintained. But in the next period our full employment output will be higher, on account of the increase in the working population and in productivity of labour (as a result of technical progress). Thus to maintain the degree of utilization of equipment the capacity of the latter must expand proportionately to the increase in working population and productivity of labour. This gives us the clue to what should be the level of private investment. *Private investment must be at a level adequate to expand the capacity of equipment pari passu with the increase in working population and productivity of labour, i.e. proportionately to full employment output.*[2]

In the case of an increase in working population this statement is obvious, but it requires perhaps some explanation in the case of a rise in the productivity of labour. Imagine that an old machine is replaced by a new one requiring less labour to produce a given output. The supply of labour thus increases proportionately to the rise in average productivity, and if full employment is maintained a proportionate expansion in the capacity of equipment is necessary if no increase in the degree of its utilization is to occur.

---

[1] In so far as changes in net profits will result from a deliberate policy of redistribution of income, care will have to be taken to neutralize the negative effect upon investment by appropriate measures (cf. p. 54).

[2] If the working population is decreasing, but the rise in productivity is higher than the decline in population, the resulting full employment output will rise more slowly than the productivity of labour. The capacity of equipment must expand in this case also proportionately to full employment output.

Regulating Private Investment

To establish private investment at the level conforming to the above rule a variety of methods may be used. It is known that a reduction (increase) in the rate of interest causes *ceteris paribus* a rise (fall) of the rate of private investment because it raises (diminishes) the expected net profitability of investment. The same is true of the rate of income tax. Thus when private investment tends to be 'too low' it may be stimulated by a reduction of the rate of interest and the rate of income tax, and conversely.

The operation of either of these methods, however, involves serious difficulties. To bring about an appreciable change in the *long-term* rate of interest—which is relevant for influencing investment—is rather a slow process.[1] Moreover, what is more important, there are limits to the reduction of the long-term rate because (in longer periods) this rate always exceeds the short-term rate by some margin and the short-term rate cannot fall below zero.

Changes in the rate of income tax involve in full employment a redistribution of consumption, and it is inconvenient that the attempt to influence investment should be tied up with it. For instance, the application of this method involves a redistribution of consumption from the lower to higher income classes whenever private investment is to be stimulated.

The best method seems to be to replace a part of the existing income tax by the 'modified income tax,' described on pp. 45-6, which does not affect the net profitability of investment. (Replacing of income tax by a capital tax may be used for this purpose also.) If, for instance, the standard rate of income tax at a given moment is 7s. in the £, we may make 3s. of it subject to the modification. This removes the adverse effect of income tax on the net rate of profit. Thereby we shall leave only 4s. to exert the normal pressure on investment. The larger the shift from the normal to modified income tax, the more will investment be stimulated.

State Enterprise

In addition to stimulating or discouraging private investment direct Government intervention in the sphere of private investment is possible and may be useful.

The curtailment of private investment may be done by direct con-

---

[1] If the reduction of the long-term rate of interest is carried out by means of reducing the short-term rate a considerable time lag is involved. This difficulty may be overcome by large-scale open market operations. However, a quick fall in the long-term rate of interest would have undesirable consequences (cf. p. 113).

rols, for instance by licensing of investment. This will be of special advantage as compared with the 'global' methods described above if investment is much 'too high' (i.e. creates large excess capacities) in a particular sector. On the other hand, if private investment is inadequate, the deficiency may be made good by the Government itself taking a hand in this sphere. State-owned enterprises may be created which will fulfil this task to the extent to which private enterprise is unable to do so. This method is also of particular advantage when the deficiency in private investment has a pronounced sectional character.

A good example is provided by slum clearance. The Authorities withdraw gradually from occupation a certain number of obsolete buildings and raise thereby the level of investment necessary to maintain the housing capacity. They then fill the gap themselves by building new houses instead of stimulating private building activity.

Public Investment versus *Subsidies to Consumption*

The long-run level of the rate of investment in the private sector, discussed above, has an important bearing upon the size of Government expenditure which is required to achieve full employment at the existing tax rates.[1] The Government spending programme must be on such a scale that it will establish full employment in combination with investment adequate to expand productive capacity *pari passu* with the increase in population and productivity of labour.

Let us now consider in turn how the spending programme should be divided between public investment in the strict sense (roads, hospitals, schools, etc.)[2] and subsidies to private consumption. It is frequently maintained that the spending programme should be fully devoted to public investment, and there is no objection to this view from the aspect of generating sufficient effective demand. But the gap to be covered by this Government expenditure may be so large that public investment will soon become entirely, or at least nearly, useless. In such a case it would be absurd to restrict the Government spending programme to public investment when a higher standard of living can be achieved by devoting a part of this spending to increasing consumption. The general principle must be that social priorities should decide the nature of the Government's spending programme. It will have to be decided, for instance, whether it is more important to

---

[1] It should be remembered that only a part of the increase in Government expenditure will be finally financed by borrowing, because a part is covered by the increase in tax revenue resulting from the rise in incomes (cf. p. 40).

[2] Housing, whether carried out by public agencies or by private entrepreneurs we include in the sector of private investment.

provide in a given year more swimming pools or more milk for children. Such decisions may be to a great extent affected by political factors. However, the principle of social priorities will in any case eliminate such projects as building five bridges over one stretch of the river for the mere purpose of providing employment.

It should be added that if investment in the 'private sector' (in which, however, the Government may participate, cf. p. 49) increases, say as a result of slum clearance, the amount of Government spending on 'pure' public investment and subsidizing consumption necessary to achieve full employment will be *pro tanto* reduced.

II. STIMULATING PRIVATE INVESTMENT

The Process and its Consequences

We shall now consider the stimulation of private investment as a way of achieving and maintaining full employment. In this conception private investment is to be stimulated (by one of the methods described above, cf. p. 48) to such a degree that the effective demand caused directly and indirectly (multiplier effect) by it establishes full employment. We have already shown that if full employment is achieved by deficit spending measures to stimulate private investment may be necessary. However, this assistance to private investment did not have the purpose of creating effective demand—this task was fulfilled by the deficit spending—but was necessary to ensure that the level of investment expanded productive capacity proportionately to the long-run increase in full employment output. Now, there is no *a priori* reason for this long run 'equilibrium' rate of investment to be just equal to that rate of investment which is necessary to generate sufficient effective demand to obtain full employment. We have so far assumed that where this latter level is higher—which seems to be a likely case—the difference would be made good by Government loan expenditure. In the conception considered now, the level of private investment is pushed up to the point at which it provides effective demand adequate to secure full employment. It is clear that if this level exceeds that necessary to expand productive capacity proportionately to full employment output there will be a continuous fall in the degree of utilization of equipment and thus a continuous rise in excess capacity. A part of private investment will thus prove abortive.

Moreover, the fall in the degree of utilization of equipment will be reflected in a decline in the rate of profit which will tend to depress private investment. In order to prevent the fall in the rate of investment, which without compensation by Government spending would entail a cumulative slump in output and employment, it is necessary to provide a new stimulus to investment (i.e. to reduce further the rate of interest or income tax, or to replace to an increasing degree the normal income tax by a modified income tax). But after a certain time the trouble will reappear. Another reduction of the rate of interest, or some other measure, will be necessary to stimulate investment. We thus come to the conclusion that to achieve full employment by stimulating private investment only, it may be necessary (if the level of investment creating effective demand is higher than that level of investment which expands equipment *pari passu* with full employment output) to stimulate it in a cumulative way.

The 'Deepening' of Capital

Some economists may object that to push investment beyond the level necessary to expand productive capacity *pari passu* with full employment output will not create excess capacity, but rather lead to more capital being used in relation to labour. And, so they would argue, this will result in an increase in the productivity of labour and consequently in the standard of living.

The idea that the reduction of the rate of interest stimulates the application of more capital per worker is based on the assumption that the planned *output* of the investing entrepreneur is given. On this condition a lower rate of interest makes it profitable to use more capital and less labour. If we assume, however, that the *capital* available to a firm for financing investment is given, the reduction of the rate of interest has no influence on the choice of the method of production when planning investment, because it affects the expected net profits equally whatever the method of production adopted. In fact the actual conditions are probably represented by something intermediate between these two alternatives, because the imperfection of the market for products limits to some extent the planned output and the imperfection of the capital market limits the available capital. Thus the reduction of the rate of interest would, in theory, tend to induce more capital intensive investment, but by no means to such an extent as is frequently assumed. In practice even this influence is doubtful.

The main stimulus to use more capital per worker is provided by new inventions. The advantage offered by them is usually so high that it will be taken whatever (within a wide range) the level of the rate of interest. This explains why factories built in backward countries, where the rate of interest is high, are usually as modern as in old capitalist countries where the rate of interest is much lower. In such conditions it is doubtful whether moderate reductions in the rate of interest will stimulate the application of more capital per worker to any considerable degree.

We have so far assumed that investment is stimulated by the reduction in the rate of interest. However, it has been previously shown (cf. p. 48) that this method is not very effective because the long-term rate of interest changes rather slowly and (what is more important) because it cannot be reduced below a certain limit. For this reason we suggested earlier that a more effective way of assisting private investment would be to reduce the pressure of income tax, in particular by replacing it by a 'modified income tax' or a capital tax (cf. p. 48). It is now easy to see that if investment is stimulated in this way there is no influence upon its capital intensity whatsoever. Indeed, whether the output planned by investing entrepreneurs or the capital available for financing investment is given, the reduction of the income tax pressure will not affect the choice of the type of equipment. For the method of production which yields the highest profit before taxation will also yield the highest profit net of income tax.

We have tried to show above that a reduction of the rate of interest or of the pressure of income tax is not likely to contribute significantly to the 'deepening' of capital. An acceleration of the increase in the productivity of labour can be achieved, however, by subsidizing the modernization of equipment, for instance, by granting cheap credit for projects submitted for the approval of a Government agency. Nor is this the only way to achieve the required modernization. Modern State-owned establishments may be created, in order to force through competition an improvement in the methods of production of private firms. But such activities should not be governed merely by the wish to achieve full employment through investment in the 'private sector.' It is only to the extent that the acceleration of technical change has a social priority over public investment (in the strict sense) and subsidies to consumption that such schemes should be put into operation.

The Deficiencies of the Method

The difficulties encountered in achieving full employment by stimulating private investment reflect the fundamental error of this conception. The proper role of private investment is to provide tools for the production of consumption goods, and not to provide enough work to employ all available labour. There is a close analogy between this problem and the question of public investment *versus* subsidizing consumption in a Government spending programme. Both public and private investment should be carried out only to the extent to which they are considered useful. If the effective demand thus generated fails to provide full employment, the gap should be filled by increasing consumption and not by piling up unwanted public or private capital equipment.

In addition to this fundamental point a technical but important disadvantage of this method should be mentioned. Government spending can never fail to achieve immediately the desired employment effect if it is on a sufficiently large scale, because it generates effective demand directly. The effects of stimuli to private investment depend, however, on the reaction of entrepreneurs, and it is quite possible that when they are in a very pessimistic mood they may not respond even to considerable inducements. This may happen, for instance, if they do not feel confidence in the political situation.

We thus conclude that, both for fundamental and for technical reasons, a policy which attempts to achieve full employment in an industrial country exclusively by stimulating private investment cannot be regarded as satisfactory.

III. REDISTRIBUTION OF INCOME

Redistribution and Effective Demand

Redistribution of income is the third way frequently suggested to achieve full employment. The underlying idea is that when income is shifted from higher to lower income earners total consumption is increased, because the poor have a higher propensity to consume than the rich. If, for instance, we increase the income tax on the rich and at the same time reduce indirect taxation on necessities or semi-necessities to the same extent, or pay an equal amount of family allowances, we increase the average propensity to consume.

The complicating factor which is often left out of consideration is the depressing influence of the rise in income tax upon private investment. We shall take account of this effect in the subsequent argument.

It should be noted that if the proceeds of the increased income tax are used, not for subsidizing private consumption, but for public investment this also increases effective demand, provided private investment is not affected. For while a part of the income affected by the new tax was saved, all proceeds of the tax are spent on investment goods. Thus demand for investment goods increases more than the demand for consumption goods falls.

The Use of the 'Modified' Tax

We start our considerations from the fact that we know in advance what should be the level of private investment in full employment. It must be such as to raise the capacity of capital equipment *pari passu* with the increase in population and in the productivity of labour. It is now easy to see that two conditions must be fulfilled in order that full employment be achieved by the imposition of a higher income tax: (1) Income tax on higher incomes must be fixed at such a level that its stimulus to effective demand, in conjunction with the level of private investment as specified above, produces full employment. (2) In order to maintain private investment at the specified level, either the rate of interest must be fixed sufficiently low, or rather—as this may be difficult —a sufficient part of the income tax must be put on a modified basis (or replaced by a capital tax). Imagine, for instance, that the joint increase in population and productivity of labour is 2.5 per cent per annum. Thus our target in private investment must be such that it expands the capacity of capital equipment by 2.5 per cent per annum. Imagine further that this level of private investment being in existence, an income tax of 10s., out of which 5s. in the £ are put on a modified basis, will establish effective demand adequate to secure full employment. Moreover, the 'modification' of income tax to the extent of 5s. will, let us suppose, allow for the maintenance of private investment at the required level. It is clear that in such a case our problem is solved.

The Limits of Taxation

We see that a sufficiently high income tax provides a workable solution of the full employment problem, on condition that an appropriate part of it is put on a 'modified' basis (or replaced by a capital tax). It should be noted that the amount of Government expenditure necessary to create full employment is *ceteris paribus* higher under the 'income tax system,' as compared with the case where deficit spending is applied. For taxation, as opposed to deficit spending, tends to reduce consumption of the people taxed, and thus stimulates effective demand only to the extent to which it falls upon savings.

The advantage of the 'income tax system' over a 'Budget deficit policy' can be seen in the fact that it not only secures full employment, but at the same time it renders the distribution of incomes (after taxation) more egalitarian. But precisely for this reason, 'full employment through taxation' is likely to encounter a much stronger opposition than a 'Budget deficit policy.' One cannot, therefore, make any definite choice between the Budget deficit and the income tax method. Income tax may be pushed as far as practically possible, but after this has been done, one should not hesitate to have in addition such a Budget deficit as is still required to achieve and maintain full employment.

The Wage Question

The problem of wage increases in excess of the rise in the productivity of labour is, in a fully employed economy, closely connected with the matters discussed in this section.

Imagine that we start from a position where, in addition to the influence of the existing income tax, some Budget deficit is necessary to maintain full employment. Imagine further that an increase in wage rates greater than the rise in productivity of labour has taken place. In order that prices should remain stable subsidies to offset the rise in wage costs are granted. These subsidies are financed by income tax. It is easy to see that there will nevertheless be some increase in consumption. For the consumption of wage earners will increase more than the consumption of high income earners (affected by income tax) will be reduced, because the propensity to consume of the latter is lower than that of the wage earners. In other words: the redistribution of income from higher to lower income classes increases effective demand. On the other hand the supply of consumption goods can be increased in a fully employed economy only at the expense of investment which, however, may be assumed to have been fixed at the level considered necessary for the normal progress of the economy. Thus in order to counteract the tendency of consumption to increase, the new income tax must be higher than is necessary to finance the subsidies alone; and to the extent of this excess the budget deficit will fall. The increase in wages with prices maintained at a constant level will cause a shift from the 'Budget deficit policy' to the 'income tax system.' The increase in income tax must, of course, be accompanied by measures to prevent private investment from being affected.

This discussion shows that wage bargaining is likely to change its character in full employment. It will have to be linked with 'bargaining' for higher income tax on larger incomes and thus will relate the policy of trade unions more closely to general economic policy. We shall see below that this is also true when prices are kept constant not by subsidies but by price control.

The 'Squeezing' of Profit Margins

We have so far considered the redistribution of incomes by taxation. However, it is also possible to redistribute income before taxation by price control. If prices of consumption goods are reduced, while wages remain constant, there will be a shift from real profits to real wages, roughly equivalent to that which would obtain if prices of consumption goods were constant and wages correspondingly increased. Thus such a policy, provided it is accompanied by measures to maintain private investment at an appropriate level, will be as effective as income tax in achieving full employment. Applied, however, as a *general* policy this method will, from the administrative point of view, be inferior to the redistribution of incomes by taxation, which settles the problem at one stroke. On the other hand, if industrial monopolies come under price control there will be ample opportunities for reducing their profit margins, which—as far as it happens in the sector of consumption goods—contributes towards the solution of the problem of full employment. The task left to income tax and Government loan expenditure in securing full employment will then be correspondingly smaller.

Profit margins may be cut not only by price reductions but also by raising wages while prices are kept constant. On p. 55 we considered the problem of wage increases in a fully employed economy and assumed that prices were kept constant by subsidies financed by income tax. An alternative is to keep prices constant by price control. Its disadvantage is that pressure for higher wages is not likely to be restricted to industries where profit margins are relatively high, and therefore to keep prices constant, without subsidizing them, may frequently be difficult. We can imagine, however, a mixture of the two policies, and it is therefore important to see what will be the implications of wage increases with prices kept constant in a fully employed economy.

As in the previous case, where prices were maintained by subsidies financed by income tax, a redistribution of income from higher to lower income groups will take place: wages will rise and profits will fall *pro tanto*. This will tend to increase effective demand and therefore, under full employment, it will be necessary to curtail the consumption out of higher incomes. Thus, in addition to the shift from profits to wages an appropriate income tax must be imposed which will reduce *pro tanto* the budget deficit. There is here a perfect analogy with the alternative case of subsidies offsetting the wage increases. To the shift from payers of income tax (by which the subsidies are financed) to wage earners, there corresponds, in the case now considered, a direct shift from profits to wages. To the *excess* of new income tax over the level necessary to finance subsidies, there corresponds the imposition of income tax in *addition* to price control. In either case the budget deficit is reduced by the amount of 'extra' income tax which has to be imposed in order to offset the effect of redistribution of income upon consumption. The present case also involves linking up trade union bargaining with general economic bargaining. For (*a*) prices must be prevented from rising by price control, although costs have risen; and (*b*) income tax must be imposed in addition.

CONCLUSIONS

Government expenditure on public investment and subsidies to mass consumption, either in the shape of 'deficit spending' or financed by an increase in income tax, is always capable of securing full employment. The expenditure must be larger in the latter case because of the pressure upon the consumption of income tax payers. In practice income tax financed expenditure—which has the advantage not only of securing more employment but also of reducing the inequality in the distribution of incomes (after taxation)—should be pushed as far as politically possible, and, if this is not enough to secure full employment, expenditure should be expanded as much as is necessary by means of borrowing. Cutting profit margins—either in the form of price reduction of consumption goods or wage increases with constant prices—undertaken within the framework of price control will also increase effective demand and thus make the task of Government expenditure to secure full employment easier.

Private investment must be pushed up to the level sufficient to expand the productive capacity of capital equipment *pari passu* with the increase in population and productivity of labour. This may be done by making a part of income tax subject to a modification which eliminates its adverse influence upon net profitability (or by replacing a part of income tax by a capital tax).[1] Moreover, it may be advantageous or

---

[1] We do not, of course, exclude the possibility that the Government may have to keep private investment *down*, by restrictive measures.

even necessary for the Government to take a hand in investment in the private sector (e.g. slum clearance).

Government expenditure on public investment and subsidies to mass consumption (financed by income tax or borrowing) must be such as to create full employment in combination with this level of private investment. The division of Government spending between public investment and subsidizing consumption should be based on the principle of social priorities.

PART III

THE STABILITY AND FLEXIBILITY OF FULL EMPLOYMENT

by G. D. N. Worswick

THE point of departure of this study is that the level of employment can be effectively varied by changes in taxation, in the spending policy of the Government or by other means. In the last decade we have indeed passed through all stages, from the deepest depression to a state of over-employment, where economic stability can only be maintained by instituting rigorous direct controls over the use by entrepreneurs of labour, materials, equipment and factory space. Not only has the tremendous armament production banished involuntary unemployment, in the sense that no worker who is in any way employable can remain for more than a few weeks out of a job, but it has been necessary to compel many people to enter industry who would not have come forward voluntarily, given the existing leve of wages in the industries concerned. Further, the special character of the war-time expansion, the concentration *à tout prix* upon the increase in the supply of war materials, creates a tremendous inflationary pressure which can only be held in check by drastic direct controls of personal expenditure. It is tempting to conclude that a price will have to be paid for full employment after the war in the form of direct controls, especially of labour, and that the higher the level of employment aimed at, the stricter these controls must be. It is also suggested that a high level of employment is inherently unstable, the economy being pushed to the brink of a cumulative inflation. A further set of problems arises out of the fact that plant and labour are in varying degrees *specific*, both in their location and in the purposes to which they can be put. Thus, it is commonly argued, if employment expands, bottlenecks of plant or of labour will be encountered while the total number of workers unemployed is still high, and special measures will have to be taken to deal with these bottlenecks. We try here to analyse these questions of stability and flexibility.

59

I. STABILITY AND THE WAGE PROBLEM

Reserves in General

Let us consider first the case when labour is perfectly mobile. There will be four main labour reserves:

(1) involuntary unemployment (due to insufficient effective demand);
(2) increased working time;
(3) 'voluntary' unemployment;
(4) disguised unemployment (e.g. labour at present wastefully used).

This classification of reserves is not rigid. A reduction in working time, effective demand remaining constant, would reduce the *numbers* of involuntary unemployed. Many women not at present insured might be willing to work for the present money wage if there was a job. Nevertheless, it is likely that after the war either custom, legislation or negotiation will set a fairly definite level of normal working hours per week, while custom also will fix a reasonably clear line of demarcation between those who may be regarded as employable and those (especially married women with children) who may be considered for practical purposes outside the field of paid employment. The fourth category of reserves includes workers who, from a social point of view, are wastefully employed because of the existence, for example, of excessive selling costs in some industries. We shall see later how price control may reduce 'disguised' unemployment: for the time being we shall ignore it.

It is obvious that in any actual expansion of employment, the extra labour will be drawn simultaneously from all four categories of reserves. Let us suppose, however, that in the expansion only the involuntary unemployed are drawn in to begin with, and that no overtime is worked until the first reserve has been completely drained. The Government will try to maintain effective demand at just this level where involuntary unemployment vanishes. What will happen if, when all normally employable workers are working normal hours, an error is made and effective demand overshoots the mark? Two cases arise: (1) If no one will work overtime, the rise in effective demand will cause a rise in prices, which will be mitigated only if workers not normally employable (Category 3) can be drawn into employment, or if productivity is proportionately raised. This case is, however, somewhat unlikely. Provided that a sufficient bonus is paid for overtime, it is reasonable to assume that the expansion of effective demand will lead to an increase in working hours.

(2) Suppose that overtime is paid uniformly at time-and-a-half. To illustrate this case we make some further assumptions. First, that there

is a closed economy, i.e. in this context we do not consider the complication of imported raw materials. Secondly, that in forming their prices entrepreneurs add to average prime cost a certain percentage, which we call the 'gross profit margin,' which does not change in the short period. Although this theory of prices is different from the classical competitive theory (price = marginal cost) it agrees closely with the theory of monopolistic competition (marginal revenue = marginal cost). Moreover, it seems to accord with business practice, in so far as entrepreneurs use average-prime cost as a first approximation to marginal cost. It is obvious that, with our first assumption of a closed economy, this means that if all wage costs (per unit of output) are raised, prices will rise proportionately.

The effect of overtime working will be to raise *average* prime cost, and prices will rise proportionately. Thus real wage rates will fall. But, although real wage *rates* fall, the total real earnings will increase. Moreover, hourly money earnings will rise proportionately to average prime cost (being two sides of the same coin), so that, if there is no decline in productivity due to the extra hours, average real *earnings* per hour will remain constant. Thus if the overtime is spread uniformly, the fall in real wage rates will be compensated by the rise in real earnings per week (say), proportional to the increase in hours of work. Even if productivity falls somewhat (if the normal working week is relatively short, say forty-four hours, a considerable fall is unlikely) weekly real earnings will still rise.

If in this situation workers do not press immediately and strongly for an increase in money wage rates, it appears that a rise in effective demand of at least 10 per cent could quite easily be absorbed by overtime working. It is most unlikely that the errors of judgement of the Government[1] in controlling effective demand would be of this order of magnitude, so that with our assumptions full employment (i.e. the absence of involuntary unemployment) would be stable: there would be no danger of an inflationary spiral. General overtime working would be a signal of the need to reduce effective demand.[2]

[1] In practice Governments may tend to undershoot, rather than overshoot the mark.

[2] On our assumptions the curve of average prime cost has the shape shown in the diagram. The jump occurs when 'involuntary' unemployment disappears. The curve is then an upward sloping straight line followed by a gradually steepening slope as productivity declines due to excessive hours. The slope of the linear part of the supply curve is easily determined. Suppose the normal working week is 44 hours and that x hours are worked overtime, paid at time-and-a-half. The earnings are $w(44+\frac{3}{2}x)$ where w is the normal wage rate. Average wage costs per hour are $w(44 + \frac{3}{2}x)/(44 + x)$

If we remove the assumption of a closed economy, the conclusion is little different. A rise in effective demand now has a smaller effect on home employment but increases imports. Real wage rates do not fall as much as before, because there is no reason to expect a rise in import prices, and real earnings increase more than proportionately to the hours of work.[1] From this point of view errors in determining effective demand are even less likely to start an inflation. Moreover, the pressure on the trade balance is, *ex hypothesi*, temporary, and will raise no problems if there are adequate reserves (cf. p. 158). A further stabilizing element is introduced if the expansion of employment draws in labour from the third category of labour reserve: if, for example, women hesitating to seek employment make up their mind when it is clear that there is a job available near at hand.

If the productivity of labour declines when employment increases, i.e. if we have the 'classical' case of employment of inferior labour with expanding output, there would be a tendency for costs, and hence prices, to rise slightly[2] as employment expands. Even this rise can be mitigated if piece-rate is made the basis of wage payment, for then labour costs per unit of output would be constant. The above argument is, of course, dependent upon the assumption that there are always adequate reserves of equipment to employ all the labour available. In the long run we are correct in assuming this to be the case.[3] In the short period specific shortages may arise; this problem is considered later.

If we apply these conclusions tentatively to the real world, it would seem that, if labour is sufficiently mobile, and if the average normal working week is relatively short, say forty-four to forty-eight hours, so that some overtime working does not cause a sharp fall in productivity, *and* there is stability of money wages, then full employment, in the sense of the absence of involuntary unemployment, is stable. That is to say, random fluctuations in effective demand, due to errors in the Government control of effective demand, would not immediately push the economy into inflation.

$= w(1 + \frac{x}{88})$ approximately. If employment is measured in terms of hours worked per week, the slope is $\frac{1}{88}$. An increase of x hours leads to a price increase of $\frac{x}{88} \times 100$ per cent, e.g. 4 hours extra leads to a rise in prices of less than 5 per cent.

[1] Still more so if some raw materials are imported, for average real earnings will now rise more than proportionately to prime costs.

[2] Prices, following *average* prime costs, would not rise sharply. Time-and-a-half pay for overtime is equivalent to a rise in marginal cost of one-half (or a fall in marginal productivity of one-third).

[3] Cf. Kalecki above, p. 47.

Wage Policy

The argument so far has been concerned with *changes* in the level of output at or near the level of full employment (due to errors in controlling effective demand). Such changes, we have argued, do not bring with them any new difficulties. But once a high level of employment is established, the fact must be faced that Trade Unions may, and probably will, press for higher money wages. This has nothing to do with *changes* in the level of employment, accompanied by changes in prices and real wage rates; it is a function of the state of employment itself. The arguments on this point are too well known[1] to require detailed repetition here. On the one hand the Trade Unions are in a strong bargaining position; the fear of under-cutting of wages by non-union unemployed is absent. At the same time any one employer can only increase his staff by reducing the staff of another, and he may try to entice labour by offering higher money wages. 'When labour is scarce not only are Trade Unions very powerful, but employers themselves throw their weight into the scale of rising wages.'[2] The loose co-ordination of Trade Unions with regard to wage questions adds a further complexity. If one single body bargained for wages for all workers the effect of a rise in money wages upon prices would be immediately obvious; but in fact each Trade Union bargains for its own membership[3] and this masks the ultimate result of a set of separate wage increases.

The ultimate effect of money wage increases upon real wages is, in fact, very difficult to trace.[4] An increase of money wages in one industry only will lead to an almost proportionate increase in real wages in that industry: for though the price of the product concerned may rise, it will, in general, constitute only a tiny part of the expenditure of the workers in the industry. There will be a rise in the price of *one* item in the cost-of living, but only a tiny rise in the cost of living as a whole. Even if we assume, for the moment, that the price of a particular product always increases in exact proportion with the rise in money wages, it is natural for Trade Unions to continue to press for higher money wages. For Trade Unions have different degrees of

---

[1] Cf. Joan Robinson, *Essays in the Theory of Employment*: first essay on 'Full Employment.'
[2] Op. cit., p. 15.
[3] Not exclusively: a 'sympathetic' strike may sometimes be classed as bargaining by workers in one industry or occupation for higher money wages in another.
[4] Cf. Kalecki, *Essays in the Theory of Economic Fluctuations*, pp. 75 *et seq.*

organization and power, and wage bargains are not made simultaneously. So each section of the workers can, for a time, obtain higher
real wages, until all other workers have caught up. (If there is *no alternative*, the best way to see a football match is to climb on your neighbour's
shoulders, even though the next man in turn will try to climb on to
yours.) Moreover, if the supply of imported raw materials is fairly
elastic home prices of manufactured goods will not rise in exact proportion to wages, but somewhat less. Add to this the fact that certain
prices, e.g. rents, are fixed or rather sticky over long periods, and it is
clear that an all-round increase in money wages may bring a slight, and
long-lasting, improvement in real wages.[1] A continuous upward
pressure on money wages must, therefore, be expected, in the form of
a succession of discrete upward movements in different industries and
trades. The crucial question is how rapid this rise will be. If productivity rises, say by 2 per cent every year, then an annual rise in money
wages of 2 per cent will have no effect on prices, for it will simply serve
to keep labour costs per unit of output (in money terms) constant.[2]
Such a rise may seem very small, but if it takes the form of a 10 per
cent increase in money wages for 20 per cent of the workers each
year, it may appear somewhat greater. Nevertheless, it would be
quite unjustifiable to assume that Trade Unions and employers would,
in a multitude of separate negotiations, hit upon just the right average
increase.

If the rate of increase in money wages is less than the rate of increase
in productivity there will be some fall in prices. To the extent that
some prices are sticky and do not fall proportionately to the reduction
in unit money costs, there will also be a decline in effective demand.
For while it is reasonable to suppose that the greater part of any increase
in real wages will be spent it is much less likely to be the case for
increases in other incomes: the solution is, of course, a further expansion
of effective demand by the Government. If this case were to occur in
practice we might fairly say that there would be no 'wage problem'
in full employment.[3] We must, however, consider the alternative case
where money wages tend to rise *more* rapidly than productivity. This,
as we shall see, raises a number of complicated issues. In order to

---

[1] With a corresponding deterioration in the real income of rentiers, etc.

[2] Actually the rate of increase could be slightly greater with a consequent slight rise in prices,
if the consequent fall in the real income of rentiers does not create great opposition. There would
be a continuous relative shift of real income from rentiers to entrepreneurs. This is a special
case of the redistribution of income discussed below.

[3] Although certain difficulties would be raised by a fall in prices, e.g. the increasing real burden
of debts.

avoid excessive repetition we shall for the remainder of this section suppose that money wages will in fact tend to rise more quickly than productivity.

1. If there is considerable unemployment there will be a general downward pressure on money wages; if there is full employment the upward pressure is too great. There must, it might be argued, be a unique level of employment which will bring out precisely the 'correct' rise in money wages, which does not lead to a steady rise in prices. Could not effective demand, which we assume can be controlled by the Government, be set at this precise point? But this 'critical' level of employment, even if it could be found and kept under control, which is doubtful,[1] may be relatively low, and so involve considerable waste of resources. We must therefore reject this solution as being incompatible with full employment.

2. Under conditions of full employment we assume that money wage rates will rise more rapidly than the productivity of workers. We have already pointed out that, even if prices are uncontrolled, this may lead to a certain, once-for-all, rise in real wages of workers, offset by an equivalent relative[2] fall in the real income of rentiers, earners with fixed or slowly rising salaries, unemployed pensioners, etc. In other words, the steady rise in money wages will bring about a redistribution of real income, though not necessarily of the most desirable kind, for the rise in prices may inflict considerable hardship on certain classes.[3] The steady devaluation of the currency which would be necessary in an open economy would create additional difficulties.

In the previous article Mr. Kalecki outlines two solutions to the problem, which we shall now consider in greater detail.

3. According to the first method:

(i) The cost of living is pegged throughout by subsidies.

---

[1] The pressure on wages is partly a function of the strength of Trade Unions, and of the willingness of employers to meet their demands. Both of these factors are indeed affected by the level of employment, but they may change (with any given level of employment) for a host of reasons which cannot be fitted into any systematic pattern. And although, according to the theory, at any given moment there is a 'correct' level of effective demand from our present point of view, in practice this point would have to be found empirically. The Government would in fact be attempting to pin down, by adjustments in its fiscal policy, a critical level of effective demand subject to random changes, with the continuous threat that if it overshoots the mark the spiral of wages and prices will be set in motion. Taking into account the problems of diagnosis and the inevitable lapse of time before appropriate adjustments can be made, this does not seem a very practical proposition.

[2] Not necessarily an absolute fall. If the rise in money wages only slightly exceeds the rise in productivity the real income of rentiers may also rise, though less rapidly than productivity. An absolute fall in the real income of the latter, however, seems to be most likely.

[3] On recipients of Social Insurance benefits, especially, unless the benefits are related to the cost of living.

(ii) As money wages rise, income tax[1] is raised to a greater extent to cover the increase in the cost of subsidies and to allow for the fact that a given amount of tax will not reduce consumption *pro tanto*, because it falls partly on savings.

(iii) The taxation must be designed so as not to interfere with the incentive to private investment.

Under this scheme real wages would rise continuously, in proportion to money wages, while the real 'available' income of non-wage earning classes would be correspondingly reduced by taxation. In addition, the budget deficit would also be continuously reduced. If the rise in money wages is not too rapid, the method might indeed be said to combine the virtues of gradualism, fiscal orthodoxy, and social justice! It is clear, however, that even if the incentive to private investment is preserved by the appropriate tax system, this continuous redistribution of available real income must, sooner or later, raise social and political issues of profound importance. Before discussing this in any detail, we shall consider the alternative method of tackling the wage problem in full employment.

4. Instead of keeping prices constant by means of subsidies (which means, in fact, that there is a gap between the 'producer's price' and the 'selling price') we now suppose that all prices are frozen by law, at a given date, and we assume further that no hidden price increases occur in the form of deterioration of the quality of goods. This is not, as we shall see, the best way to operate price control in practice: but we are concerned here with principles. With a price stop a rise in money wages is accompanied by a proportional rise in real wages. If this rise is proportional to the increase in productivity in the same period (a year, say) then real wage-rates will rise each year in the same proportion, while real wages and real profits per unit of output will be constant. Again, however, we must anticipate pressure for a higher rate of increase in money wages.[2] If prices were free to rise, we argued (p. 63) that employers might 'throw their weight into the scales of rising wages,' but if the price stop is held, the employers will throw their weight heavily in the opposite direction. For now rising money wages will mean rising real labour costs, and so eat into the 'gross profit margin' between price and prime cost of production. This means

---

[1] To peg the cost-of-living index by financing the subsidies out of indirect taxation on mass luxuries, e.g. drink and tobacco, which are underweighted in the index, would, of course, leave real wages unaltered. Although many Trade Unions take into account the cost-of-living index in wage negotiations, in the long run bargaining power is likely to count for more than statistical finesse.

[2] Although, just because prices are fixed, this rate will not be so great as when prices are free to rise; the same applies when prices are pegged by subsidies.

that employers must either (*a*) reduce real costs as wages rise, or (*b*) they must sacrifice part of profits proper, i.e. allow the 'net profit margin' to be reduced.

(*a*) There is considerable scope for the reduction in costs. The price stop will tend to drive out the marginal producers in any industry, so that its immediate effect is the curtailment of supply. Now under conditions of imperfect competition the 'intra-marginal' producers have surplus capacity; they are therefore technically able to expand output. It seems likely that buyers who used to get their goods from the marginal producers will now switch their demand to one of the remaining producers. Apart from the consequences upon the efficiency of an industry as a whole, the price stop will also affect the individual firm. Each firm will attempt to take up any slack in its own productive organization. It will also tend to cut down its selling costs, for two main reasons. In the first place the evidence tends to show that in the past firms have always economized first on selling costs[1] whenever trade becomes worse. Secondly, full employment will, by guaranteeing a steady market, reduce the need for excessive competitive advertising.[2] This reduction will occur in any case, but the pressure of wage increases may accelerate the process. The price stop, in so far as it hits *costs*, will thus bring about an all round rise in the productivity of labour: in addition it may accelerate the *rate* of technical progress, by compelling firms to react more quickly to improvements for fear of becoming the marginal producer. This is not all. As wages increase, effective demand increases; but the reduction of costs releases the labour to provide the output necessary to meet the increased effective demand. Thus, in so far as the price stop operates on costs the wage problem is not rendered more difficult by wage increases.

(*b*) To the extent that entrepreneurs cannot compensate for rising wages by reducing costs, the price stop must bring about a redistribution of gross incomes (i.e. incomes before taxation); there will be a shift from profits proper to wages. This will lead to an increase in effective demand, since the propensity to consume of wage-earners is higher than that of capitalists. Progressive taxation must therefore be increased (or the deficit spending on public investment reduced) to bring effective demand back to the full employment level.

The working of the price stop is thus rather complicated, and

[1] That this was not always based on sound economic reasoning does not matter: so long as firms regard advertising as a 'semi-luxury' item of cost we may expect this reaction. For a discussion of this question see K. W. Rothschild, 'A Note on Advertising,' *Economic Journal*, April 1942, pp. 119-21.

[2] This may be one reason for less intensive competition. Another is the increasing difficulty of getting labour to expand output when there is little or no unemployment (cf. p. 77).

difficult to forecast. It is likely to cause: (*a*) a rise in productivity due to the pressure on costs, with possibly also an increase in the rate of technical progress, which eases the wage problem, and (*b*) a redistribution of gross income, the effect of which must be compensated by increased taxation.

Certain practical difficulties are bound to arise both in the subsidy method and with price control. It is obviously administratively convenient to limit subsidies to a few important commodities, e.g. bread, meat, clothing, and housing; but if this is done the structure of relative prices will be fundamentally altered. Or again, it is quite arbitrary to freeze all prices at the level ruling on a given day. Consider, for the sake of example, two industries A and B. In the former we will assume high efficiency and low wages and profits, and the latter low efficiency and high wages and profits.[1] The scope for profit 'squeezing' in the former is very small, so that a rise in wages would have to be met by a subsidy, if the cost of living is to be pegged. On the other hand there is plenty of scope for a rise in wages in the latter, even though wages are relatively high: in this case indeed a price reduction would be more appropriate than a wage increase. These instances show that the wage problem is likely to require a rather complicated system of price controls and subsidies, operated together industry by industry in such a way as to produce the over-all stability of the price level.

We have considered four methods of attacking the problem of rising money wages in full employment. The first, of reducing effective demand, we rejected because it implied the abandonment of full employment. The second, merely allowing wages and prices to chase one another, is also rejected because of its undesirable social and external repercussions. The other two methods, of subsidizing prices by means of increasing taxation, or of controlling prices by law, both present technical difficulties, but at any rate in theory would preserve the stability of the economy through a continuous redistribution of income. A solution combining both methods can, however, only work on certain conditions.

At present the wage policies of Trade Unions are sectional, each Union negotiating separately on behalf of its particular members; such co-ordination as does exist is very loose. Now the success of the stabilization of full employment depends upon hitting an *average* rate of increase of wages which is not more than can, in the existing circumstances, be compensated by increases in taxation on non-wage earners. It is improbable that the outcome of a multitude of separate

[1] Due, for example, to monopoly.

wage-bargains will prove to be just right. In full employment, indeed, Trade Unions may have two functions. Sectional bargaining for increases in money wages will continue to obtain relative advantages for the members of a particular Union. But, as we have seen, such bargaining for money wages *by itself* will not lead to an overall increase in real wages if prices are free to rise. If, therefore, Trade Unions wish to translate increases in money wages into increases in real wages they will have a second task. They will have to press for increases in taxation on non-wage earners (to finance subsidies and to control total effective demand), in order to permit of a rise in the real consumption of workers. Clearly this second function cannot be fulfilled upon sectional lines.

To make this point clear let us imagine that the average increase in money wages in a given period (which is the result of a number of independent sectional bargains) is greater than the increase in productivity in the same period. If the Trade Unions, acting together, can ensure that taxation on non-wage earners is increased to reduce their consumption sufficiently, then the rise in money wages will be reflected fully in a rise in real wages. What if they do not, or cannot, obtain the necessary increase in taxation upon non-wage earners? Then, either the stabilization policy will be abandoned, and prices *will* be permitted to rise; or, taxation will be extended to cover wage-earners as well. In either case part of the increase in money wages will be nullified. If, indeed, taxation *is* extended, in a progressive way, to cover wage earners, there will be no danger of inflation: but in this case wage anomalies are more likely to arise. Thus this second function of Trade Unions in full employment, the function of pressing for increases in the consumption of workers as a whole, is bound to react to some extent upon sectional bargaining. It is desirable that sectional policies should be co-ordinated sufficiently to ensure that the *average* rate of increase in money wages is not more (nor less) than can be compensated by increases in taxation upon non-wage earners. Ideally, a central body, presumably the T.U.C., would draw up a scheme of priorities for wage increases. Such a central body might, for example, exert greater pressure for scaling-up the wages of the lowest paid workers, than, say, for further improving the standards of the relatively well-to-do skilled workers. It would be for the Unions themselves to determine the degree of freedom which can be left to individual Unions for modifications of wage-rates within the general framework. In preparing its wage policy the central body will want to know, and have to know, more about the financial position of industry than has been made known in the past, and this may involve certain institutional modifications in the conduct of industry.

The second point concerns the effect of steadily rising money wages (and hence, with price control, reduced profit margins) upon the expectations of entrepreneurs. On the one hand, the elimination of fluctuations in output, by maintaining full employment, will reduce the risk of enterprise:[1] on the other hand, if an entrepreneur anticipates still further wage increases in the future, this factor will assume larger proportions in his mind (precisely because the risk is lower). The two factors of falling risk and the anticipation of lower profits may, of course, just offset one another. In any case the assistance provided by the modified income tax is available to keep private investment at the requisite level. In practice, however, if the rate of increase in wages is very rapid, technical difficulties may occur and these will set a limit[2] to the wage increases which can be obtained by this method.[3]

How great the pressure for wage increases will be cannot be foreseen. Obviously the rate of increase of money wages, when prices are controlled, bears no relation whatever to the rate of increase when prices are left free, so that there is a 'quasi-inflation' of wages and prices chasing one another. But whatever the actual pressure, it is clear that in the conditions outlined above wage bargaining becomes direct bargaining for the distribution of real income. To be effective, money wage increases have to be combined with price control and increased income tax. The outcome of such wage bargaining is thus decided by the relative strength of economic pressure groups.

Conclusion

To sum up, the pressure for rising wages under conditions of full employment can be dealt with by means of a combination of subsidies and price control, which keep prices constant. Apart from the effect of price control in increasing efficiency, the solution involves a gradual redistribution of available real income. The ease with which the policy can be carried out and the extent of the redistribution of income will depend upon: (1) the effectiveness of Trade Unions in pressing for profit 'squeezing' and for increases in taxation on non-wage earners.

---

[1] It will also raise the *rate* of profit: for the abolition of fluctuations will permit a higher average utilization of equipment.

[2] This is, of course, to look at the economy as a whole. If profits cannot be squeezed further in any *particular* sector, it is always possible to keep prices constant by subsidy.

[3] Even if no further redistribution of income from capitalists to wage earners is possible, wage *adjustments* can still be made, by 'concentrating' the whole of the wage fund made available by the increase in productivity on the lowest paid workers. Thus if the average annual increase in productivity is 2 per cent, this would allow of a 10 per cent increase in wages for 20 per cent of workers (other wages remaining constant) without creating inflationary tendencies.

(2) The degree to which pure 'sectionalism' is modified by the co-ordination of wage policies of separate Unions.

Wage bargaining in full employment is, in fact, a political problem, and will be settled on the political plane.

II. BOTTLENECKS AND MOBILITY

So far we have assumed that labour was homogeneous and perfectly mobile, and that there was no shortage of equipment in any sector. In practice, when employment expands, bottlenecks will be encountered in some sectors while there are plentiful idle resources in other sectors. Further, even when full employment has been established, there will still be subsequent shifts from one industry to another, due, for example, to changes in taste, which may again give rise to temporary shortages of labour. We may distinguish three principal types of bottleneck: (1) Scarcity of raw materials, (2) scarcity of equipment, (3) scarcity of labour in a particular sector.

In this section we shall examine first scarcities of particular materials and types of equipment, and show that, while a violent expansion or shift from one industry to another may call for special measures, in the longer run the breaking of these bottlenecks depends upon the mobility of labour, which we shall then discuss in detail. We shall find that while the problem of mobility is unlikely to cause difficulties in the period of expanding employment, i.e. when there are still pools of unemployment, some trouble may arise when there is already full employment and a particular firm or industry wishes to expand production in competition with others. Finally, we shall discuss briefly the relation between 'reserves' and 'planning.' The special case of the control of the location of industry is treated in the following section.

1. *Scarcity of Raw Materials.* If, as employment expands, a particular raw material becomes scarce, its supply can first be increased out of stocks. If demand continues to expand, production, or imports, must be increased. The expansion of imports is treated separately in a later study (p. 126): here we consider only home-produced materials. Production can be increased next by working overtime the existing labour and equipment.[1] The running down of stocks and overtime working will, between them, provide a considerable elasticity. Further increases in supply require, of course, an increase in labour and plant. We are assuming here that the equilibrium between demand and supply is restored by increasing output. In the case of many raw materials,

[1] If there is no surplus capacity in the raw material industry there will be a 'derived' bottleneck of equipment (see the following paragraph).

however, the disequilibrium may lead to a sharp rise in prices, and this will be accentuated if there is speculation. In principle, prices ought only to rise to cover an increase in *long run* marginal costs. But if there is no control the initial rise in prices may be accentuated by over-ordering on the part of consumers, and this in turn may lead to over-investment in plant, so that the subsequent fall in prices will be violent. In cases where this is likely to occur (actually it has affected in the past mainly imported materials and agricultural products) it is desirable to fix statutory maximum prices, subject to long-period readjustment, or even to institute (or maintain) a full-scale State trading concern which buys and re-sells the material and can hold sufficient stocks to meet normal fluctuations in demand.

2. *Scarcity of Equipment.* Normally an expansion of output, by taking on additional labour, or working overtime, is possible without increasing the amount of plant and equipment. In a rapid expansion, however, equipment may become a bottleneck. The elasticity of supply of this equipment, in the short period, depends in turn on whether additional labour can be put to existing plant in the industry producing the particular equipment. If it can, the original bottleneck will not persist: it will be broken as quickly as labour can move into the equipment producing industry. If not, we get a 'derived' bottleneck which carries us back a stage further in the productive process. It should be stressed that a certain elasticity is introduced at each stage by the element of overtime working, and in an open system by imports. Apart from violent transitions we can reduce the persistence of all bottlenecks to a function of the mobility of specific types of labour.[1]

3. *The Mobility of Labour.* Let us begin from a state of affairs in which there is already normal full employment, e.g. every worker has a job and is working the normal number of hours each week. Demand now changes so that one industry will begin to expand in relation to the others.[2] Where will it get its labour?

The first source of additional labour is overtime working, and, as we have already seen, if the normal working week is fairly short this source supplies a reserve of 10 to 15 per cent in man-hours. Short

---

[1] Even the import bottleneck can ultimately be reduced to mobility of labour, either into export industries in the case where an expansion of exports is possible, or into substitute production where exchange considerations dictate it.

[2] There is little evidence to support the argument that these shifts in demand will be frequent and violent. For example, in *The Times* of March 2, 1943, a correspondent wrote: 'The immobility of labour between trades is great and growing. Both abroad and at home, where we are spending a rising proportion of our income on quasi-luxuries, demand will shift from one article to another with growing rapidity.' Rapid changes of *fashion*, e.g. women's clothing, do not, in general, call so much for the movement of labour, even between firms, as for the adaptation of the product itself.

period *fluctuations* are therefore easily handled. If the expansion is permanent, then the higher earnings and possibly also wage-rates (depending upon the general wage policy) will act as an attraction to workers outside the industry. The next source of labour for readjustments are juvenile entrants. According to statistics of 1927-31 'juvenile entrants make a far greater contribution to the readjustments of labour between industries than do the new entrants aged 16 to 64.'[1] The average unemployment in these years was high, and it is not unexpected to find juveniles accounting for most of the readjustments; there was little need to re-train workers from other industries, or occupations. 'But on the supply side the population situation means that for a number of decades the ratio of new recruits to the existing labour force in industry will be low, and this deprives us of our easiest means of readjusting the numbers employed in each trade to the changing demand for its products.'[2] This forecast seems unduly pessimistic. It is of course risky to refer to the pre-war experience in this respect, because of the existence of general unemployment. It is likely, however, that employers in expanding industries were more anxious to draw in new juvenile labour which is more adaptable, than to draw on existing reserves of middle-aged unemployed. And there is no evidence that any trades were snapping up all the juvenile workers they could and clamouring for more. Nevertheless, the decline in the number of juvenile entrants does mean that the flow should be more carefully directed than in the past, by providing a wider knowledge of expected industrial requirements for the juveniles themselves, by developing a flexible technical education, and perhaps equally important, eliminating 'blind-alley' occupations.

In the event of a continuous and rapid expansion of a particular industry (accompanied *ex hypothesi* by a contraction elsewhere) it will be necessary to draw upon workers hitherto employed in other trades and other occupations.[3]

[1] 'Studies in the Mobility of Labour' by H. Makower, J. Marschak, and H. W. Robinson, *Oxford Economic Papers*, No. 2.
[2] *The Times*, March 2, 1943. The Correspondent proposes a kind of voluntary industrial Commando, in which the worker would be paid a full wage if he were unemployed but 'as a *quid pro quo* for the security provided, the worker would have to be willing, as occasion required, to change his trade and even the place of his home.'
[3] The only statistical work on mobility on any wide scale which has been done in this country are the 'Studies in the Mobility of Labour,' *Oxford Economic Papers*, Nos. 1, 2 and 4. Unfortunately it is not possible to use numerical results arrived at in these Studies, since they are based upon data collected in years when there was an *average* unemployment of over 10 per cent, with much greater proportions in the depressed areas. Even the fact that mobility is—over the range of unemployment percentages studied—positively correlated with the level of employment cannot be applied without some qualification to conditions of full employment. Our attempt to foresee the difficulties arising in full employment conditions is bound, therefore, to be rather speculative.

There are two aspects of the problem which can be conveniently taken separately: (1) The technical obstacles to movement, and (2) the incentive to move.

(1) *Occupational mobility* appeared even in peace-time to be very high,[1] and may be expected to remain high in full employment. Workers of all types appear to be versatile. It is likely that recent industrial trends have been such as to demand less specialized skill and more skill of a general character. In some cases what has happened is that the installing and maintenance of machinery is a job of very rare skill, while the operation of the machinery itself requires relatively little training.[2] Rigid Trade Union regulations can, of course, act as a very strong brake upon occupational mobility by the closed-shop principle, by insisting upon long apprenticeship as a condition of membership and by refusing membership to certain categories of workers (e.g. women). These barriers were broken down at the outbreak of war, and 'dilution' to any required degree voluntarily accepted for the duration of the emergency. Without going into a detailed examination of Trade Union policy, it seems reasonable to suppose that the anxiety of Trade Unions (especially craft unions) to restore regulations which hinder occupational mobility will be in inverse proportion to the success of the Government in maintaining full employment.[3] On the other hand, it should not be overlooked that, in general, craft restrictions are strongest in precisely those trades where technological conditions still allow it. Thus an expansion of employment, or an adjustment due to a change in relative demand (total effective demand remaining constant) might be hampered, if the expansion or the change required an additional supply of labour in a particular craft with strict regulations. In such conditions it should not be difficult to obtain the relaxation of the restrictions, provided certain guarantees of economic security for existing members were given.

What has been said so far about mobility from one *occupation* to another applies to movement between industries where the technique of production is not widely different. Some industries, e.g. coal mining,

[1] Cf. Dennison, *Location of Industry and the Depressed Areas*, pp. 154–6.

[2] This would explain the remarkable productivity of many women in 'skilled occupations' in war industry after only a few months in the factory.

[3] Discussing this point in *The T.U.C. in War-Time* (February 1944) Sir Walter Citrine writes 'It may be necessary to arrange for some relaxation of trade union demarcation rules. These demarcation rules were imposed by the Unions because of economic insecurity. It was the fear of unemployment which made the Unions insist upon many practices which it would in some cases be difficult to logically defend.'

are, however, highly specialized,[1] so that it will not always be easy to re-employ directly the labour rendered redundant by changes in demand. The solution, leaving aside the question of incentives, lies in the provision on a sufficiently large scale of training facilities in industry, or, when necessary, Government training centres at which workers are paid an adequate wage.[2]

The purely technical obstacles to shifts between industries and between occupations do not appear likely to cause any trouble in full employment,[3] provided there are adequate facilities for retraining. *Spatial* mobility is another question. In the years before the war there was a large-scale migration of population from the depressed areas, in which were concentrated the declining industries, to the expanding districts of the South and the Midlands.[4] Despite the migration the concentration of unemployment in the declining areas was most marked. In October 1937,[5] for example, the average unemployment of insured workers aged 16 to 64 in Great Britain was 9.9 per cent. In London, the South and the Midlands the percentage was between 6.0 and 7.3 per cent, but in Northern England and Scotland the percentages were 16.2 and 14.5 respectively, while in Wales unemployment was still 21.3 per cent. Yet 1937 saw the peak of the recovery—before rearmament. The strategic location of munition factories in depressed areas, with the concomitant rise in prosperity of ancillary industries, has reversed the pre-war 'drift to the South.' The depressed areas are, for the time being, prosperous.[6] But the prosperity is based upon war production, either directly through munitions or indirectly through the revival of heavy industry, especially shipbuilding. What the post-war prospects of the depressed areas are depends on a complex of political and strategical factors; upon the size of the peace-time armed forces, upon U.S. post-war shipbuilding, upon exports of capital goods and so on. How ever these matters are settled, a situation in which there

---

[1] Here again a qualification must be made. Some part of the 'specialization' of mining is due simply to the geographical concentration of mining, so that whole mining communities, with powerful traditions, have grown up. Miners have not been slow to take up other jobs when they were offered during the war.

[2] Pre-war experience of training centres throws little light on our problem, because of the existence of general unemployment. The war-time experience is more to the point.

[3] Cf. Mandelbaum, p.198.

[4] 'From 1923 to 1936 London and the Home Counties and the South-Eastern and South-Western divisions of the Ministry of Labour made a net gain of 2,400,000 inhabitants, the North-East, North-West, Scotland, and Wales lost 2,200,000, and the Midlands showed almost no change.'—'Britain's Town and Country Pattern,' *Nuffield College Social Reconstruction Survey,* pp. 22-3.

[5] Taken as the first month for which the July 1937 count of insured workers was available.

[6] Cf. 'Turnover and Population Movements,' *Bulletin of the Institute of Statistics,* Vol. 3, No. 10, p. 213, and 'A Survey of Industrial Development in Great Britain Planned since the Commencement of the War,' by P. W. S. Andrews, *Oxford Economic Papers,* No. 5, June 1941.

are pools of relatively heavy unemployment in certain areas is by no means impossible. Thus there might be something like full employment in, say, the South and Midlands, while there is still heavy unemployment in the depressed areas of Scotland, South Wales, Tyneside and so on. But, provided there is a Government policy of expanding effective demand, this state of affairs could not last very long: one reason why the pre-war depressed areas appeared so intractable was precisely the lack of such a policy. Although there were many unemployed workers who, because of family ties, or because they owned their own house, were relatively immobile, there was a large number of younger workers who throughout the pre-war years were ready to go almost at an instant's notice to any part of the country where there was a vacancy with any prospect of lasting more than a few weeks. Clearly the greater security of employment in a district away from home, which would exist under conditions of full employment, would tend to make these younger workers move even more quickly. There may, however, remain some obstacles to movement for other workers. These obstacles can be reduced by: (*a*) the State financing the transfer of families; (*b*) increasing the number of houses which can be *rented* at low cost in all parts of the country;[1] (*c*) extending the information services of the Labour Exchanges. We shall argue later that, although the expansion of effective demand may be expected to drain the 'surplus' workers from depressed areas in a relatively short time,[2] it is not necessarily the best way of dealing with them. Once we reach the state of affairs in which nearly every worker everywhere has a job, the problem of spatial mobility is very different; for the repellent power of destitution no longer operates.

(2) *The Incentive to move.* In the past one of the strongest incentives to the worker to change his trade or leave his home has been prolonged unemployment. This incentive will no longer exist under conditions approaching full employment. Shifts in demand will, however, bring about at once differences in earnings. In the expanding sector there will be overtime working, while in the contracting sector either some workers will become temporarily unemployed, or there will be short-time working. The incentive to move is clearly somewhat stronger in the former case than the latter. Whether there will be short-time working is difficult to say, for there will be two opposing forces at work. On the one hand, if there is an adequate unemployment benefit, there will be less moral pressure on employers to maintain their

[1] Cf. G. D. H. Cole, 'The Building Industry after the War,' *Fabian Quarterly*, January 1944.
[2] Cf., pp. 79 *et seq*.

full personnel on short-time. On the other hand, employers may wish
to retain workers on their pay-roll in anticipation of the recovery[1] or to
use them for new lines of production. Even if short-time is worked,
the differences in earnings may under certain circumstances be sufficient
to attract workers from the under-employed to the over-employed sector
of industry. A further financial incentive can and should be provided
by adjustment of the relative wage-rates. This reinforces the earlier
argument for a central wage policy: such a readjustment might, of
course, be expected to come about in time by the normal process of
sectional bargaining, but it might well be slow. If we assume that there
is a great improvement in the provision of information about employment prospects in other industries and occupations, this, together with
the financial incentive, ought to ensure the required mobility of labour.
There may indeed be some people who are at the moment working
short-time, and who know there is a better paid job going in another
firm with normal working hours, and still do not wish to leave their
present job. In such cases there does not seem to be any cause for
special action.

But there is a real difficulty when we turn to the attitude of *employers*
in a full employment economy. What will happen to competition?
Suppose that there is already full employment in the strict sense of
every one being in a job working normal hours. A firm of soap
makers, A, now finds an improvement in soap making which it wishes
to exploit in competition with other manufacturers. If A reduces his
prices, he will attract a certain custom from all the other producers.
Where will he get the labour for the increased output? In theory, from
the other firms, whose output will drop. But unless these firms are
very near to his this is difficult. Thus the abolition of the reserve of
actual unemployed will act as a brake upon competition. To put it in
more formal terms, the abolition of unemployment, by reducing
mobility, will increase the degree of monopsony in the labour market;
labour will be less responsive to changes in wage-rates in any particular
industry or firm. As a result the spread between price and prime cost
will tend to rise, and bring about a redistribution of income opposite
to that necessary for full employment itself.[2] This latter effect can be
prevented by price control, which we have already advocated as one

---

[1] There were instances of this during the war when the first sharp cut in civilian production
was enforced.

[2] Unless the increase in the degree of monopsony of the employer is accompanied by a corresponding increase in the strength of Trade Unions, who could prevent the individual employer
taking advantage of the relative immobility of his workers by depressing their wages (or not
raising them as much as would be necessary if labour were more mobile).

of the ways of handling the general problem of wages in full employment. This still does not find the employer his labour. To get it he will have to make greater use of the facilities provided by the Employment Exchanges, and will have also, as has happened in many factories in war-time, to study more carefully the utilization of his existing labour resources.[1]

This particular difficulty concerning competition is, in fact, one instance of the general rule that planning and reserves are complementary. The less there are of the latter the greater is the need for the former, not only on the part of the Government, but on the part of private employers. The Government must, on our argument, control the aggregate of demand, and hence to a greater or less extent it must be controlling its constituents. Aggregate demand will in fact be made up of: (*a*) Demand for specific goods and services financed directly by the Government, e.g. public investment, schools, health services and so on; (*b*) private demand for consumption, whose character will be determined by the general policy with regard to income distribution and Government subsidies, and by consumer's choice; (*c*) private investment which in turn will depend upon the private demand for consumption goods. In the long run it will be the policy of the Government to allow supply to adjust itself to demand. But in the short run, since adjustments of supply take time, the Government may deliberately stimulate demand in a particular sector, e.g. by strictly temporary subsidies. Suppose, for the sake of example, that the demand for coal is falling very sharply (due to the use of other fuels). It might take some time before the unemployed miners can be reabsorbed into other trades; in this case, rather than leave them unemployed it would pay to subsidize coal prices temporarily, while at the same time taking steps to transfer labour and capital to meet the change in the structure of demand. In the same way the Government might refrain from spending too heavily on a service, e.g. education, where there are difficulties of expanding supply in the short period. The private employer in his turn will also have to a much greater extent to plan his output in advance, and also fit his individual plans within the general economic plan. Probably the most important single case where planning should replace reserves as a means for the adjustment of industry is in its location, and in the final section of this article we consider this question in some detail. Before doing so it may be useful to summarize the argument of this section.

[1] The response of the employer to labour shortage by rationalization was very marked in Germany. Cf. p. 199.

Conclusion

In any expansion of output, either a general expansion or in a particular sector, particular shortages of materials, equipment and labour will be encountered. The effect of these shortages will be delayed by running down stocks, by working overtime, and by the 'spreading' of orders. In certain cases, where supply is inelastic in the short period, e.g. in the case of raw materials, it may be necessary to institute price control or to establish a State trading concern which buys the material for re-sale and holds stocks. The overcoming of all shortages can, however, be reduced ultimately to the problem of the mobility of labour.

With regard to mobility in full employment certain difficulties may be expected to arise, in particular with regard to competition between firms. There are various lines of attack upon these difficulties, especially the extension of the information service concerning vacancies provided by Labour Exchanges, and provision of adequate facilities for re-training. Nevertheless, it is clear that the reserves of idle labour which exist in unemployment must be replaced by planning. This last point, incidentally, brings out the difficulty of *defining* full employment in any way which is suitable for practical application. The smallness of the number of persons actually without work on any particular day in the future will depend on the extent to which the information and re-training facilities are developed and upon the ability to anticipate changes in demand and to make appropriate plans to meet them.

III. CONTROL OF THE LOCATION OF INDUSTRY AND POPULATION

Until a few years before the war 'industrialists have been free to choose those sites for their enterprises which seemed to them most suitable, and it can probably be taken for granted that in so far as there has been conscious choice of location, and businesses have not grown up in a particular locality from more or less accidental causes, that choice has been determined almost exclusively by business motives, and the site has been selected which appeared to afford the greatest balance of advantage to the particular enterprise.'[1] Where there is a *deliberate* choice between sites for a new enterprise—and the fact that many firms and industries are now where they are mainly as a result of 'accidents' should not be overlooked—the entrepreneur has in the

[1] Memorandum of Evidence of the Board of Trade before the *Royal Commission on the Geographical Distribution of the Industrial Population*, 1937.

past minimized *private* cost of production, or more correctly (since the choice of site may affect the scale of production) maximized his proceeds. It is often argued, it was in fact strongly argued by the Board of Trade in 1937, that the consequence of locational *laisser-faire* is that 'in general the present distribution of the industries of the country approximates very closely to the distribution which enables each of these industries to operate most economically and efficiently and *there is therefore reason to suppose* [our italics] that this distribution is well adapted to serve the economic interests of the country as a whole.'[1] But this argument is fallacious. In the first place, there is the whole complex of locational 'imperfections,'[2] analogous to the imperfections of the market, which implies that whole industries might have been differently placed if more detailed knowledge of alternative sites had been available.[3] Secondly, and this is of far greater importance, each new industrial development *itself* disturbs the previous locational balance of industries, by drawing labour away from old-established industries, by creating a new market in a new locality, and in other ways. This tendency is strengthened by the fact that much industrial expansion takes the form of extension of *existing* plants. There is therefore no reason whatever to suppose that the sum of a number of unco-ordinated individual decisions to maximize private proceeds, taken at different times, will produce the optimum use of resources from the point of view of the community as a whole.

Now in one sense this may not be important. Since it is impossible to foresee with any degree of accuracy the technical developments of the future, it follows that even if it were possible to lay out to-day's industry entirely afresh in order to make the best use of to-day's resources, from the point of view of the national economic interest, the very fact that to-day's location is the optimum makes it unlikely that, as a result of uneven technical development in different industries, to-morrow's location could be as good as if the whole of industry was

[1] Ibid.

[2] In his Memorandum of Evidence submitted to the Barlow Commission, Mr. Mobbs, Chairman of the Slough Trading Estates, who had acquired a vast experience of location problems, wrote: 'The owner or manager of a light factory, whether small or large, has a totally different education and social position to that which he had fifty years ago; so has his wife. They are not inclined to live in the climate of the North of England, and this climate is unalterable by human effort. They are not inclined to lose the social life which has developed in the South of England, educational, cultural and sporting. This is alterable by holding the Wimbledon Championships in Yorkshire, removing the Royal Academy to Lancashire, and paying the heads of Government Departments and the Bank Managers in Northumberland as much as they are paid in London. It is unlikely to be altered.'

[3] No one planning the location of British light industry *ab initio* could have produced the disorderly 'conurbation' which is known as London!

once more re-planned in the light of the new technical knowledge. Thus one can only proceed from day to day—though the further it is possible to foresee future developments the better. But even on this day-to-day basis the optimum location of a new enterprise from the point of view of the community as a whole may not be that which the entrepreneur would choose, looking only to private profit. 'It is misleading to speak of a conflict between economic and "social" considerations. The real issue is not between "natural" economic location for industry and arbitrarily enforced uneconomic location, nor is it even between economic and social considerations: it is between locations which may be economic for the individual or small group in the short run, and those which are economic for the community as a whole in the long run.'[1] Wherein lies the difference between social and private cost? Of the measurable items the principal are the cost of public utilities, social services in the area concerned, drainage, roads, water supply, etc. Thus if industries are set up in a new area the social cost of production will include the provision of these services, mainly carried out by public authorities. Who actually carries the cost depends upon the details of local and national taxation, but whatever they are the cost is carried by the public. Let us take as an example a depressed area 'Wales' and an expanding area 'London.' Suppose that in 'London' there is already a high level of employment and that new enterprises requiring extension of housing and public utilities are to be set up. Now private cost may be lower in 'London' than in 'Wales,' but net social cost in 'Wales' would be little higher than private cost: for it is likely that unemployment of labour will be accompanied by surplus capacity in fixed public equipment (the latter having been designed to serve industries which are no longer active): there may be no housing shortage (though this excludes the question of the *condition* of houses in depressed areas). Social cost in 'London,' however, might be much higher than private cost, because existing public utilities, etc., would probably be already fully used. Quite apart from this, extensions to public services, etc., may be cheaper in 'Wales' than in 'London'; to take only one example, new industrial development in the latter may mean costly additions to the Underground. Thus for the community as a whole it would pay to instal the new enterprise in 'Wales.'[2]

A second consideration of great importance, though less susceptible to measurement, is the undesirability of breaking up communities. Migration is not uniform with regard to sex and age groups. The

[1] P.E.P. *Report on the Location of Industry*, p. 17. This is, of course, true only if 'economic for the community as a whole' is interpreted in the wider, welfare, sense.
[2] In the long run it would probably pay the entrepreneurs as well.

younger workers are more mobile than those already settled in a district with family responsibilities, and possibly owning their own house. While no one would argue in favour of maintaining fully the *status quo* in the location of population, it is equally unwise to take no account of the 'community' factor. Moreover, there is a difference between attracting workers away from one area to another, from worse paid to better paid employment, and forcing them to leave by sheer economic necessity.

It was a common observation that the districts which escaped the worst features of the slump were those in which there was a *variety* of industries. The spreading of industries is also an insurance against any single area being unduly hit by non-cyclical changes in demand (we rule out here cyclical changes, assuming that Government policy will be successful in maintaining effective demand as a whole). Moreover, once the decline of a particular area (and exactly the same applies to the growth of a new area) has set in, the process is cumulative. The labour itself in most cases constitutes part of the market for the industries: this applies more to the growing light industries than the declining heavy industries. As the area declines some of the previous external economies become less effective in their operation. It seems, in the light of the foregoing, that Government control of location of industry is essential if the optimum use of economic resources is to be achieved.[1]

In practice it is likely to prove most convenient to intervene in the location of those enterprises for which *private* cost differs least in different parts of the country. Recent investigations have shown that for a great number of light industries the locational factors exert a much smaller pull than before, the principal cause being the decline in transport costs, both absolutely and in relation to manufacturing cost. Cost of production (to the firm) would not differ very much wherever many enterprises were located, provided that transport and power were readily accessible. The obverse of this fact is the growing importance

---

[1] The arguments used, for example, by the Board of Trade in their Evidence to the Royal Commission against control fall to the ground once the principle of maintaining a high level of effective demand is accepted. 'It is thought that it would rarely, if ever, be found desirable to prevent the expansion of an established undertaking, and any efforts to control the development of industry would therefore probably be directed almost wholly to factories about to be established. . . . When it becomes necessary for an industrialist to consider finally whether or not to start the new business, it may be that the effect of a decision to prevent him from starting in a locality which seems to him for whatever reason to be the most suitable will assume in his mind an undue importance.' (Evidence before the Royal Commission.) In any case this argument suggests that it is the *last* straw which breaks the camel's back. The same argument could be applied to wage increases rises in interest rates, increases in material costs, etc. To the camel *every* straw counts.

in the minds of the entrepreneurs of 'access to the market.'[1] And it is precisely this accessibility to markets which is most dependent upon the location of industry itself. To instal a large number of new enterprises in a depressed area would itself generate both primary and secondary employment which would *create* a large part of the market for the products of, at any rate, consumers' goods industries.[2]

The practical difficulties of controlling location only arise where industry is conducted in the main by private enterprise. In a socialist economy the planning authorities would be directly concerned with social cost of production as well as with the 'private' cost of a particular enterprise. But control of location is practicable in a capitalist economy provided private cost does not differ widely in different parts of the country. As we have seen, for a wide range of light industries the choice of location has been fortuitous or else determined on the grounds of proximity to the market. Thus for the State to control the location of new enterprises (and even extensions into new lines of production by existing companies) will not put these enterprises at a serious disadvantage with respect to their competitors. It might indeed be argued that the State should carry the difference in cost (e.g. by subsidy) where it instructs a firm to set up a factory in a place other than that which would be chosen by the firm itself: if there is a wide system of price control, which we have shown to be desirable for other reasons, it would be relatively easy to do this by allowing regional differences in profit margins. But too much should not be made of this point in an economic system in which market imperfections are such that there already exist the widest differences in the efficiency of 'competitive' firms. It would be absurd to reject control of location on the grounds that it would be impossible to achieve full 'justice' between firms with regard to competitors.[3] Nevertheless, it is clear that the best time to introduce control of location is when there is a great pressure on the part of entrepreneurs to expand production as quickly as possible, because of an excess of demand over supply. Such a situation will exist immediately after the war. Entrepreneurs will be far more concerned with starting or re-starting production of consumer's goods, which the pressure of demand (even though it will be controlled by rationing) will enable them to sell without difficulty, than with the delicate balancing of costs of production in different locations. Moreover, in

[1] Cf. Dennison, *Location of Industry and the Depressed Areas.*

[2] We have neglected throughout the *strategical* considerations. These are heavily in favour of control. The pre-war 'drift' was a drift to the areas *most* vulnerable to bombardment.

[3] The control will be lighter according to the extent to which practical schemes can be devised to put part, or all, of the burden of social cost, associated with a particular enterprise, on the shoulders of the entrepreneur.

the immediate post-war years the State will be obliged to retain other controls, such as the control of raw materials, which it can use effectively to control the location of new enterprises.

Conclusion

At the end of the discussion on the mobility of labour, it was pointed out that full employment, by reducing the volume of reserves, would raise certain difficulties which can only be overcome by a greater degree of advance 'planning.' Even in the absence of such planning mobility is probably sufficiently high to prevent the recurrence of long-period depressed areas, provided there is a policy of generating and maintaining sufficient effective demand. This last section has in effect made the same point with regard to capital. Private capital is in the modern industrial system highly mobile, in the sense that its earning power is not very much altered wherever the firm or plant is actually located: at any rate for a wide range of light industries. But although both labour and capital are mobile, if neither is ordered in any way, considerable, if temporary, pools of unemployment may arise from time to time. To avoid this waste of resources it is necessary to introduce positive planning. Two lines of approach are possible. The Government might ask the entrepreneurs: 'What are you going to produce and where are you going to set up your factory?' and then proceed to assist the labour to move to the site chosen, and to help in re-training it. The other way is for the Government to plan, to a greater or less extent, the location of new enterprises in relation to the existing, or desirable future, location of the working population. The latter approach has two important advantages. In the first place there is little direct interference with the lives of individual persons, while migration often involves considerable personal hardship. Secondly, the Government, in planning the location of industry, can take account of social costs, with which the private entrepreneur is not concerned. Such planning is, of course, easier where the industry or enterprise concerned is publicly owned: nevertheless, the fact that private cost does not differ much for many industries as between different localities makes planning practicable where industry is operated by private enterprise.

PART IV

PUBLIC FINANCE—ITS RELATION TO FULL EMPLOYMENT

by E. F. Schumacher

'THE characteristics of the special case assumed by the classical theory happen not to be those of the economic system in which we actually live, with the result that its teaching is misleading and disastrous if we attempt to apply it to the facts of experience.' These words were written by Mr. J. M. Keynes (now Lord Keynes) in 1935. His book, *The General Theory of Employment, Interest and Money*, produced—or rather brought to a head—a revolution of economic thought. It is the purpose of this paper to apply the results of this 'revolution' to another field—the field of Public Finance.

Every general theory of economics has as its natural corollary a theory of Finance which translates the principles of the former into money terms and into practical financial principles. Such a translation is necessary because, no matter how strongly one is convinced that it is the *real* things that matter, all these real things must somehow be added together and compared with one another, and this can be done only with the help of a common denominator which, in an exchange economy, is supplied by the social invention of money. Financial theory can never be more than the 'reflected image' of general economic theory,—unless, indeed, it is wrong and misleading. Thus there is nothing wanton or deliberate in translating the principles of modern economic thought into principles of finance: if the result occasionally appears paradoxical or provocative, this is due to the fact that the Keynesian analysis itself has produced results which—measured against the classical doctrine—represent a revolutionary departure.

THE PRINCIPLES OF PUBLIC FINANCE

The Classical Theory

The classical doctrine, it will be recalled, assumed that supply creates its own demand, from which it follows that there can never be more than frictional unemployment or more than sectional overproduction. Private enterprise, it was assumed, tended always to employ all available factors of production, provided that wages. and prices were sufficiently flexible. It was by no means overlooked that one man's income depended on another man's outlay and that, if some people should refuse to spend a part of their income, this would automatically reduce some other people's income. But it was believed that this, in fact, could never arise: the real resources left over by the former would always and inevitably be used by some business man for the creation of additional capital equipment.

To-day we know that this is far from inevitable. Some people may wish to save, with no one willing to use the resources left unused by them. Decisions to save are not linked by any automatic mechanism with decisions to invest; they are ruled by a different set of motives, and the rate of interest does not work as a co-ordinating force.

The logical corollary of orthodox economics is orthodox finance. If it is believed that all factors of production are normally and inevitably utilized by private business, it follows that the State can obtain the use of such factors only by preventing private business from using them. In financial terms this might mean two things: the State might use its prerogative of 'creating' money and compete with private business for the use of the available factors of production; the result would be that the prices of all factors would rise under the pressure of this additional demand;—in other words: inflation. Or the State might use its prerogative of commandeering a part of the income of the citizens by way of taxation, in which case its own expenditure—balanced by tax revenue—would no longer *add* to the total demand for productive factors but would simply be substituted for private expenditure. From this it follows that the first principle of 'sound' Public Finance is that the budget should be balanced.

But many other principles follow as well.

First, that the State cannot increase the level of business activity,—a truism when we start from the assumption that private business automatically maintains that level at 'full employment.'

Second, that the best budget is the smallest budget,—since taxes always to some extent impinge on private saving; a reduction of private savings being assumed to imply a reduction of private investment, taxes have to be looked upon as an impediment to the accumulation of productive capital.

Third,—and this follows from the last paragraph—that the most undesirable and destructive taxes are those that impinge most heavily on private saving, namely death duties, super-tax, business taxes,—in fact all taxes on the wealthier classes. Indirect taxes, on the other hand, could be taken as impinging primarily on consumption and could thus be considered economically harmless, albeit socially—perhaps—somewhat objectionable.

Fourth, that a budget deficit—necessitating State borrowing—leads possibly to inflation and certainly to a reduction in the accumulation of private capital. It leads to inflation if it is financed by the issue of 'paper money' or of short-term Government debt, because then the rate of interest does not rise sufficiently to produce a fall in private investment which offsets the increase in State expenditure. And if it is financed by the issue of long-term Government bonds, such bonds are simply substituted for the bonds or shares which private business would otherwise have been able to place.

Fifth,—and this follows by implication—that a budget deficit, even though financed in a way which avoids inflation, must lead to a reduction in the rate of progress (because it derives from the savings of the community which would otherwise all have produced new real capital) unless the Government uses borrowed funds exclusively for the creation of capital equipment at least as important as private capital.

These principles follow logically from the original proposition of classical economic theory, namely that private business automatically maintains full employment. They may be summed up in the following precepts:

1. Keep the budget small.
2. Keep the budget balanced.
3. Tax consumption, i.e. mainly the poor, rather than saving, i.e. the rich.
4. If a deficit cannot be avoided, issue long-term bonds.
5. Borrow only for purposes of 'productive' investment.

These precepts—with the exception of (1) and (3)—happen to be exactly the same as those that guide the private business man. It is therefore an easy and most plausible conclusion that the principles of Public Finance are identical with those of private finance. The similarities, at least, are much more striking than the differences. The differences, however, should not be overlooked—and have not been overlooked. Private finance has no place for precept No. 3 because it has no power to tax. Nor has it a place for precept No. 1: on the contrary, its very essence is expansion of turnover. A private business man, moreover, cannot normally create inflation even if he wanted to, but the Government can. And the private business man cannot extricate himself from a temporary difficulty by 'creating' money for his own purposes,—but the Government can, at the cost, perhaps, of inflation. Thus there are important theoretical differences even on orthodox theory. The statement that Public Finance is just ordinary finance written with a capital 'F' has never been true.

If it had been true, Governments would not have been able to contract the amount of indebtedness which in fact they have contracted Nor would they have been able to run into debt for unproductive purposes. There has always been a *qualitative* difference between Public Finance and private finance which has been more than a difference in quantity.

For a private business man a debt is a burden, and nothing but a burden. For the Government, which represents the community as a whole, a debt is not, in this sense, a burden. Being the representative of the community, it owes money to the same body which it represents. The community as a whole owes money to itself. A National Debt, therefore, when considered for the community as a whole, is not a burden in the same sense as a private debt is a burden on the debtor. This, of course, has been said innumerable times before. It is repeated here for the purpose of emphasizing that it is as true under the assumptions of 'classical' as of modern economics The view that a National Debt is a burden on the whole community, or that it represents a mortgage on the future, has always been erroneous. Under the assumptions of classical economics, however, the National Debt *did* represent a 'deadweight,'—not in the sense of a mortgage, but in the sense of a wasted opportunity. It did measure the extent to which the State had— up to date—prevented the hard-earned savings of the community from augmenting the real capital of the nation. And a reduction of the National Debt was—on these assumptions—logically tantamount to a 'making good' for the extravagances of the past: an artificial augmentation of current savings and thus of current private investment.

To the five precepts of orthodox finance listed above, we can therefore add a sixth:

6. Pay off the National Debt as fast as you can, by increasing all taxes which impinge upon current consumption.

This precept, like the others, is inherent in the classical assumptions

The Impact of the General Theory

But what happens to our theory of Public Finance when the modern (Keynesian) theory is substituted for the classical approach?—Abstention from consumption no longer leads straight to an accumulation of capital. The attempt to save, on the contrary, may lead to unemployment, a fall in the National Income, idle capacity and thus to a retardation of capital accumulation. It is no longer possible to say: 'What we don't consume, the business man uses for investment.' It is necessary to say: 'Unless we consume, the business man refuses to invest.' Under the 'classical' assumptions it looked as if society had a choice between consuming more and investing more; that consuming less meant a more rapid accumulation of capital, and that consuming more meant a reduction in the rate of advance. Now we discover that, on the contrary, private investment cannot normally rise except when consumption is rising too (or expected to rise presently) and that a reduction in consumption, far from speeding up investment, kills it. To the classics, who treated total income and outlay as given, it seemed clear that consumption and investment could only grow one at the expense of the other. But to the moderns, who have no longer any right to assume that total income and outlay are unchangeable, it has become apparent that, if there is movement at all, consumption and investment can only rise or fall together. (The reader will appreciate that this applies only to *private* investment, i.e. to the production of means of production. It obviously does not apply to the production— either private or public—of non-marketable durable goods, like roads, hospitals, armaments, etc.)

How does this profound change in the general theory of economics affect the principles of Public Finance?

As soon as we admit the possibility of a proportion of the productive resources of the community not being utilized by private business, we must also admit the possibility of the State claiming these resources through means other than taxation. Or to put it in another way: as soon as we admit that the outlay of the community may be insufficient to absorb all productive resources, and thus insufficient to produce a maximum national income, we must also admit that an increase of the outlay of the State beyond its revenue can increase the national income. The notion, therefore, that a balanced budget is desirable in all circumstances falls to the ground as soon as we abandon the classical assumption of automatic full employment.

But this is only the beginning of the revolution which the abandonment of this assumption produces in the theory of Public Finance. There are many further changes of a more subtle nature which we shall now try to follow up.

Let us first consider the principles of Public Finance on the assumption that it is the duty of the State to ensure full employment without increasing the National Debt, that is to say: with a balanced budget. This case is taken first because it lends itself to a discussion of the principles of taxation under modern conditions. The case of a full employ-

ment policy through budget deficits (and hence through a rising
National Debt), which necessitates an elucidation of some more
complicated problems of financial technique, will be considered later.

A Balanced Budget?

Unemployment implies that a certain margin of the community's
productive resources is not claimed by any private citizen or firm.
It remains left over and must run to waste unless measures are taken
which enable either the citizens of the State or the State itself to claim
it. What measures could be taken to enable the citizens to claim it,—
to produce, in other words, the very condition which classical theory
has always assumed to exist *ipso facto*? If a given National Income
exists at a certain historical moment, it will continue to exist as long
as that income is currently expended and thus re-creates income.
Such a continuous re-creation of the National Income, however, may
fail to materialize owing to the attempt to save more than the amount
for which investment outlets can be found.

The volume of savings does not depend merely upon the size of the
National Income; it also depends upon the distribution of incomes. All
available evidence goes to show that a more even distribution of
incomes would increase the average propensity to consume and thus
reduce the danger of investment outlets being insufficient to absorb
all the savings people plan to make at full employment. A Government, therefore, which is intent on ensuring full employment without
incurring budget deficits must so redistribute the National Income that
the community will never attempt to save in excess of current investment opportunities. Since private investment opportunities, however,
are themselves not a fixed quantity—for reasons which cannot be
discussed here[1]—the redistribution of incomes necessary to assure permanent full employment would probably have to go rather far, and
a continuous policy of adjustment, through variations in the weight and
structure of taxation, subsidies and price control, would be required
to keep the economy on an even keel.

But we need not pursue this point for the purpose of our argument.
Any redistribution of incomes towards a smaller inequality is bound
to reduce private saving and may thus contribute to the solution of
the unemployment problem.

Once it is realized that the ultimate cause of unemployment in
modern society is to be found in the prevailing distribution of incomes,
the most logical course of action that suggests itself would be to go

[1] Cf. p. 54.

to the root of the matter and to alter the conditions which determine the distribution of gross incomes, i.e. incomes before taxation. But these conditions are of such a fundamental nature and are created by the whole structure of distribution of property, by inheritance, imperfect competition, and the very design of present-day capitalist society, that a discussion of them in this paper would be out of place.

The gross distribution of incomes might be left as it is—or altered to the extent which general conditions permit—and taxation may be employed for the purpose here under discussion. Taxation, therefore, appears here in a function which is somewhat different from the function normally attributed to it: its object is 'redistribution' rather than merely the raising of cash for the State.

REDISTRIBUTIVE TAXATION

The Purposes of Taxation

It may be useful at this point to recall that the concept of taxation as a method of income redistribution is foreign to the theory of Public Finance that derives from classical economic thought. It is foreign in the sense that it has no economic merit—although it may have merits on the grounds of social justice. To use taxation for the purpose of transferring income from the rich to the poor appeared to the classical economist as tantamount to sacrificing progress to current enjoyment. Social reformers were in a dilemma: greater social justice appeared to be obtainable only at the price of retarding the accumulation of capital, and any plea for it could be answered by the question: Is it not better to cease worrying about the distribution of the cake and to concentrate on increasing its size?

But now it is different. Inasmuch as depression and unemployment and indeed long-term stagnation can be traced to inequality of income distribution, redistributive measures commend themselves not merely on the grounds of social justice but pre-eminently on the grounds of economic reason. A classical economist was being logical when he recommended taxing the poor rather than the rich. But a modern economist is logical when he recommends taxing those able to save rather than those anxious to consume.

The argument of social justice and the economic argument have thus become amalgamated in modern theory. The old dilemma of the social reformer has been resolved. But a distinction between the two functions of redistributive taxation can nevertheless be made. One function is the reduction of private savings; the other, the equalization of living standards. The former is relevant to the problem of how to achieve and maintain full employment; the latter is relevant to the problem of what 'content' is to be given to full employment. A redistribution of incomes for purely economic reasons, in other words, may be pressed up to the point that must be reached in order to abolish unemployment; but it may also be pressed further for reasons of equity. To say that redistributive taxes are no longer inimical to technical progress and the accumulation of capital does not mean that some kinds of taxation may not have economically destructive effects. It merely means that there is now a *prima facie* case in favour of a large measure of redistributive taxation, both on economic and on social grounds, which was not the case as long as the classical assumptions held good.

The question arises: What are the limits of redistributive taxation? Or, to put it differently: What margins can be created by taxation between gross incomes and net ('available') incomes without interfering grievously with the economic process? What happens when the available income of the rich is substantially smaller than their gross money income? And: What happens when the income of the poor is substantially augmented through State expenditure?

No definite theoretical answer is possible to these questions. Too much depends upon the reactions of the public, historical evidence of which is as yet scanty. But a few general considerations may not be out of place here.

Limits of Redistributive Taxation

Taxation, when strained beyond a certain point, creates a new set of economic motives which may have far-reaching economic effects. Every tax, of course, creates different motives, and we cannot do more here than to single out a few typical cases.

Surtax creates the inducement for owners of business establishments to leave their profits in the firm, as reserves or 'undistributed profits.' There they escape surtax, being taxed merely at the standard rate of income tax. This may become an important factor in firms in which a few wealthy persons are the principal directors determining dividend policy. Rather than distribute to themselves and to the other shareholders large dividends, they will prefer to accumulate such profits within the firm and use them for buying up other firms or buttressing a monopoly position. Such a policy may increase the net savings of the community as long as investment outlets are plentiful; but it will cause increased unemployment when investment fails. The undistributed profits of companies are the principal source of (potential) savings in this country in peace time and thus hold a position of key importance with regard to the general level of employment. A tax structure which puts a premium on leaving profits undistributed necessitates larger budget deficits for full employment than would be necessary if such a premium did not arise.

High direct taxation generally puts a premium on every kind of tax evasion—legal or illegal. The prevention of illegal tax evasion can be left to the Attorney-General and does not concern us here directly. But it is necessary to realize that no system can be considered satisfactory which puts too high a reward on breaking the law. Legal tax evasion is even more important. A high income tax, imposed for the purpose of redistribution, is subject to the law of diminishing returns in more senses than one. It leads to a situation in which every item of expenditure that can be booked over 'expense account' is automatically subsidized by the State at the rate of the standard tax. It leads to an attempt on the part of business men to charge as much as possible of their private expenditure over the cost account of the business they control. Rather than drawing substantial salaries, they will try to obtain as much real consumers' value 'in kind' as possible. The firms themselves will employ tax experts and lawyers—their salaries being chargeable to cost account—to exploit every possible loophole in the tax structure. The wit of the tax collector is continuously pitted against the wit of the ablest legal and accounting talent which money can buy. Advertising, high pressure salesmanship, 'prestige' expenditure—anything that reduces taxable profits and provides satisfaction to the owners or high executives of the firm is automatically subsidized by the State. The more 'progressive' the scales of taxation, the smaller, at the same time, is the reward obtainable by business men for extra effort and risk-taking. In a free society the 'limits of taxation' deserve the closest study.

It is perhaps worth emphasizing that these limits have nothing to do with the concept of 'taxable capacity.' This latter concept has no intelligible meaning when used as an argument in favour of State borrowing instead of taxation. Whether the State borrows from the rich or taxes them, it is practically the same funds which are gathered in. Only the motives and incentives created by these two different courses are different.

If the above arguments are accepted it follows that taxation, as a redistributive device, must be handled with care, and that there is no justification for neglecting the *gross* distribution of incomes on the grounds that it can always be modified by taxation. The greater the gap between the gross and the net distribution, the greater is the distortion of the economy which a tax-free cost account produces and the greater the dis-incentive to enterprise. There is little doubt that full employment in this country might in the long run be brought about by means of redistributive taxation alone, i.e. without permanent budget deficits. But it might be associated with a marked decline in entrepreneurial efficiency and would not affect the real luxury consumption of the owners and controllers of business as much as might be thought according to the statistical evidence of net incomes. All measures which by-pass the gross distribution of incomes are only a second-best as compared with measures applied directly to profit margins, interest, rent, salaries and fees.

The Incentive to Invest

Income and surtaxes, however, do not affect saving (mainly undistributed profits) and consumption alone. They also affect the incentive to invest. In the business man's language: they make the State a partner in profits, when the investment turns out to be a financial success, but not a partner in losses in case of failure. They thus reduce the reward of risk-taking without reducing risks. This argument has often been contested on the grounds that income tax reduces the net returns of all investments equally and that a person with £100 of savings will thus suffer the same percentage reduction, whether he uses his savings on a safe or on a risky venture. But it is not the percentage reduction that matters, it is the absolute reduction. Assume the standard rate of income tax to be 10s. in the £. An investor contemplates putting £10,000 into a risky venture which he expects to yield twenty per cent profits, or £2,000 a year. Taxation reduces this amount to £1,000 net. He concludes that if all goes according to expectations he will have earned profits equivalent to his initial outlay in ten years. If there had been no tax on profits, his profit would have amortized his investment in five years. The risk he incurs is largely a function of the length of the engagement, and income tax increases the length of the engagement.

As against this, it has been argued that the risk incurred by investing a given sum of savings is itself reduced by the fact that all 'unearned' income is taxed at 10s. in the £. The investor's risk, so the argument runs, is not measured by the possibility of losing a given amount of capital, but rather by the amount of net income he would have obtained by putting his money into a safe investment. The very risk of investment is thus held to be cut in half by taxation, inasmuch as taxation is cutting in half the net yield obtainable on any alternative investment. This argument implies the view that the value of a given capital sum is fully expressed by the net income obtainable through it without taking a risk—a view which is clearly erroneous. A capital sum is 'valuable' even if held in cash: it is a claim on immediate goods, not merely a claim to a future income. Even if income tax were at the rate of 20s. in the £ on 'unearned' income, money capital would not thereby become worthless: it would still command current goods. But it could no longer be used for buying an income. Such a rate would destroy the incentive to invest for profit, but it would not reduce the value of money over goods.

Thus it appears as incontestable that income tax (and surtax in the case of one-man businesses) reduces the incentive to invest, and this sets another limit to the amount of income tax which may be levied in a private enterprise economy without seriously disturbing the economic process. But this limitation can be overcome without great difficulty, as Mr. Kalecki has shown,[1] by a modified form of income tax. At present depreciation allowances are tax-free, whether they are re-invested or not. Investments beyond depreciation allowances (new investment) are subject to tax. If all actual investments were made (wholly or partly) chargeable to cost account—depreciation allowances without actual replacement not being so chargeable—income tax, at whatever level, would cease to have any direct effect upon the incentive to invest.

So far we have considered only one aspect of redistributive taxation —taxation as a means of reducing excessive incomes. A redistributive fiscal policy, however, does not merely decrease the income of the rich; it may also increase the absolute income of the poor.[2] Such an increase may take the form of money—when produced by old-age pensions, family allowances, and other social security payments,—or it may be brought about 'in kind'—free services and amenities,—or finally by State subsidies employed for the purpose of reducing the cost of living.

It is sometimes argued that the augmentation of small incomes, through State expenditure covered by taxation on the large incomes, must reduce the incentive to work. If every citizen is entitled to a certain share of the national output, not on account of his contribution to such output, but simply on account of his being a citizen, is there no danger of slackness and decay? This line of reasoning ceases to be

[1] Cf. pp. 45-8.
[2] A *relative* increase in their income is effected even if the State expends revenue obtained from the higher incomes in a way of no direct economic benefit to either rich or poor.

convincing when it is considered that work, in any case, is not the only, or even the predominant, source of income for that section of the community which carries the greatest responsibility and on whose energy and wisdom the fate of all most directly depends. But we need not go into these arguments here. If they have any truth in them at all, they can only apply to certain forms of redistribution—free services and cash payments. They cannot apply to subsidies paid to reduce the prices of essential consumers' goods. To apply them to subsidies as well would imply the view that every rise in the standard of living of the masses is *ipso facto* undesirable.

Instead of subsidizing prices, of course, it is always possible for the State to desist from levying indirect taxation and thus to lower prices. Every tax on goods consumed by the masses leads to a curtailment of their general consumption, and every subsidy leads to a general expansion. The specific effect of tax or subsidy depends, of course, on the elasticity of demand for the article in question. But it appears that the demand for most goods of mass consumption, while elastic in response to income changes, is relatively inelastic in response to small price changes.

Taxation in pre-war Britain, although more 'progressive' than in most other countries, was redistributive only in the sense of reducing large incomes; not in the sense of augmenting the absolute incomes of the poor. 'The amount of taxation paid by the "under £250" class was very nearly as large as their receipts from the Government's social expenditure. There cannot, in any case, have been any great difference between the two amounts (estimated for 1937 as £460 millions and £520 millions respectively). It is therefore hardly right to describe that expenditure as a "transference from the rich to the poor," a description commonly used. . . . What is true, however, is that the lowest income group had been almost entirely relieved of the necessity of making a contribution to the general expenses of government. . . .' (Hicks, *The Social Framework*, pp. 187-8).

Consumption versus Investment?

Modern economic theory, as we have seen, forces us to look with favour upon redistributive taxation. It thus leads us to adopt a position which is directly opposite to the position that follows from an acceptance of the 'classical' assumptions. Redistributive taxation, far from reducing the rate of capital accumulation, is likely actually to increase it—provided only that it is levied in such a way as not to restrict unduly the incentive to invest.

This may still sound extremely paradoxical to economists (and others) educated in the classical tradition. The notion that Investment and Consumption are opposites, and that every increase in expenditure on consumption implies a decrease in expenditure on investment, dies hard. But it is a notion which has no place in a capitalist economy, except when there is in force a system of direct rationing and allocation of labour and raw materials. One way—in fact the most sensible way—of increasing private investment, of inducing a more rapid accumulation of privately owned productive capital, is to stimulate the consumption of goods for the production of which such capital is required. Generally speaking, an increase in consumers' demand, no matter to what point it is carried, is not likely to cause a curtailment of private investment; just as a decrease of consumers' demand, although it leaves productive factors 'free' for investment, is not likely to be accompanied by a rise in the rate of capital accumulation under conditions of free capitalism. The normal reaction of a private business man is to expand his plant when faced with a rising demand for his products, and not to expand it when demand for his products flags. Even after full employment has been reached, it will not be investment that suffers from a further expansion of consumers' purchasing power.[1] Investment will go on, but prices will rise, and the larger money outlay of consumers will fail to secure them a larger real income. The system as a whole will run into inflation. The reason for a deliberate curtailment of consumers' demand at any given moment does not derive from the fact that Consumption would otherwise encroach upon private investment: it derives from the entirely different consideration that inflation would otherwise destroy the value of money and disrupt the stability of the economy as a whole. The propensity to consume, as such, is not inimical to the propensity to invest, but a pre-condition of it. Redistributive taxation, employed for the purpose of raising the propensity to consume for the nation as a whole, promotes private investment as long as the taxes themselves are so designed as to allow such investment to remain profitable.

The propensity to consume, however, may itself be so high as to create inflationary dangers. If Consumption could always expand at the expense of private investment, this danger would be remote. The danger is a real one *because* Consumption and private investment are closely linked together and a sustained rise in Consumption produces a derived demand for private investment goods. The supreme objective of fiscal policy should be to keep the economy as a whole on

[1] Unless that expansion is financed by a kind of taxation which destroys the incentive to invest.

an even keel: to avoid Inflation as much as Deflation. The tax weapon therefore—coupled with the policy of State expenditure—must now be considered for its anti-inflationary potentiality.

Anti-Inflationary Taxation

In a modern economy there is, as experience shows, little danger of private expenditure on consumption and investment causing inflation. When such a danger appears it can normally be traced to exceptional circumstances—an exceptional and non-recurrent propensity to consume and to invest in the aftermath of war. It is thus not private expenditure which need engage our attention in this connection as much as State expenditure. If the spending programme of the State itself is of exceptional dimensions, inflation may arise on that score. When the problem of full employment is considered in isolation, it is normally assumed that the *raison d'être* of State expenditure is solely or primarily the achievement or maintenance of full employment. But this, of course, is an unrealistic abstraction. In a modern society, collective activities, necessitating large expenditures of public funds, possess a high, and often the highest, priority. If the distribution of *gross* incomes were so arranged that the public's spontaneous demand for consumption and private investment were always sufficient to employ all available resources,—that is to say, if the basic assumption of classical theory were realized,—taxation would still be required so as to free real resources for the use of the State.

Fiscal policy thus appears in a double function. It appears in its traditional function of preventing private citizens from utilizing resources which the State itself wishes to utilize for collective needs. And it appears, in addition, in the function of modifying the distribution of incomes. These two functions, of course, overlap to a considerable degree. The economic motive (as distinct from the social motive) of progressive taxation is to effect a reduction in the propensity to save. The economic motive of anti-inflationary taxation is to effect a reduction in the propensity to consume. Taxes designed to impinge on savings do not, to the extent that they fulfil their design, free real resources for the use of the State (assuming that the incentive to invest is not impaired). But taxes designed to impinge on private consumption do reduce the public's use of resources and can therefore be justified only if these same resources can be shown to yield a higher return in welfare when collectively used. It is possible to argue that the State is under a greater moral obligation to make a wise use of funds derived from consumption taxes than it is with regard to funds derived either from loans or from taxes impinging upon private savings. In the former case it commandeers resources which the public would otherwise have used for itself. In the latter case it commandeers resources which might have been left unused.

These complications did not arise under the assumption of classical theory. Any kind of tax was assumed to serve equally the purpose of freeing real resources for collective use. A difference was indeed made between taxes affecting savings and taxes affecting consumption. But the conclusions drawn from this distinction were of a very different character. Since all private savings were assumed to lead automatically to the creation of private capital, taxes impinging on private saving were viewed as being inimical to economic progress. Inasmuch as it was considered inconceivable that any substantial real resources might be left in idleness altogether, the anti-inflationary effect of all taxes was treated as equal, and there remained only the choice between curbing current consumption and curbing current capital accumulation.

Modern economic theory puts a different complexion on the matter. The anti-inflationary effect of different taxes can no longer be taken as equal. Assume that the State—after full employment has been reached—raises its revenue exclusively from death duties and surtax,—that is to say, in a form which impinges most directly upon savings. Assume further that all State revenue is expended on goods and services furnished to the consumer free of charge. The increase in general consumption creates an increase in private investment,[1] thus augmenting further the total outlay. An inflationary rise in prices leads to increases in profits and thus to an increase in the revenue from surtax. But the ever-swelling flow of State revenue is not a brake on the inflationary spiral: it is simply the result of inflation taking place.

This example may serve to illustrate the fact that the precepts of 'sound' finance are no longer a guide even to deflationary policies. It is no longer true to say that it is safer to finance, say, 60 per cent of State expenditure out of taxation, and only 40 per cent out of borrowing, rather than the other way around. Everything depends upon the *kind* of taxation applied. Everything also depends upon the kind of borrowing. A scheme, for instance, such as Lord Keynes advocated at the beginning of this war, whereunder a large part of war expenditure would have been financed out of borrowing, would not have produced inflation on that account, since the funds to be borrowed would have come from incomes which otherwise would have gone

[1] If income tax is modified so as to leave the incentive to invest unaffected.

almost wholly into consumption. If the Chancellor of the Exchequer tells us the proportion of State expenditure which is covered by taxes and by borrowing respectively, this information may be of interest in some respects, but it does not enable us to draw any conclusions as to the effects of financial policy with regard to inflation, unless we know also the source of the taxes and the source of the borrowing (savings).

Only such taxes are effective as an anti-inflationary weapon which directly impinge upon consumption or private investment. This is not to say that even such taxes could under all circumstances be screwed up to a level which would effectively stave off inflation. If, as in wartime, there are large unsatisfied demands, taxation fails as an anti-inflationary weapon, because spending can be financed out of past savings, and recourse must be taken to a direct control of expenditure through rationing, etc.

DEFICIT FINANCE

The Burden of the Debt

So far, we have discussed some of the economic effects of various types of a balanced budget. We must now turn to the effects of an unbalanced budget: effects upon the National Debt and upon such things as the volume of money in circulation, the liquidity of financial and other institutions, and the rate of interest.

Assuming, then, that a quantitatively sufficient adjustment in either the gross or the net distribution of incomes cannot be obtained and recourse must be had to 'unorthodox finance' to secure full employment, what are the consequences?

Every budget deficit adds to the National Debt. Two questions arise here: Is there any limit to the size of the National Debt which a community may carry without harm?—a question of quantity; and: In what form should any necessary additions to the National Debt be made,—in long-term bonds, short-term paper, or cash?—a question of quality.

That there is a profound difference between the significance of 'national debt' and that of 'private debt' is now generally understood. A national debt—internally held—is a debt which the community owes to itself. Saying this, however, does not dispose of the matter altogether. There remains the fact that not all members of the community are equally the creditors of the State,—that indeed the Government securities, notes and deposits which represent the National Debt are largely concentrated in the hands of a small section of the population.[1]

---

[1] The part played by the banking system is discussed on pp. 116–120 below.

Assume for a moment that the National Debt—of (say) £24,000 million—were evenly distributed amongst the 48,000,000 citizens of this country. The holding per head would amount to no more than £500. An average holding of this size, earning something like £10 to £15 interest (subject to tax) per annum, would serve as no more than an 'emergency reserve' of purchasing power. It would neither create rentiers nor diminish the incentive to work. It is clear that every citizen is, in fact, eligible under present conditions for a 'minimum income' of a much larger size—quite irrespective of whether he works or not. He gets it by way of Unemployment Insurance, Health Insurance, Pension—even Charity. If he received it by way of interest on his share in the national debt, some of the other payments might become unnecessary; in any case the granting of such an income 'by right' could not be considered a burden on the community in any valid sense. But where would the money come from? Let us assume it were raised by means of social security contributions—and it is at once clear that the final effect of such a national debt would be very similar to that of many of the social security schemes which are now in operation. It has never been suggested that such schemes must be limited in scope because of the 'transfer burden' they involve. They may be criticized on other grounds (rightly and wrongly), namely that the way the money is raised may place an undue burden on some groups and that the way it is expended may not be in sufficient accordance with current ideas of social priority. This is also the only way in which it is possible to criticize the economic effects of the national debt: that it involves taking money from people from whom it ought not to be taken, and giving it to people who ought not to receive it.

The concept of 'transfer burden,' therefore, obscures the important issues at stake: it suggests that the size of the national debt, as such, imposes a definite burden, and that the larger the size, the greater the burden. But this is incorrect. A national debt is 'burdensome' only in a special sense which derives not from its size, but from the distribution in the ownership of the debt. The mere collection and redistribution of money has been technically perfected to such a degree that it imposes no appreciable inconvenience. But a national debt, held by a small minority of citizens, which necessitates the yearly transfer of considerable amounts of money to persons already wealthy becomes a stumbling block in any policy—undertaken on social or economic grounds—of reducing the inequality of incomes.

The yield of income tax in 1936, at £257 million, only just exceeded the cost of the National Debt Service, at £224 million. Income tax, at the rate then current, therefore, might be said to have had no substantial redistributive effect as between the income tax payers, taken as a group, and the others: if there had been no national debt and no income tax, the position would have been much the same. Surtax, in 1936, brought in only £53.4 million. Alone, it covered no more than 24 per cent of the cost of the National Debt Service. Inasmuch as a very large part of the national debt is owned—directly or indirectly—by surtax payers, they certainly paid less in surtax than what they received in interest on Government bonds. We found in our discussion of taxation that there are certain limits to the usefulness of taxes as a redistributive device. If a considerable rate of taxation has to be imposed just to offset the enhanced inequality of incomes which the national debt service produces, less is left over for redistribution proper. This, it seems, is the fundamental problem posed by the national debt,—a problem which does not become apparent as long as we talk simply about the 'transfer burden.'

Before we go any further, however, let us consider the quantitative importance of the problem we are here facing. Our immediate concern is not the effect of the national debt which already exists (or will exist at the end of the war), but the soundness or unsoundness of pursuing a full employment policy by means of deficit finance.

The maintenance of full employment in Britain after the war may necessitate an annual budget deficit of something like £300,000,000. This figure is based on the assumption of a return to pre-war rates of taxation and of a final price increase of not more than 40 per cent over the pre-war level. The average rate of interest payable on war-time indebtedness is about 2 per cent. At this rate, the annual increment in the interest burden would not be more than £6 million. Income and surtax reduces this amount to probably less than £4 million—assuming 1938 rates of taxation. A part of the capital value of the national debt, and thus also of the annual increment, goes back to the State in the form of death duties. Thus the problem is reduced to a matter of a few million pounds net per annum,—an amount which, although cumulative,[1] cannot be said to present a serious problem. If it

[1] If all other factors remain equal, the deficit itself will have to increase every year by the same amount as was paid in interest during the previous year. That is to say: the interest payable on the yearly increments of the national debt would itself have to be borrowed. If the consumption of the bondholders shows a tendency to increase owing to the increase in their interest claims, additional taxation must be imposed upon them. The motive behind such taxation would not be merely the desire to prevent the national debt from rising at a compound interest rate, but rather to prevent an expansion of luxury consumption at the expense either of State outlay or of the private outlay of the poorer classes. The greater the luxury expenditure of wealthy savers, the smaller the need for a budget deficit. Yet, employment created in this way would have a low

is compared with the total amount of 'unearned' income—profits, interest and rent—which amounted to £1,853 million in 1938 and rose to £3,054 million in 1943, it is seen to be of small quantitative importance. The sums involved may add up to a considerable figure over a prolonged period of time, but they are entirely overshadowed by other factors in the economy which have a far more powerful impact upon the distribution of gross incomes,—such as inheritance laws, interest rates, imperfect competition, etc. The 'transfer burden' of the national debt is only one subsidiary aspect of the much larger problem of income distribution in present-day society—albeit a factor working in the wrong direction.

Are we then to conclude that the size of the national debt—apart from its effect upon income distribution—does not matter at all?

Ownership of Government bonds,—like the ownership of any other form of capital, real or financial,—is a claim to wealth, not merely a claim to an annual income. A steady increase in the national debt means a steady increase in the volume of financial claims held by a small section of the community. Even if taxation is so adjusted that, for the group as a whole, a growth of their holdings does not lead to a growth of their net incomes, there remains the growth of their holdings. Such an accumulation will become increasingly futile. It may ultimately lead to an undesirable rise in the number of rich rentiers and to an equally undesirable increase in 'conspicuous consumption.' That is to say, the propensity to consume of the wealthy may gradually rise to such an extent that their savings—and consequently the very need for further deficit finance—disappear. This would indeed solve the problem of unemployment, but it would give to 'full employment' a content which could hardly be defended on moral or social principles.

Let it be remembered, however, that this accumulation of somewhat meaningless money titles is not due to the fact that full employment is being created by budget deficits: it is due to full employment as such, coupled with the existing distribution of incomes. If private investment produced (and were able to maintain) full employment, the

social priority. A large deficit, as such is not an evil, if it is spent on communal needs of high social value.

The quantitative relationship between the whole national debt and its yearly increment, however, is such that even a very small fall in the rate of interest reduces the interest burden sufficiently to 'make room' for a substantial increase in the debt. Such a reduction, of course, exerts its effect only to the extent that conversions of old bonds became possible. It needs time to bear fruit. But the cumulative effect of the steadily growing debt upon the interest burden also needs time to gain quantitative importance. If the average rate of interest payable on the national debt were reduced by one-tenth of 1 per cent every two years for a period of twenty years—i.e. by 1 per cent in all—the capital sum of the national debt could rise at the rate of £400 million a year without increasing the total interest 'burden.' (The rate of interest is discussed below.)

result would be not better but worse. The total volume of negotiable assets within the community would not be smaller, nor would it increase at a slower rate,—only private debt would take the place of Government debt. The income of rentiers would be even larger, and would rise at a higher rate, because private debt cannot normally be financed at interest rates of 2 or 3 per cent. In a society in which the bulk of current saving is done by the wealthy, there is an inevitable tendency for the wealth of rentiers to increase.[1] Those who predicted such a development in the past have not been in error, as far as the logical deductions from their basic assumption are concerned. But their basic assumption—the assumption of classical theory, that full employment is always maintained—has falsified their prediction. Full employment, consciously pursued, would make their assumption come true and, consequently, justify their prediction. In the past, it has been one of the functions of recurrent depressions to wipe out a proportion of these accumulations at regular intervals. Depressions have never directly destroyed 'real capital'; but they have destroyed 'paper capital'; they have deflated the value of money titles by bankruptcies, defaults, 'capital re-organizations' and Stock Exchange slumps. They have cruelly and indiscriminately brought down the structure of private indebtedness. If depressions—a high price to pay for such a purpose—are avoided, the structure of paper indebtedness—public or private—and the volume of money titles in our society will grow without visible limit.

The Direction of Deficit Spending

The volume of indebtedness, obviously, is not influenced by the way in which borrowed funds are expended. A debt of £100 is a debt of £100, whether it has arisen in connection with buying armaments, machinery, beer, or roads. Nor is the interest payable on it different according to the object of expenditure. The problem of income distribution, as intensified by the interest payments on the national

---

[1] Not only the wealth of rentiers, but also the inequality of property distribution itself is likely to increase. If all income groups saved the same proportion of their income, the degree of inequality would remain constant. But there is every reason to believe that—in conditions of general stability—the proportion of income saved rises with a rise in income. The high income groups, in other words, not only save a larger absolute amount per head than the low income groups, they save a higher *proportion* of their higher incomes. This generalization does not necessarily apply to a society in which there are sudden changes in the relative position of the various classes. The experience of Britain during the inter-war period does not conform with this pattern as far as personal incomes are concerned. It does conform fairly well when undistributed profits' are included in the incomes of the owners of industrial equities. The figures on Consumers' Expenditure and Savings in U.S.A., made available by the National Resources Planning Board for 1936, afford an excellent confirmation of the generalization.

debt, is therefore not directly affected by the purpose for which the debt has been incurred.

The State has complete freedom as to the purpose to which it decides to devote borrowed funds. It may devote them to roads, hospitals, free milk, or consumers' subsidies. The decision is not dictated by economic reasoning, but should be dictated by social priority.

Considerations of social priority[1] may indicate that the most desirable object of State expenditure is the creation of durable assets, like roads, schools, hospitals, etc. Or it may indicate that a greater need will be satisfied if expenditure is directed so as to increase the consumers' outlay of those in want. The latter course can be pursued along one or both of two lines: directly—through subsidies which cheapen certain selected consumers' goods, or indirectly—through cash payments made to consumers' in need. In either case there results not only an absolute increase in consumption but also an absolute increase in the stock of productive capital. The demand for (say) textile machines does not exist independently of the demand for textiles: it is simply derived from the latter, in much the same way as the demand for textile fibre is no self-subsistent entity but a function of the demand for the finished products. The connection between the demand for consumers' goods on the one hand and the demand for raw materials or productive capital equipment on the other is naturally an elastic one. Expectations of profit may induce business men to accumulate stocks or to expand capacity before an expansion of consumers' demand has actually set in. It falls outside the scope of this paper to discuss the precise relationship between these factors under varying circumstances. The only point of importance here is that private net investment activity is a *derived* phenomenon; it needs the stimulus of profit expectation which, in turn, can arise only out of an actual or anticipated increase in the demand for the ultimate product. The ultimate product of private industry is consumers' goods and services, for which consumers are able and willing to pay. This, of course, does not apply to communal investment, i.e. the creation of durable goods of a non-marketable kind: roads, schools, etc. With regard to these there does exist a freedom of choice, and the Government may decide to push consumption at the expense of communal investment, or *vice versa*. But no such freedom of choice exists as between consumption and private investment, once the period of direct rationing and allocations has passed.

The 'derived' character of private investment is overlooked by

---

[1] Also: considerations as to what real resources are unemployed and can be mobilized without undue difficulties.

writers who propose to stimulate private investment *as a means* of maintaining full employment. There is no doubt that relief of taxation and subsidies can be, in principle, granted on a sufficient scale to induce capitalists to maintain their net investment expenditure permanently at boom level. But the accumulation of investment goods, which are merely a means to the increased production of consumers' goods, lacks economic purpose, unless there is an equivalent expansion in consumption, i.e. in the purchasing power of consumers. The mere subsidization of private investment, therefore, cannot solve the problem in the long run. It may be useful for the purpose of raising the level of employment out of depression; but it cannot serve to maintain full employment without leading either to a crisis or—if subsidies rise at a cumulative rate—to a purposeless accumulation of idle capacity.

It is however pointed out that this particular difficulty would not arise if the effect of tax-relief and subsidy were the 'deepening,' rather than the 'widening,' of capital equipment; if it were in the nature of 'rationalization' rather than expansion. Yet, rationalization leads to fewer workers producing the same output, which—unless accompanied by expansion—must lead to unemployment. If full employment is to be maintained, there must be 'widening,' i.e. new equipment for the displaced workers, alongside with 'deepening' and thus an expansion in the output of marketable goods. The old problem, consequently, recurs. In addition, it would be necessary to consider how such 'rationalization' can be brought about by State action in privately owned industry. A certain 'deepening' will indeed occur automatically during any period of recovery, for the relative shortage of labour consequent upon the expansion of effective demand presses the entrepreneur to obviate labour shortage by rationalization. But as full employment is reached, any further pressure of demand,—any intensification in the shortage of labour,—would soon lead to inflation. Under full employment conditions, in other words, rationalization cannot be enforced merely by increasing consumers' purchasing power,—whether that increase be brought about through wage bargaining or through consumers' subsidies. The general method of attaining a 'deepening' of capital in privately owned industry, then, is to institute a system of price control with the object of exerting pressure on profit margins and thus forcing entrepreneurs to seek to maintain their profits by rationalization. Otherwise, there only remains the method of State interference with the management of private industry: compelling severely undercapitalized industries to re-organize and providing assistance, in special cases, with State guarantees, cheap credit, and so forth. In all cases, however, there stands out the general fact that private net investment cannot continue for long without becoming purposeless, unless accompanied by an expansion in consumers' demand, and that that expansion, under conditions of full employment, is not automatically brought about.

The new theory does not demonstrate that, by tax concessions or subsidy, it would be possible to maintain full employment through maintaining private investment permanently at boom level. On the contrary, it demonstrates that private net investment in the long run depends for its continuance on an expansion of consumers' demand. It shows, on the other hand, that the State can achieve and maintain full employment irrespective of the volume of private investment— by tax policy or deficit finance. It demonstrates, further, that no limitation is imposed by economic reasoning upon the choice of objectives towards which the State might direct its expenditure. To suggest that such a limitation exists with regard to loan expenditure can only serve to induce the Government to depart from the relevant considerations: considerations of social desirability and need.

We have suggested that the size of the national debt (to the extent that it arises out of the pursuit of a full employment policy) is a factor causing concern only on account of its influence upon the distribution of gross incomes and upon the volume of money titles which it allows to accumulate in the hands of a small minority. We must now consider the question which immediately suggests itself at this point, namely, whether a large national debt—or for that matter a large accumulation of private debt—must not lead to inflation.

National Debt and Inflation

The mere existence of money or of money claims does not create inflation; only expenditure does. Does the existence of money or of money claims in the hands of the public affect expenditure?

By far the most important factor determining expenditure during any given period is the amount of income earned during the preceding period. But it is not the only factor. A proportion of income is currently saved; a rise in consumers' expenditure is always possible if they attempt to spend the whole of their previous income. A further rise is possible if they attempt to 'dis-save,' i.e. to finance current expenditure out of past accumulations.

There is therefore always a possibility of an inflationary development. This possibility does not depend upon the existence of past accumulations of money or money titles. It exists in any economy that does not spend the whole of its current income on consumption. Any sudden increase in the propensity to consume spells inflation in a fully employed economy, unless it is compensated by an equivalent decrease in the volume of real resources used by the State. The inflationary effect of a sudden increase in the average propensity to consume is intensified by the strong link which, as stated above, exists between an increase in consumers' demand and the private demand for capital goods.

Since an inflationary development can always arise out of an increase in the propensity to consume, and since this development can take place without any 'dis-saving' taking place, it is clear that the existence of a large national debt, in itself, cannot be considered an 'inflationary' factor.

The average propensity to consume is likely to be abnormally high after the war. It would be abnormally high even if the war had been financed wholly by taxation and there had been no increase in the volume of cash in circulation, the volume of deposits, the floating debt, or the national debt as a whole. Even if people do not touch their war-time accumulations and merely insist on spending all their current income on consumption, private investment activity will cause inflation. The necessity for war-time controls to be continued for a suitable period in peace arises, not out of the existence of past savings in a more or less liquid form, but out of an abnormal propensity to consume. It must be continued until the propensity to consume and the current supply of consumable goods have returned to something nearer normality.

In a normal peace-time economy no pressure is exerted to induce people to save, and all such savings as are currently made are voluntary savings in the fullest sense of the word. The act of saving does not leave behind a condition of 'pent-up demand,' as it does in war-time. Some individuals, indeed, save with a definite 'spending purpose' in mind: they save up for a house, for a holiday, for children's education, or for retirement. But there is nothing which could lead us to expect that they act as a group. That is to say, some of them will always be saving while others are using their savings. The millions of individuals in question each make their separate plan, and the result is a steady stream of expenditure emanating from the group as a whole. The low-income group, comprising something like 80 per cent of the population of this country in peace time, in any case does not accumulate any substantial amounts of financial claims. Although it accounts for some of the net savings of the community, it is itself the investor of such net savings—

investing them mainly in durable consumers' goods, above all: houses.

What about the savings of the other (say) 20 per cent of the population? They enjoy far larger current incomes per head, and their saving habits are consequently somewhat more volatile. Their savings are largely of the nature of a residual item: money left over after all current needs have been satisfied. If full employment—achieved by budget deficits rather than by income re-distribution—stabilizes their incomes at a high level, their average propensity to consume may rise, but there is no reason to suppose that it will be subject to sudden fluctuations. And even if there should be some fluctuations, affecting the group as a whole, these are not likely to be so large as to lead to actual dis-saving. It would be fanciful to assume that this group would, during one period, save a large proportion of their income and, during the next, not only cease to do any saving out of the same income, but, in addition, supplement their current consumption by a liquidation of past accumulations. The experience of the past, at least, suggests nothing of the kind, although this group has always been in the possession of considerable financial resources (past savings).

We conclude, therefore, that consumers' expenditure in ordinary peace-time conditions can be taken as fairly steady—as long as incomes are steady. The mere existence of a large amount of negotiable financial assets, in itself, is not likely to make it any less steady. Some fluctuations in the total of consumers' expenditure there might well be, but they will be covered by those parts of current income which are normally saved. They can occur even in a society in which the volume of negotiable assets is extremely small. Two cases, however, deserve mention where this conclusion may have to be modified. The first relates to expenditure on investment and the second to expenditure induced by sudden changes in the value of capital assets.

Past experience indicates that investment spending, indeed, is extremely irregular. This irregularity has been generally recognized as the direct cause of the trade cycle. The question is: Will private investment continue to be subject to extreme fluctuations once a full employment policy has been inaugurated and has stabilized incomes? Mr. Kalecki, in the second study, has already given the reasons for answering this question in the negative. But even if some irregularity remains—e.g. owing to the sudden appearance of new inventions—will it be made *more* irregular by the existence of a large volume of financial assets? Will it be greater when the national debt is high than when it is low? There is no reason to assume that it will. An exception, however, may have to be made for investment abroad. The sudden appearance of a Stock Exchange boom in another country may lead to sudden movements of speculative capital, and it is at least arguable that such movements are likely to be larger when investors hold a large volume of easily saleable securities than when they hold a small volume. A control of international capital movements is therefore likely to be necessary for this reason; but it is necessary for a great number of other reasons in any case.[1]

A second case deserving special consideration in this context is that of the behaviour of capitalists when there is a sudden appreciation in the money value of their holdings. Such capital appreciation may be the result of a sudden drop in the long-term rate of interest and will be considered later on. At the moment, it is sufficient to note that it may have an unsettling effect upon consumers' expenditure, since it produces windfall profits, not just for single individuals, but for the group as a whole. These profits, although merely 'on paper,' i.e. not by way of income, may indeed induce an increase in the propensity to consume even to the point of dis-saving. And while this possibility has of course always been present in a capitalist society, its importance would be greater with a large national debt than with a small one. We shall argue later on that a sudden drop in the rate of interest should be avoided also for other reasons.

Barring these two rather special cases, we can find no reason to assume that the mere size of the national debt[2] is a factor of potential inflation—as long as the savings represented by the national debt are 'voluntary' savings in the above-mentioned sense. With reference to the supposed danger of inflation there is no discernible limit to the internal debt a community can carry. The statement that the size of the national debt 'does not matter' is broadly speaking true.

Methods of Financing

Public debt, however, can take various forms. The quantitative aspect, which has occupied us so far, is closely linked up with the qualitative aspect. Even if it be agreed that the mere size of the national debt (or, for that matter, the volume of private debt) does not produce inflation, can it be shown that inflation may be the result of the particular method of financing employed by the Government? Is it true that, for instance, finance through Ways and Means Advances is more 'inflationary' than finance through 'floating debt'; that the latter is

---

[1] Cf. pp. 173 *et seq.*

[2] As distinct from the size of the budget deficit which, of course, must be currently adjusted to the 'unclaimed margin' of real resources.

worse than finance through long-term loans; and that the worst is finance through the printing of notes?

This brings us into the field of monetary policy,—a field which is normally dealt with as something quite apart from general economics. From what has been said before, however, it should be clear that this field, like that of Public Finance, is ruled by principles which are not independent, but merely a derivation of general economic reasoning.

It is outlay—public and private taken together—which is relevant to inflation. Not, of course, outlay all by itself; but outlay in relation to potential production. To the extent that outlay is determined by income, the problem of inflation is the problem of the management of total income. To the extent that outlay breaks the fetters of income —dis-saving or loan expenditure—the problem of inflation is connected with the problem of the management of money, credit and negotiable assets.

We have seen above that, in an otherwise stable economy, inflation could be produced by the public only through sudden bouts of spending on consumption or on investment. But we have found little reason to assume that such bouts will actually occur,—at least not as long as past savings are predominantly held in the form of interest bearing long-term securities (or 'equities'). There have always been enough negotiable assets in private hands to finance such bouts of spending; there has always also existed a margin of savings which might have financed them—and yet they have not occurred. Our question at this point is the following: If Government debt should be financed to an increasing extent on a short-term basis (or even by the creation of cash), or if other changes took place which made long-term assets more easily convertible into ready cash,—would this lead to an instability in the spending habits of the community which did not exist before?

Let us first take the case of changes in financial practice that would have the effect of making long-term assets easily convertible into cash. The way to turn a bond into cash is to sell it. If a Government bond, i.e. a bond which carries no specific risk, could always be sold at the purchase price, at a moment's notice, there would be no point for any saver to hold more than a convenient minimum of his funds in cash or short-term paper, since by putting them into long-term Government bonds he could earn long-term interest without any risk whatever. As it is, the prices of Government bonds are not absolutely stable and reliance cannot be placed upon the possibility of always selling such bonds without loss. Thus there is a risk factor in holding long-term bonds: the risk of depreciation. The long-term rate of interest is a reward mainly for this risk.

Depreciation of Government bonds, however, means a rise in the rate of interest, and appreciation, a fall. Since the only risk incurred in holding Government bonds is the risk of depreciation,—the risk, that is to say, of a future rise in the rate of interest,—we find that the long-term rate of interest is a reward for taking the risk that the long-term rate of interest may rise in the future. It follows that a complete stabilization of the rate of interest would remove the very risk for the taking of which the rate of interest is the reward.

No Government could confidently embark upon a policy of maintaining full employment by means of deficit spending, unless it were certain that the rate of interest was under its own control and could not be raised against it. The Government, like the investor, is therefore interested in developing a financial technique which prevents the rate of interest from rising,—because any such rise means an increased cost of new borrowing to the Government, and a capital depreciation on old bonds to the investor. But if the Government succeeds in developing such a technique, the very justification of a long-term rate of interest disappears, except for the cost and inconvenience of buying and selling Government paper. And not only would the long-term rate of interest cease to have any justification as a reward for risk-taking: the very difference between the liquidity of cash, short-term paper and long-term bonds would tend to disappear, because a money title that can always be sold for cash at a fixed price is almost as good as cash.

We thus come to the following propositions:

1. In order to be able safely to finance full employment the Government must stabilize[1] the long-term rate of interest.

2. The stabilization of the long-term rate of interest, as such, increases the liquidity of Government bond holders to practically the same extent as if, instead of bonds, they had been accumulating cash or deposits.

3. The stabilization of the long-term rate of interest deprives the rate of interest of its principal *raison d'être*.

4. If propositions 1 to 3 are correct, the very practice of issuing long-term bonds instead of cash would appear to lose its *raison d'être*.[2]

[1] Against a rise; not necessarily against a fall.

[2] In an economy with a highly egalitarian distribution of incomes the long-term rate of interest may acquire a new *raison d'être*, namely that of regulating the volume of spontaneous saving attainable without either inflation or deflation. The classical idea of 'reward for waiting,' which has no place under existing conditions, may come into its own again. But even then it remains doubtful in what way savings and the rate of interest are correlated,—whether a high rate is, in fact, an incentive or a dis-incentive to saving.

Our argument seems to drive us to the conclusion that budget deficits might just as well be financed by printing new notes (or by borrowing from the Central Bank) which carry no interest as by printing new long-term bonds which carry interest. But before we jump to any conclusions let us consider the effect of abolishing—or of suddenly reducing—the long-term rate of interest.

There are at least two practical difficulties. (1) Insurance companies, trust funds, and other institutions have made contracts with a multitude of persons which are based on the assumption that liquid funds can always be invested, without appreciable risk, to bring in a few per cent of interest per annum. If this assumption ceases to be fulfilled, these contracts may have to be revised. If they cannot be revised, the companies will be forced into losses or even into default. The banking system, too, is adjusted to being able to invest a substantial proportion of customers' deposits in interest bearing securities and to use this income partly to cover costs and partly as a source of profit. A disappearance of the rate of interest—or even a sudden reduction of the rate below its present level of about 3 per cent (long-term)—would necessitate far-reaching and often difficult readjustments with a great number of financial institutions. There is no doubt that such adjustments can be made. The question is rather whether they are worth making, or, if they are, how much time should be allowed for them.

(2) The second difficulty is of a more serious nature. We have seen above that a full employment policy, as such, will stabilize profits at something like a boom level. It will greatly reduce the risks of business and thus the risk element in long-term private investments. The normal yield basis of commercial bonds and shares will therefore decline,—which is another way of saying that capital values will rise to even higher levels than those which boom profits would justify on the present yield basis. If, in addition, the yield basis is further reduced by an elimination of the rate of interest on Government bonds, capital values will rise to still higher levels. This applies not only to 'financial' capital,—stocks, shares and bonds. It applies also to real capital, such as houses and land. A sudden reduction or complete disappearance of interest on bonds would affect the real estate market in a way the short-term results of which are difficult to foretell.

These considerations point to the conclusion that any sudden reduction of the rate of interest on Government bonds would probably create more difficulties than it solves. Those who argue that there is no justification for the Government paying interest for the privilege of borrowing the savings which its own spending has created should reflect that the long-term rate is already extremely low; that the amount of interest payable on new borrowings is of small quantitative importance; and that a sudden reduction in the rate would have after-effects upon the structure of capital values that are quite out of proportion to the saving achieved.

But have we not ourselves argued that a stabilization of the rate of interest would destroy its very justification? Yes; once the financial community comes to place absolute reliance in the fact that the rate of interest, though it might fall, will certainly never rise (not even after a fall), it will no longer wish to hold a substantial volume of short-term notes or Treasury Deposit Receipts, but put all funds that are not needed for day-to-day transactions into long-term Government bonds. Such a development, however, is not likely to occur for a considerable time. The signal for the long-term rate of interest having lost its justification would be a widespread attempt on the part of holders of short-term paper to exchange this into long-term bonds. If such an attempt should be made, the Government would have the choice of either letting the long-term rate of interest drop further or of discouraging such a movement from short to long by levying a charge on the buying and selling of long-term bonds. The latter course might—in the short run—be preferable to the former; it would affect the liquidity of bonds and thus make them less attractive as an investment opportunity for short periods.

But we have yet to answer one question which may be uppermost in the minds of those who point to the fact that the rate of interest, surely, is determined by the lender rather than the borrower: How can the Government, being the principal borrower, exercise sovereign control over the terms on which it is to borrow?

This control, indeed, is not exercised by the Government in its capacity as a borrower. It is exercised by the Government in its capacity as controller of the Central Bank. In any given situation, the Government, like any other borrower, has to accept the terms of the 'market.' But the Government, unlike any other borrower, can always change the situation of the market. It can always create a plethora of cash, or a stringency of cash. During this war the Treasury has developed something like an automatic mechanism for this purpose. Long-term bonds of various maturity dates, at a stable rate of $2\frac{1}{2}$ to 3 per cent, are no longer 'placed' in pre-determined amounts: they are sold 'on tap.' Assume that the Government wishes to spend £1,000 million beyond its revenue. If subscriptions to the 'tap' issue amount to only (say) £500 million, the rest is financed partly by

Treasury Bills and Deposit Receipts and partly by Ways and Means Advances. Thus the market itself is able to decide in which form it holds the savings which the Government's deficit expenditure has brought into existence. With this technique, the long-term rate of interest can be kept absolutely stable.[1]

Let us assume that this method is maintained in a full employment economy. The budget deficit, let it be remembered, is nothing more than an offset to private savings which would otherwise find no offset, so that a depression would ensue. The funds, therefore, which the Government requires for its deficit are, so to speak, potentially idle in the hands of the public. Now, the public wishes to hold them in four different forms: in cash, in bank deposits, in short-term paper, or in bonds. Its preference is determined by a number of different factors. First, its preference for cash and deposits is determined by the volume of business, taking into account the level of prices, in short, by 'turnover.' Once full employment has been reached and prices are kept stable, 'turnover' has reached its maximum (for the time being). The preference for cash and deposits has also reached its temporary maximum, and there is no reason to suppose that the community would wish to hold more than a small fraction of its newly accruing savings in the form of additional cash deposits. The demand for these, in other words, becomes satiated; practically all savings accruing thereafter must go into either short-term or long-term paper. Secondly, what determines the division between short-term and long-term? Since the latter earn a higher rate of interest than the former, they would attract all new savings if it were not for the afore-mentioned risk of capital depreciation. This risk, as we have seen, consists in the danger of the long-term rate of interest being allowed to rise. If the method of issuing long-term bonds 'on tap' becomes firmly established, at a fixed rate of interest, this risk disappears, and there will be a tendency for all available funds to go into long-term.[2] But as long as some uncertainty as to a possible rise in the future long-term rate persists, financial institutions and business firms will tend to maintain some sort of proportion between their short-term and long-term holdings, and will adjust their subscriptions to tap loans accordingly. The floating debt, consequently, will rise in a certain proportion with the long-term debt.

[1] The application of this technique does not depend on the Government incurring a deficit. If subscriptions to the long-term 'tap' exceed the amount the Government wishes to raise, this is an indication that the long-term rate of interest can be allowed to drop. If the price of long-term bonds tends to fall, the Government can always buy such bonds and finance itself by Ways and Means advances.

[2] This tendency might even become a rush, if the rate is firmly expected to fall, since every fall in the rate entails a windfall profit for the holders of old bonds.

The Rôle of the Banks

So far we have pushed ahead with our argument without making any mention of the fact that Government bonds and short-term paper may be held by the banks. Does not this fact change the whole picture? Do not the banks 'create credit,' which they place at the disposal of the Government, and is it not objectionable that they should earn interest on something the creation of which costs them nothing? These, and many similar, questions are so frequently raised to-day that a discussion of the place of banks in our economy becomes necessary.

What is the function of the banks?

First of all, it should be made clear that throughout this paper we have treated the Central Bank as a part of the Government machine. We cannot here enter into a discussion of whether or not this *de facto* position of the Bank of England should be formalized by a change in its *de jure* position. In the following, we are concerned only with banks other than the Central Bank.

Their function is a double one: to manufacture liquidity and to store liquid funds. They do this by interposing themselves between debtor and creditor. A glance at a bank's balance sheet will confirm this view.

The biggest item on the liability side is 'deposits.' These deposits are past savings of the deposit holder himself or the proceeds of funds the deposit holder himself has borrowed. For the deposit holder, they are an equivalent to cash—merely a more convenient way of holding cash. On the asset side of the bank's balance sheet, we find that the biggest item is 'Investments' and 'Advances.' Actual cash is only a small item, normally equivalent to 10 per cent of total deposits. What does this mean? It means that each individual bank accepts 'money' which the public cares to deposit with it, keeps 10 per cent of such 'money' as a 'reserve' against the deposit thus created, and employs 90 per cent of it on making advances to industry or purchasing long-term or short-term securities. Thus, whenever a bank accepts 'money' into a deposit, it acts as a mere 'cloak room' for 10 per cent of it, but accepts a banker's risk by lending out the remaining 90 per cent. It gives a promise to its creditor (the depositor) that he may withdraw his deposit whenever he pleases, but does not extract a similar promise from its debtor (the business man, who receives a bank loan, or the firm or Government whose securities the bank has purchased) to repay his debt on demand. The bank, therefore, takes the risk of becoming illiquid—if its creditor should demand cash while its debtor cannot be called upon to furnish cash. As a reward for taking this risk, the bank earns interest on its investments in exactly the same way as any person in the possession of cash—whether his own or somebody else's—earns interest when he foregoes his liquidity and safety and puts such funds into a less liquid form. If there were no banks, the savers in the community would have to deal directly with those who intended to borrow; as most of the latter would want to have money for a definite (or indefinite) period, most of the former would have to part with the control over their money for a definite (or indefinite) period. Such direct transactions, of course, take place. Normally, however, the banks enable savers (i.e. their depositors) to keep their funds in a liquid and riskless form, while at the same time enabling borrowers to obtain funds for a definite (or indefinite) period. This is the traditional function of banking; the creation of additional liquidity.

Yet, although this function is extremely simple and clear-cut, it is all too often misunderstood. The misunderstandings arise from the fact that while each individual bank never does more than lend out 90 per cent of what it has received from its depositors, the banking system as a whole can lend out nine times as much as any new cash it may receive. The explanation of this paradox is simple. When £100 of new cash are deposited, the bank, as stated above, keeps £10 in reserve and lends out £90. But these £90 find their way back into the banking system and reappear as a 'new' deposit with Bank No. 2. £9 are now put into the cash reserve, and £81 are lent out, etc., etc.[1] The final result of this process is that cash reserves increase by £100; investments and advances increase by £900, and deposits increase by £1,000. The banks expand *both sides* of their balance sheet by £1,000. This process is normally called an 'expansion of credit.'

It might be well to emphasize three points in connection with such an 'expansion of credit.' Firstly, since the banks themselves cannot create new cash, their ability to expand credit is determined by the agency which does control the creation of new cash, i.e. the Central Bank. Secondly, the banks' ability to expand credit depends, in addition, upon the willingness of the public to hold their 'money' in the form of deposits. If, for some reason, the public should prefer to hoard notes rather than hold deposits, the power of the banks to 'expand credit' is destroyed. Thirdly, the ability of expanding, in favourable

---

[1] The formula for this geometric progression is as follows:

$$a \times \frac{9}{10}\left(1 + \frac{9}{10} + \left(\frac{9}{10}\right)^2 + \ldots\right) = \frac{a \times \frac{9}{10}}{1 - \frac{9}{10}} = 9a$$

circumstances, both sides of the balance sheet, is inherent in all business and is not a special privilege enjoyed by the banks.

It should hardly be necessary to emphasize that a 'creation of credit' by the banks is something entirely and fundamentally different from a 'creation of incomes' undertaken by the Government.

Since the Central Bank controls the cash basis of the banking system, it controls the private banks' ability to 'create' credit. There is no sense in saying—as is often being said to-day—that the banks have 'usurped' the prerogative of creating money and that this prerogative should be recaptured by the State.

It is quite true that the profits of banking may increase when the State, by providing a larger cash basis, enables the banking system to expand both sides of its balance sheet. But if the State does *nothing else* but increase the cash basis, any consequent increase in the profits of banking is likely to be short-lived, because the increased liquidity of the banking system depresses interest rates and thus, while allowing an expansion of the banks' portfolio, depresses the average rate of earning obtainable on their investments. If, however, the State does *more* than merely increase the cash basis of the banking system: if it raises the National Income by means of a budget deficit, then the profits of all private enterprise increase, not only those of banking. Those who maintain that there is no justification in the profits of banking increasing as a result of State action should be consistent and apply their criticism also to the increase in the profits of other enterprises. If the rise in the National Income is brought about by State expenditure, it is possible to argue that all the resultant profits should belong to the State. But it is not possible to argue that only the resultant profits of the banking system should belong to the State.

The part played by the banks in our economic system is one of severely limited significance. The banks can create credit only when the Central Bank allows them to do so. They cannot, by themselves, create additional savings or a rise in the National Income. They can only assist. Savings and the National Income rise only if somebody outside the banking system—a private citizen or the State—is prepared to spend. If no one is prepared to do any additional spending, the banks—no matter how large a cash basis is provided for them—cannot do more than reduce the rate of interest, which, unless accompanied by a proportionate increase in their interest-bearing assets, leads to a fall in their income.

Why should the Government have to pay interest on its borrowings from the banks? This is a question which agitates many minds. The answer becomes simple if we look at the matter as follows: A budget deficit implies that the Government has spent beyond its revenue. It has purchased goods and services (or enabled—say—old-age pensioners to purchase goods and services) against an IOU. These instruments of indebtedness must take the particular form which those who have supplied goods and services against an IOU (ultimately: the 'savers') wish them to take. If they want to hold them in Bank of England notes, notes must be printed; if they wish to hold them in short-term paper or long-term bonds, such paper or bonds must be printed. But they may not want to hold all of them in any of these forms. They may—and are indeed likely to—want to hold some of their savings in a form which is as safe and as liquid as Bank of England notes, but at the same time more convenient: deposits with a bank. In that case the banks step in and satisfy this demand. They take some of the IOU's of the Government and give to the *real* creditor of the Government a deposit in exchange. They do this because, although it involves them in a risk, it enables them to make a profit. This is a perfectly legitimate procedure.

It might, of course, be argued that banks should not be allowed to use the funds deposited with them by their customers for the purchase of Government bonds. They might be forced to hold non-interest bearing Government paper, i.e. currency notes or Bank of England deposits, instead. This would mean to single out the banks for discriminatory treatment, depriving them of a right which everybody else in this society enjoys: namely the right of any one to choose freely the form in which he wishes to hold the funds for which he is responsible. It would have to be shown why it is equitable, desirable, or indeed necessary to make such a discriminatory arrangement.

Bank profits, as we have seen, can rise only if the State allows the rate of interest to rise—for which there is no justification, or if the National Income expands. With a stable rate of interest, the volume of deposits—and thus the size of the banks' interest earning assets—is determined by total turnover, i.e. the level of output and the level of prices. Once both become stabilized, deposits cease to expand except with the secular trend. Bank holdings of Government paper will then also expand only with the secular trend. The *real* savers, i.e. the public, will find their demand for cash and deposits satiated and will put their current savings directly into short-term or long-term Government paper, without needing the interposition of the banks. The banks, as manufacturers of liquidity, will obtain no additional business and will expand their balance sheet no further, once the public's need for deposits has become satiated. They, like private business in general, will then depend upon the secular trend for any further expansion of their balance sheet.

Methods of Finance—Concluded

After this digression, we can now return to our main problem. If Government expenditure beyond revenue (deficit spending) is necessary for the maintenance of full employment—is one method of financing such deficits more 'inflationary' than another? We can now say that this question is wrongly put. The particular method employed should be adjusted to the preferences of the Government's creditors. The deficit itself creates the savings necessary for it. As long as these savings are purely voluntary savings—in the sense that they are a residue remaining after all individual consumers' wishes have been satisfied—they do not represent 'pent-up' demand and, barring some special cases, are not likely to lead to sudden bursts of spending, either on consumption or on investment. If the Government refused to give the savers what they wanted—if it insisted on financing the deficit exclusively by the issue of long-term loans—it would drive up the rate of interest to no purpose. If it insisted (for the purpose of keeping interest charges low) on financing the deficit mainly by Ways and Means Advances, it would so increase the cash basis of the banking system as to produce a sudden break in the structure of interest rates—with consequent effects upon capital values which we have already discussed. Neither of these courses is desirable. Neither possesses any merit. The present long-term rate of interest is, for the time being, a convenient rate. Dearer money would only do damage to private investment activity; ultra-cheap money, suddenly introduced, would only do damage to the structure of capital values, and might lead to an inflationary (and socially undesirable) increase in luxury expenditure. The financial technique, as evolved under war-time conditions, is ideally suited for a full employment economy. Both long-term and short-term Government paper should continue to be offered 'on tap,' and any balance not covered by subscription to the tap issues made up by Ways and Means Advances. It is not necessary to apply force or persuasion to the banks or to the public with a view to getting higher tap subscriptions than are spontaneously forthcoming. Only if there should develop a tendency towards converting a large part of the existing floating debt into long-term bonds, might it be advisable to let the rate of interest drop or to introduce an artificial margin between the buying and the selling price of long-term bonds,—a margin analogous to the 'gold points' under the old Gold Standard.

The time has passed when it might have been possible to control private investment activity by variations in the rate of interest. If a sudden investment boom or a sudden rush of consumers' buying should develop owing to the appearance of altogether abnormal conditions, the inflation thus threatening ought not to be counteracted from the side of money. A rising rate of interest or a policy of monetary deflation (reducing the cash basis of the banking system) would have little effect if pursued hesitantly and would do great damage if pursued vigorously. Inflation must be counteracted by heavy progressive taxation or even more direct methods—rationing and direct control of materials. Such measures will then be justified by the emergency which has produced the necessity for them. They need not be contemplated in the economics of stable full employment.

BUDGETING FOR FULL EMPLOYMENT

The New Economics demonstrates that it is within the power of any Government of a well-organized modern society to ensure a full utilization of resources. This power rests upon two traditional prerogatives of Government: first, to commandeer part of the income of citizens and to spend the proceeds of taxation, and, second, to print IOU's of whatever kind the citizens may desire to hold as a vehicle of their savings. This second prerogative derives its importance from the fact that one kind of governmental IOU, namely currency notes, are legal tender in Law and generally accepted 'money' in Custom.

Either one of these prerogatives may be employed for the purpose of a full employment policy. Such a policy, in other words, may rely exclusively or primarily upon 'redistributive' taxation, or it may (with any given level and structure of taxation) rely exclusively or primarily upon budget deficits financed in the way described above.

Either policy, while feasible in itself, possesses certain disadvantages. Redistributive taxation, designed to impinge heavily upon private savings, tends to create economic motives which lead to considerable waste and to weaken economic incentives upon which a private enterprise economy depends. Budget deficits, designed to 'mop up' private savings (which, if not 'mopped up,' would not come into existence and would express themselves in unemployment), tend to aggravate the mal-distribution of incomes and of private wealth and thus to enhance the very need for redistributive taxation later on.

Either policy alone, and particularly a mixture of both policies together, can be applied so as to lead to full employment, but neither policy, nor even the mixture of the two, is likely to be fully satisfactory unless the underlying problem is solved: the problem out of which most of the other difficulties arise—the *gross* distribution of incomes.[1]

The New Economics demonstrates not only that the level of employment is within the power of the Government to control, but also that the rate of interest is within its control and that the 'euthanasia of the rentier,' of which Lord Keynes spoke—at least the euthanasia of the rentier who bears no risk—can be brought about even before capital equipment ceases to be scarce.

An application of the New Economics, therefore, would have far-reaching consequences, socially as well as economically. There is no necessity that it should impinge upon the freedom of the individual. Governments used their power to tax before the advent of the New Economics, and they also used their power to borrow. The departure suggested now is that they should use both these powers under the guidance of a new set of rules. The new rules, in fact, give them a greater freedom of choice than they had previously thought to possess. But strict rules nevertheless remain.

The first rule is that the Government should reconsider the established system of taxation and distinguish between the different taxes as to their effect upon private consumption, private investment and private savings. This will bring to light the effect of taxation upon the size of the 'unclaimed margin' (which is indicated by the volume of unemployment).

The second rule is that the Government should use taxation for the purpose of altering the size of the 'unclaimed margin'—increasing it if there are communal needs exceeding the available margin that possess a higher social priority than needs satisfied by private expenditure; and decreasing it if the resources required to satisfy communal needs of high social priority are smaller than this margin of (otherwise) unused resources.

The third rule is that, whatever margin remains after the decisions under the second rule have been taken, the Government should mobilize these (otherwise) idle resources and claim them for its own communal purposes by means of deficit finance.

This policy necessitates a new conception of the budget. The traditional budget is built up on a conception of Revenue and Expenditure which is largely accidental and primarily legal. The new budget must be built up on an economic conception of Revenue and Expenditure.

[1] Cf. pp. 92 *et seq.*

Revenue, in other words, should comprise all payments made to the Central Government, to Local Government, or to any Government Fund. It comprises the profits of Government-owned enterprises as well as ordinary taxes, the income of unemployment and pension funds as well as local rates. Only pure transfer payments should be separated, i.e. payments made in purchase of a Government-owned asset or of an IOU issued by the Government or any of its branches. Expenditure, at the same time, counts as economic expenditure only to the extent that it is incurred in payment for current goods and services. Regular transfer payments to pensioners, creditors, etc., must be excluded because they do not (in the first instance) constitute a claim on real resources. Irregular transfer payments, i.e. payments made in purchase of privately owned assets or of an IOU (whether private or public) do not count as economic expenditure.

We can now see how Public Finance can be fitted into the general framework. It is necessary, first, to estimate the volume of total outlay required to reach full employment; once this figure has been obtained, it is possible to estimate the volume of private outlay on consumption and investment likely to be forthcoming under conditions of full employment and a full National Income, assuming any given level and structure of taxation. Next, an estimate is made of essential or desirable State expenditure. State outlay, added on to private outlay, must result in a total commensurate with full employment. If there is an excess—an 'inflationary gap'—taxes falling mainly on consumption must be increased or State outlay reduced. If there is a deficiency—a 'deflationary gap'—taxes falling mainly on consumption must be reduced or State outlay increased. The comparison between State revenue and State outlay then shows either a budget surplus or a budget deficit. The surplus or the deficit can be increased or decreased by altering taxes which fall primarily on savings.[1] An increase of such taxes increases the surplus or reduces the deficit. A decrease of such taxes reduces the surplus or increases the deficit.

It follows that there are two main sets of decisions that have to be taken: economic decisions, concerned with managing the size of the National Income and the distribution of real resources between the Government and the citizens; and financial decisions, concerned with the increase or decrease of the national debt and with the rate of interest. The variable and controllable factor as regards the economic decisions is taxes reducing consumption and private investment; the variable and controllable factor as regards the financial decisions is taxes

---

[1] Or capital taxes imposed on the owners of wealth without regard to current income.

reducing private savings. Assuming that there is agreement with regard to the economic decisions, there remains a choice between 'orthodox' budgetary policy, involving high taxation on all incomes[1] out of which savings are likely to be made, and 'unorthodox' finance, involving a rise in the national debt. Since all taxes impinge partly on savings and partly on consumption—although to a varying degree—the economic and the financial decisions interact one upon the other. Taxes imposed for financial reasons, i.e. so as to avoid 'unorthodox' finance, must yield a larger revenue than the amount of the deficit they are designed to abolish, the excess being used to increase State expenditure. A reduction of taxes undertaken for economic reasons, on the other hand, must be accompanied by a smaller decrease in State expenditure than the amount of taxes remitted.

In conclusion, we may list the various elements of Public Finance as they affect the volume of employment:

Factors of Increase—1. Expenditure of revenue derived from funds which, in the absence of taxation, would have been saved.

2. Expenditure of borrowed funds.

Factors of Decrease—3. Use of tax revenue (impinging on consumption) for repayment of debt.

Neutral Factors— 4. Expenditure of revenue derived from funds which, in the absence of taxation, would have been spent on private consumption or investment.

5. Use of tax revenue impinging on savings for repayment of debt, provided private investment is not affected.

Assuming that full employment is maintained, we can make a similar list of factors as regards their effect on the national debt:

Factors of Increase— 1. Reduction of taxes falling on savings.

Factors of Decrease—2. Increase of taxes falling on savings.

Neutral Factors— 3. Increase or reduction of taxes falling *purely* on consumption.

Again assuming that full employment is maintained, we can say that, given the gross distribution of incomes and the propensity to consume, every tax that reduces private outlay necessitates—to that extent—an increase in State expenditure; every tax that reduces private savings reduces—to that extent—the budget deficit or increases the

---

[1] Due provision being made for the maintenance of the incentive to invest by 'modifying' income tax.

budget surplus. Those who want the smallest possible budget, must plead for the abolition of taxes impinging most heavily on the poor, whose propensity to consume is high. Those who want the smallest possible budget deficit—compatible with full employment—must plead for an increase of taxes falling most heavily on the rich, whose propensity to save is high. Those who want the State substantially to expand the scope of its own spending may plead for a high level of both.

PART V

THE INTERNATIONAL ASPECTS OF FULL EMPLOYMENT

by T. Balogh

I. THE NATURE OF THE PROBLEM

IN the previous studies the problem was considered of how to create and maintain conditions in which the resources of a closed economic system would be both fully and efficiently employed. We must now turn to analyse the consequences and implications of the fact that the world economy is not a homogeneous system. It is, and will in the foreseeable future remain, a congeries of some scores of sovereign national or regional units of widely different economic, social and political constitution, at widely different stages of economic and technical development. It does not possess common executive organs which can evolve and pursue a coherent economic policy in order to solve the problem under discussion: even if all units had identical views about the broad character of the common policy to be adopted.

The classical theory of foreign trade was based on an economic model which was supposed to function automatically in response to changes in demand and supply acting through free markets on the profit motive. Under its assumptions, foreign trade does not in essence differ from inter-regional trade. In that system *ex hypothesi* no conscious policy is needed; in that system any Government 'interference' with 'unseen' economic forces of adjustment is assumed to result in economic *malaise* only. Given these assumptions, the economic consequence of the existence of national units was taken to amount to no more than that divergences in economic changes were more marked, the relative immobility of factors, especially of labour, greater, and differences in productivity resulting from the uneven geographical international distribution of resources larger between, than within any one of the national units. It may be objected that the 'classical' theory recognized the difference in monetary adjustment between and within countries and evolved the analysis of gold movements. This is undoubtedly correct. But on the gold coin standard identical gold movements take place between and within countries. The establishment of Central Banks must, from the 'Liberal' point of view, be

126

regarded logically as the first step to 'State interference.' The really logical followers of that school, of whom Professor Mises may be mentioned, in fact advocate 'free banking' linked by gold automatism.

As soon as it is recognized that the community organized as a State can, and in certain cases must, take conscious action to secure the optimum exploitation of its natural resources and manpower, the scope of the study of international economics is completely altered. The non-existence of appropriate world organizations and executive organs immediately raises new problems: the scope of international, as contrasted with national, problems must then be defined as embracing that field of economic activity in which appropriate executive action cannot be taken without affecting relations with economic units over which the executive taking the action has no constitutional regulative or coercive power.[1]

The strength of the challenge of so-called 'Liberal Internationalism' is derived from this fact. Its slogans are clear-cut and decidedly attractive: the abstention of states from entering into commercial quarrels; the refusal to use sovereign power to grant privileges to private people by way of the innumerable methods of protectionism; the clear distinction between profits and politics—*a priori* must appeal to all who wish to further international amity and general progress. The argument that nations should be so closely knit by commercial ties that each should be unable by itself to lift the sword sounds more than plausible to a generation which has become sceptical about the efficacy of formal pacts in preventing hostilities. Free economy and free trade, however, may mean—and in the inter-war period have meant—economic dependence and insecurity for the majority of the population and a standard of life well below the potential level corresponding to the increase in productivity. If considered in this light, the moral precepts of the Liberals, however attractive at first, appear somewhat artificial and false.

In the present essay an attempt will be made to analyse: first, the conditions in which full employment can be maintained in a world economic system consisting of different national units following divergent economic policies; secondly, the methods available to a single country to enable her to pursue a policy of full employment if the prerequisites of an international full employment policy cannot be attained.

---

[1] These economic units might therefore either passively comply with the regulation or induce another equally sovereign executive to take retaliatory steps.

II. FULL EMPLOYMENT AND THE
INTERNATIONAL BALANCE OF PAYMENTS

The international balance of payments of any country can be un-balanced for two kinds of reasons. The disequilibrium might, first, be due to the failure of other countries to maintain 'full employment' effective demand; or to its own failure to do so while others maintain such demand; or finally to its own efforts to secure full employment when others fail to do so. We shall call active or passive balances which are due to this cause 'derived balances.' Balances which would persist in spite of all countries having attained full employment—balances which were the *sole* object of analysis under classical assumptions—we shall denominate 'spontaneous balances.' It is not necessary to point out that actually recorded balances are composed of both elements. Any action, moreover, taken to adjust such actual balances will have repercussions which will, in all probability, change not only the magnitude of the balance but also its composition.

Derived active or passive balances of international payments. Derived balance due to slumps abroad

Let us start from a position in which all countries are fully employed and there is equilibrium in the balance of payments. We understand under this term the position in which the short-term capital position, i.e. the liquid reserve, of a country is unchanging; any long-term borrowing, however, is offset by an increase in the productive capacity of the country.[1] If we now suppose that a slump starts in any one country, all other countries will immediately be affected—and this in two ways. With home demand sagging, industries of the depressed

[1] A country may succeed in maintaining its current account in balance and still be losing in liquidity, e.g. if the expected rate of profit is more favourable in other countries, and thus long-term capital is exported while borrowing at short-term takes place. In this case, the liquidity position having undergone a deterioration in spite of the balance in current account, in the long run forces are set in motion to check the continuance of the process. Adjustments can be undertaken only by disequilibrating the current account or by preventing the export of capital. This concept must be differentiated, of course, from the capacity to pay of a country which will also depend on the policy of other countries. Should the creditor be unwilling to pursue an employment policy which permits payment (i.e. the maintenance of over-full employment demand in the creditor country) the capacity to pay of the debtor vanishes. Our definition is unsymmetrical in the sense that equilibrium cannot be said to exist if the country is getting potentially poorer, but only if it gets potentially richer. This formal blemish is, however, good common sense. The existence of capital claims abroad will, in a free system, result in market imperfections in favour of the creditor. If, on the other hand, control over foreign trade and payments is maintained the advantage will be in favour of the debtor. These imperfections may in their turn change the terms of trade in subsequent periods. A short-term balance of the current account can obviously not be taken by itself as indication of long-run equilibrium. Under our definitions short-term equilibrium may co-exist with an intermediate and long-term dis-equilibrium.

country will increase their sales pressure abroad (after a time probably aided by a fall in money wages). The fall in effective demand in the depressed country will, secondly, mean a fall of its demand for foreign products. Thus the balances of payments of all countries will be thrown out of equilibrium by the slump, even if they had balanced before its occurrence. The depressed country will improve its balance: all others not immediately affected by the slump will experience a worsening.

Two consequences follow: first, if the deficit countries do not *increase* their home demand, the depression will automatically spread. A deficiency in the balance of payments is equivalent to a fall in demand, because relatively more goods are bought from abroad whose production does not create incomes at home, and/or relatively fewer home-produced goods, whose production would have created incomes, will be exported.[1] If, in order to stabilize employment at home, the deficiency in effective demand caused by the slump in foreign demand is offset by an expansion of home demand, while the slump abroad continues, this will mean a further worsening of the balance of trade.

If the deficit countries possess sufficient liquid reserves, they may be willing and able to tolerate the deficit without taking steps to restore the balance. If the depressed country is more or less of a size similar to that of the other countries; if the liquid reserves of the world are more or less equally distributed; and if the forces of expansion in the rest of the world are strong enough to offset the fall in the world effective demand due to the slump in any one country, the export surplus acquired by the depressed country may be sufficient to overcome the original disequilibrating force, the export surplus having replaced the original fall in home investment (or consumption). If, however, the depressed country represents an important fraction of the effective money demand of the world, and/or if the liquid reserves of the world economy are not spread evenly among all countries but are concentrated in a country which is liable to spasmodic deep depressions and is unable to achieve such internal conditions and international economic relations in which it would periodically disgorge the liquid reserves accumulated in slumps, then a deflationary bias will be imparted to the whole world economy. In that case other countries will not in the longer run be able to tolerate a loss of liquid reserves.

But if the deficit countries take measures to prevent the worsening of their balance of trade this must, for the same reasons, aggravate the

---

[1] The slump in demand will have a disproportionate effect, for the apprehension caused by it will immediately curtail expenditure. It will start a secondary deflationary spiral.

slump in the country where it started, since it was the growth in its foreign balance which had initially mitigated the fall in home effective demand.[1] A grave danger arises, moreover, that each country, because it possesses only limited liquid reserves, will try to remedy the diminution of external demand, not by measures increasing home demand, but by operating on the foreign balance, by cutting imports and stimulating exports. This beggar-my-neighbour policy[2] will extend the area of deflationary pressure to more and more countries and will reduce the maximum scope of the international division of labour at full employment. Yet because retaliation will follow with a decreasing lag as the slump deepens, such measures will fail to increase the actual employment in any one country appreciably at any given moment.[3]

Derived balance due to full employment policy

An attempt to achieve full employment at home presents to some extent identical problems. The country—which might be supposed to be in short run and intermediate equilibrium—by increasing its own effective demand will tend to export less and import more than hitherto. Unless other countries fall in with the new policy the country attempting to pursue it will be forced either to desist, or to increase its degree of self-sufficiency, or to borrow from abroad.

An attempt to increase employment accompanied by increasing self-sufficiency would, of course, not represent a beggar-my-neighbour policy because the *absolute* foreign demand of the country would remain unchanged (or might even increase) even though the ratio of its foreign to its total demand would decrease. But while in the short run this attempt would be justified, as it would increase real income, and while no retaliation ought to be feared, as increased protection in these circumstances (and other things being equal) would not involve a net increase of unemployment abroad,[4] the potential maximum real income attainable *if stable full employment were achieved all round without protection* would be higher.

[1] As would also the origination of an 'autonomous' slump in the deficit countries through the shock to expectations. The 'spilling' over of the deflation to the other country will cause more or less 'automatic' unemployment in the world system. The shock caused by this deflationary impact and the secondary autonomous unemployment caused by it might be quantitatively more important than the primary derived unemployment.

[2] Cf. Mrs. Joan Robinson, *Essays in the Theory of Employment*, p. 210 *et seq.*

[3] In the great depression Britain was for some time faced with countries which were by their financial prejudice prevented from retaliation.

[4] It might, however, involve a shift of the demand of the full employment country for foreign exports, hence of employment from one foreign country to another as the greater autarky results in an increase of import demand for certain (primary) products while it leads to the fall in demand for others. Even such shift of demand might therefore result in retaliation.

Autonomous disequilibrium and the prevention of inflation

Deficiencies and surpluses in the current balance of payments might occur even if all countries pursued full employment policies. Such a deficiency will represent a primary net 'expansionist,' and a surplus a primary net 'contractive' influence in the world system. The deficit country derives an import surplus from other countries, i.e. receives from them part of the fruits of their current productive effort. Three possible cases should be distinguished:

(i) If the maintenance of full employment is the policy of each of the member countries of the world economic system such deficits must be cancelled by a surplus which represents a voluntary reduction of effective demand (saving) in the creditor countries.

(ii) If it is not accompanied by such voluntary reduction, corresponding to consciously planned loans, the spilling over of the effective demand of the 'inflating' (deficit) country (on the basis of its gold reserves or of excessive loans) will result in true inflation in the surplus countries and in an involuntary fall in their available home real income. The inflating (deficit) country, by using its accumulated reserves, will compete with the home consumers of the (fully employed) surplus country for its home supplies, and by bidding for its own exports reduce the supplies available to the surplus country.

(iii) The export surpluses at full employment might represent the servicing or repayment of foreign loans. The deficit then is the means by which payment is effected and must be accompanied by a decrease of the effective home demand of the repaying, and an increase in effective demand above full employment level in the receiving country.

Deficiencies and surpluses in the balance of payments of member countries which do not in the first instance arise either out of international long-term development schemes or out of depressions must be dealt with by direct readjustment in the countries who have acquired an unfavourable balance themselves, with a co-ordinated policy in other countries lest the readjustment should lead to a general deflation. An attempt to deal with autonomous deficits by general monetary expansion would lead to general over-employment.

Balances in the current account of international payments and the intermediate equilibrium

Both autonomous and derived balances may be associated with long-term foreign lending. This would re-establish 'short-term' equilibrium in the sense that there would be no change in the liquid reserves of the countries concerned. Only if the long-term borrowing is paralleled by an at least equivalent increase in real productive capacity can we regard intermediate equilibrium assured, in the sense described above, that no subsequent fall in real income will be produced in the long run by the obligation to service and repay the loan. We must distinguish, moreover, between the 'capacity to repay' of a country and its 'capacity to produce real income.' If the creditor country does not accept repayment by permitting an import surplus (i.e. in all probability, unless it can maintain an over-full employment internal demand), no *a priori* criterion can guarantee that borrowing, however used, will be paralleled by at least as great an increase in the 'capacity to repay.' An effort to repay, as we have shown above, would result in a cumulative deflationary process. The second criterion is somewhat less elusive. Unless the borrowing is accompanied by an increase in the capacity of the community to increase real income, i.e. unless its productivity increases *pari passu*, either because of an increase of capital equipment or labour skill, the cessation of loans will result in an abrupt fall in the national real income.

If it could be assumed that full and stable employment is maintained in the world economic system as a whole, the problem of international borrowing would be relatively simple. International foreign lending might then be stimulated until the return on capital is equalized geographically. In any case as long as the divergence in the yield of capital investment exists in different areas (net of risk), foreign lending—whether private or collectively planned—would speed up the rate of increase of world real income. It might of course retard the change of the distribution of income in lending countries towards wages, which would tend to be brought about if, instead of foreign lending, consumption was increased by direct intervention.

The readjustments required by the eventual repayment would be made by common agreement without giving rise to economic fluctuations. Even so the problem might arise whether internal reforms resulting in a changed distribution of income, and more especially in a changed distribution of ownership of 'savings' (hence, given national income, of the direction and volume of 'investment'), might not in the longer run justify what might be termed increased 'capital autarky.' But, at any rate, no problem of increasing intermediate disequilibrium, of 'over-borrowing,' is likely to arise.

As soon, however, as we drop the assumption of general and partial equilibrium new complications arise. Which country will develop a deficit and be forced to borrow[1] will depend on the foreign trade multiplier, on the investment multiplier, and on the degree of employment. A further influence will be exerted by the historical position in the countries concerned. This will determine the rapidity with which excess capacity is absorbed by increasing employment. As long as confidence is maintained foreign investment, once it starts, will tend to justify itself. During the continuance of the upward movement the import of capital might sustain a deficit in the 'wrong' direction, i.e. by mature countries. If the 'lending' enables the surplus country to maintain its own employment and income by increasing exports, an interruption of the process would evoke resistance. Yet this lending may well result in a growing disequilibrium in the deficit country which in the longer run might lead to a sudden fall in its real income when the process can no longer be sustained.

If, however, certain rich areas were unable to maintain full employment without far-reaching reforms for which they are unprepared, induced deficit balances on the part of developing countries, if carefully directed to avoid over-borrowing, could at one and the same time decrease the discrepancy in capital intensity between different areas of the world and maintain employment, i.e. utilize for world development resources which would otherwise remain unemployed. A word of caution is necessary. Plans to stabilize full employment in rich but unstable industrial countries by periodical and anti-cyclical bursts of foreign loans will introduce an instability into the poorer areas which will not be wholly offset by the increased demand of rich countries for the products of the poorer developing areas during booms when the former near full employment under their own steam without foreign lending. The poor areas will thus periodically be forced to slow down investment and improve their balance. While they could possibly do this without having a general employment crisis, their real income would show fluctuations inverse to the cycles in the rich countries. It is questionable, moreover, whether unemployment can be avoided (without increasing autarky) as the rich countries might not increase the demand of the products which the poor developing countries begin to produce. Thus the main readjustment would have to come from a cut in imports of the poorer areas.

Readjustments in the Balance of Trade and Full Employment

In order to analyse the international implications of a full employment policy we were forced to distinguish between derived and auto-

[1] Cf. Knapp, *International Capital Movements and Verifications*. Review of Economic Studies, 1944.

nomous balances in the international payments of a country. The classical doctrine of foreign trade did not recognize this distinction because it was based on the assumption that general equilibrium, i.e. full employment, in the system as a whole would continuously be maintained or at least automatically and rapidly regained. The problem of the international repercussions of business fluctuations in any one country, i.e. the problem of international fluctuations in the employment of the system as a whole, was neglected. All deficiencies (though not equally surpluses), which may have been the result of other countries, and thus the whole world economy, losing equilibrium, were regarded as a sign of disequilibrium of the country suffering from it. So long as business cycles were regarded as an inevitable phenomenon this attitude was completely consistent. But it imparted an *a priori* deflationary bias to the world economic system.

The existence until 1914 of vigorous expansionist forces prevented this bias from exerting its basic influence. The peaceful development of the world economy enabled countries to undertake readjustments gradually. Even when these readjustments were aggravated by the cyclical fluctuations of the system as a whole there was no question of the complete reshaping of the international economic relations of important countries.

Once a model is investigated in which full employment is preserved, or restored automatically, the analysis of the problem whether certain methods of readjustment are more or less compatible with the maintenance of full employment is implicitly excluded. The classical approach by its assumptions prevents the investigation of the question which it sets out to answer, i.e. the maximization of output or welfare in a system of independent economic units. Without admitting that changes through time are not merely possible but highly likely and that they might be caused by the dynamics of the system itself, economic theory cannot provide a useful basis for determining policy. Static analysis is applicable only after all adjustments have been made and long-run equilibrium reached. In actual life, however, the establishment of equilibrium takes time and if the system as a whole or any of its parts are non-stationary a policy, the aim of which is to establish equilibrium as prescribed by the conditions prevailing at the initial moment, may result in a maldistribution of resources on account of the changes which have occurred in the meantime.[1] If the quantity and

---

[1] It may, for instance, be claimed that industrial protection in agricultural areas reduces the real income of the system as a whole and each of its constituent parts. But this conclusion follows

quality of productive resources in the system as a whole changes or if the degree of their employment alters, the classical argument cannot be applied.

We may now turn to the more systematic analysis of the ways in which a deliberate alteration in the balance of current payments can be brought about. Action can be taken to cut imports, visible or invisible, or increase exports, or both. The two general methods available for the purpose, i.e. acting through variation of total income either in terms of the home currency or of foreign currencies, are deflation and the depreciation of the currency. Specific methods to achieve the same ends are the limitation of imports and stimulus to export (*a*) indirectly through the price mechanism, i.e. by duties or subsidies, and (*b*) more directly by quotas or discretionary licensing, bulk purchase and reciprocal trade arrangements respectively.

Each of these methods will have two effects, both internally and abroad. First, they will influence employment at home and abroad. We shall term this the employment effect. This effect itself is not simple. The elimination of deficiency or surplus will in itself represent a fall or increase in the effective demand at home and abroad. This change may have an impact effect on the general employment position, i.e. start a secondary inflationary or deflationary spiral. Secondly, the readjustment will influence the direction of the productive effort at home and abroad, i.e. productivity.

The problem of minimizing the adverse effects of any readjustment both for the country undertaking it and for the world as a whole, depends therefore on (*a*) prevention of unemployment and (*b*) the minimization of the interference with the optimum international division of labour. These two effects in practice unfortunately often constitute alternatives, i.e. either unemployment can be avoided at the cost of limiting the effective international division of labour or *vice versa*. The optimum degree of the international division of labour, however, is itself an elusive concept. The state of employment and demand co-determine it. If, e.g., the demand for a country's products falls sharply and irrevocably, part of the readjustment will consist in replacing imported products by home output. It may well be, however, that the inherent sluggishnesss of reaction, monopolistic elements, the imperfection of markets, risk and other vital factors traditionally relegated from economic theory as frictions will prevent a rapid

---

only if we assume given existing resources, i.e. given existing skills and given, what is even more unreal to assume, the existing capital intensity per head disregarding, moreover, the redistribution of income which results from State interference.

readjustment. State interference in this case, though it may appear to be wanton, would, in fact, merely speed readjustment.

The danger of secondary spirals will be minimized if the extent of readjustment is minimized. The maintenance of the total short run effective demand in the system as a whole will be facilitated if the worsening of the real terms of trade is minimized by co-operative steps sustaining effective demand in the system as a whole. Thus—in the short run—the interest of the country undertaking the readjustment coincides with the interest of other countries.[1] If she is, moreover, not permitted by suitable international arrangements to undertake the readjustment partly by expanding her exports without undue worsening of her terms of trade, she will inevitably be forced to rely mainly, or even entirely, on the alternative of excluding imports.

Yet the reduction of the real income of the world as a whole will be greater if the readjustment were achieved by cutting imports rather than by increasing exports. The more favourable the terms on which a country is permitted to increase her exports (e.g. if she is permitted to use discriminating methods), the less she will rely on the decrease of her imports as a method of achieving balance. A discriminating policy thus may well result in a smaller alteration in the short run in the international division of labour and less violent repercussions in other countries. One of the most important arguments in favour of the establishment of an international currency and investment authority is that it might enable the deflationary impact of a given readjustment upon other countries to be minimized through co-operative action. The risk of cumulative retaliation would thereby be reduced. It should, of course, be borne in mind that in the *longer* run it will be more important and necessary to induce a shift of factors from obsolete industries than to prevent such shifts having deflationary effects.

(a) *Deflation.* Readjustment by deflation is obtained by reducing effective money demand in terms of home currency. This reduction will *pari passu* depress the demand curve for imports while cutting the demand for home products. Unless the degree of monopoly could be appropriately changed, or all money incomes can be reduced by general agreement and legislative action proportionately in each case, the eventual readjustment, i.e. the fall in the money cost of home products, must come through a pressure on wages, i.e. unemployment.

This method must *a priori* be excluded as a means of full employment policy. Yet, as we have seen, it is impossible to avoid at least

[1] In the long run the worsening of the terms of trade will benefit other countries. This contradiction explains the favour which import quotas enjoyed in importing countries, such as Britain, though they deliberately worsened the terms of trade.

the *primary* impact of a deflation which affected a foreign country, if *positive* steps are not taken to counteract the fall in effective demand at home which the unfavourable balance implies. The consequent fall in the expected rate of profit would in all probability start a further secondary deflationary spiral which might in the end carry the economic system further than even the depression in the country where it first started would warrant.

Under the orthodox gold standard 'rules of the game' a country suffering from an excess of out-payments had to protect its gold reserve by increasing the bank rate. If it possessed short-term balances abroad (or if the confidence in its ability to pay was unshaken) this mechanism in the short run led to a withdrawal of (or influx of foreign) capital from abroad. Provided the disequilibrium was of a minor character this influx, together with the consequences of the automatic lessening of the effects of the original relative over-investment (or increase in consumption) through the worsening of the trade balance, was sufficient to restore the short-term balance of payments without having to rely on a secondary, consciously generated, fall in effective demand. If, moreover, the long-term expectations were favourable, the increase in the short-term rate of interest did not result in a further fall in the level of effective demand.

If a further change in the current balance of payments was required it depended on a complex set of factors whether the terms of trade would be worsened or improved in these circumstances, thus increasing or mitigating the extent of the required readjustment. If the internal deflationary pressure in the depressed country was very great and the elasticity of supply low, its terms of trade would worsen sharply. Past experience, however, is no clue whatever as depressions in important countries hardly ever coincided with full employment. With falling demand which, therefore, hardly responds to price changes the terms of trade were mainly determined by the elasticity of supply.[1] In a partially fully employed world economic system changes in the terms of trade are likely to mitigate rather than worsen, from the point of view of the world, the effects of depression on the balance of payments of the depressed country. How important this effect is likely to be depends on the respective price elasticities of demand and supply and on the ratio of the effective demand of the world as a whole to the effective demand of the depressed area. In this analysis it is, of

---

[1] The terms of trade therefore went regularly in favour of industrial countries in depressions and moved in their disfavour in recovery. The United States unfortunately is not merely the strongest industrial country but also an important primary producer, so that the net effect of the depression on its balance of trade cannot *a priori* be taken as a mitigating factor.

course, assumed that the depression is not permitted to overlap into other countries, i.e. that the full employment policy continues.

The original theory of foreign trade, by assuming that purely competitive conditions can be applied to relations between countries, excludes this problem from its purview.[1] It has long been recognized that a country can, by protective devices, 'make the foreigner pay.' An analysis of the economic consequences of measures or policies which influence the volume of effective demand in a country has only recently been undertaken.[2] Even this analysis has not made it explicit that a variation in effective demand will have the similar result on foreign countries as tariffs. If the price elasticity of demand of a country for foreign products is less than unity, if its income elasticity is considerable, and if, furthermore, the country represents an appreciable part of the world supply or demand of certain commodities, the fall of its effective demand would have the same effect on its terms of trade[3] as tariffs in similar conditions. The effect on total real income of the country will, of course, depend on whether the loss resulting from the consequent decrease in employment is bigger than the increase due to the change in the terms of trade.

Measures which enable the increase of the national income of a country either by internal expansion or by technical progress, while at the same time not involving the absolute worsening in the total real income of the rest of the world, cannot be said to be exploitative. This is true even if these measures involved a worsening of the long run position of foreign countries relatively to the state which would rule if the increase in the national real income would have been brought about automatically, i.e. without a deliberate (protective or discriminatory) policy. We may thus contrast exploitative and constructive measures of protection, at least in the short run.

The exclusion of deflation as one of the methods of readjustment in a world pledged to maintain full employment does not absolve us from

[1] Without quite recognizing the fact that the subjects of international trade were countries having sovereign policies. Beginning with Mill, the monopolistic character of foreign trade became apparent. The revision of the theory began by considering the problem of tariffs. Cf. Mr. Kaldor, *Economica*, 1940, and Mr. Scitovszky, *Review of Economic Studies*, 1942.

[2] An adequate treatment of the problem can only be found in Mrs. Joan Robinson's two essays on Foreign Trade and Exchange (op. cit., pp. 183-231).

[3] The exclusion of an analysis of fluctuations has prevented classical economists, e.g. Mill, from applying the analysis of reciprocal demand to this contingency. An attempt (cf. Viner, *Studies in the Theory of International Trade*) to explain obvious disequilibria caused by the transfer of gold from one country to another by reference to differences in the final velocity of circulation had to break down because this explanation involved a change in the total effective demand of the system as a whole according to whether funds were transferred from high to low velocity areas. The resultant general fluctuation could not be analysed by the conceptual tools of orthodox theory.

analysing its consequence on the foreign demand and supply of a country. Deflation will cause an immediate downward shift in the demand schedules of the country. This will increase the price elasticity of supply of exports and potential exports given demand abroad. Conversely, once a deflationary spiral has started it may produce further downward shifts of the home demand and the supply schedule. We are here confronted not with a single demand curve but a family of demand and supply curves whose positions are determined by the level of income. Yet, these unavoidable shifts in the home demand curves for potential exports and the resultant shifts in the supply curves constitute a vital element in the situation. The shifts will be most marked in the case of capital equipment. The demand for food-stuffs and essential raw materials will be more stable. The demand for luxuries might remain inelastic to income changes up to a certain point and then fall steeply when people can no longer strive to maintain their previous standard of life.

The consequences of simultaneous changes in the degree of employment in more than one country are similar, if not identical, to those which can be observed in a closed economic system.[1] The analysis applied to the probable consequences of price and wage changes during fluctuations in business activity in a closed economy, can with increased force be used in an international system consisting of inter-connected economies, because of the greater uncertainty about the future policy and behaviour of sovereign countries. The effects on the demand for any one country's produce of a fall in price are highly conjectural. They will depend on the reactions of competitors in other countries and also on the state of expectations in each of the countries which again are inter-connected. All countries may well sink and rise together without their international balance, in distinction to the volume of total trade, altering in a significant manner. Any readjustment, therefore, which involves a deflationary shock must, because of the severe consequences and strains evoked by a fall in effective demand, be guarded against. This should be carefully borne in mind when considering the readjustment even of autonomous disequilibria. In a world economy which naturally or consciously tends towards full employment, the readjustment will be relatively easy and it is this case alone which has been analysed by classical economists. But the case in which readjustments are accompanied by foreign depression should be very carefully differentiated from cases where they are not so accompanied. The

[1] Cf. Part I.

reaction of foreign countries to an effort to increase exports will in the two cases be totally different.

(b) *Devaluation.* The second general method of readjustment consists in altering the equivalent of the total effective demand of the country by changing the value of its currency in terms of other currencies, without changing its volume or distribution in terms of the home currency. It is, therefore, a special case of a policy of export premia and import duties of a uniform proportion. If we could assume that effective home demand, as it asserts itself in the market, is a sufficient criterion from a social point of view for judging the urgency of needs, and that therefore an unrestricted play of the price mechanism will on the one hand choke off the least import demand and will stimulate the most effective production, devaluation would seem not only the fairest method of readjustment, but would also minimize the losses and maximize the gains for the community. The efficacy of devaluation as a method of readjustment will depend on whether the relative price elasticity at home and abroad is substantial enough to enable the necessary shifts in production and consumption to take place without causing *considerable* frictional unemployment.

What are the conditions for these hypotheses being fulfilled? We shall have to differentiate strictly between systems which are generally fully employed, partially unemployed and generally underemployed.

The first and not least important case to be investigated is the readjustment of autonomous disequilibria in single countries when others are fully employed. The foreign price elasticity of demand for the particular countries producing under these conditions might be assumed to be high.[1] There is no *a priori* reason under these circumstances to fear that competitive countries would immediately take steps to counteract the stimulus by the devaluation to the exports of the readjusting country. Thus, even that part of the effect of the devaluation which is due to the substitution of the commodities exported by the devaluing country for identical goods produced elsewhere will not be neutralized. Hence depreciation might be able to neutralize the effects of over-employment in any one country on the balance of payments, even if, as we shall see presently, it may not under all circumstances be an appropriate method of dealing with unfavourable balances induced by a depression abroad. This is the only case envisaged and investigated by the classical school under

---

[1] This is the most important reason why the close co-ordination of employment policies internationally through appropriate organs is so important,

their assumptions of full employment and/or automatic and quick readjustment abroad.

We must now turn to analyse the much more typical case of a country having to readjust her balance of payments without the assurance of continued full employment abroad. Here again we must distinguish between different types of countries as the foreign price elasticities, *ceteris paribus*, will differ greatly. The most favourable case is that of a country which produces for export primary commodities of a standard character which have highly organized world markets in which they do not represent a dominating fraction of total supply. In this case it is possible that the price elasticity of demand for their products might remain relatively high in spite of a general depression. Even in this case there is a danger that their competitors will immediately react against their effort to secure wider markets by devaluation. Whatever measures these competing countries take to maintain their exports, their efforts will reduce the price elasticity of demand for that part of the total world output of a commodity which the devaluing country produces.[1] If the products which the devaluing country exports had any competing commodities, the substitution effect might be so widespread that a high priceelasticity would be maintained. This fact would also spread the unfavourable repercussions of the readjustment to third countries over so wide a field that each of the competitors which it replaces may not feel aggrieved enough to take retaliatory steps. The devaluing country must not represent an appreciable fraction of the total money demand of the world, otherwise the depreciation of its currency might start a general deflationary spiral. Its internal social structure must be such that the cost of production will not rise easily *pari passu* with the increase in the price level. Finally it would seem desirable that its imports should consist mainly of durable consumption or producer goods, the internal income and price-elasticity of demand for which is high. A community like Australia, New Zealand or even perhaps Sweden or Denmark might hope to rely on depreciation as a means of readjustment without considerable friction, provided a catastrophic deflation is not raging in the most important industrial countries.

The problem of an industrial country, the last case which has to be investigated, differs greatly. Devaluation has to work in this case when

---

[1] This means that the country changes from being a 'perfect' into an 'oligopolistic' competitor. Financial prejudice in competitor countries against devaluation seems to have been an essential element in the success of some of the most important past cases of readjustment by devaluation. The rest was accounted for by the devaluing country also deflating.

there is unemployment abroad and full employment at home.[1] The full employment policy will render the economic system somewhat inelastic to the change of the foreign value of the currency, as we may assume that there will be a tendency for wages to increase if prices rise.

The effectiveness of depreciation as a method of stimulating *exports* will depend (i) first and foremost on the price elasticity of foreign demand abroad, (ii) secondly, on whether and to what extent two internal effects are likely. Of these the first is that depreciation, by increasing the internal price of potential exports, discourages home demand and thus increases the proportion of the currently produced output which is available for exports. The increase of exports is reinforced by the second effect, which consists in the investment of new resources in the export industries and in industries competing with imports.

(i) *The price-elasticity of foreign demand.* Under the conditions which have to be envisaged, the price-elasticity of foreign demand for the exports of the fully employed country is likely to be low, if for no other reason, because of the endeavour of foreign countries to exclude exports and resist further pressure on their prices. If the elasticity of foreign demand for exports and the elasticity of home demand for imports are together less than unity, then depreciation results in a deterioration of the balance of trade. If the elasticity of foreign demand is near unity, the improvement of the balance may be accompanied by such worsening of the terms of trade as to change the comparative cost relations so substantially that in the main the improvement of the balance of trade will be accomplished, even without further protection, by a substitution of home produce for foreign imports. This, however, could be more quickly and far more effectively accomplished by other, more discriminatory methods of readjustment. The income elasticity of demand which is, save for exceptional cases, high (though falling with increasing income) will always overshadow price elasticities in importance in its effects on the balance of payments. If a fully employed country is confronted with a depressed area its chances of increasing exports by price concessions are limited. The argument that the elasticity of demand for the produce of any *one* country is high, is based on the assumption that employment elsewhere is unaffected by the depreciation of exporters' currency. If wages are flexible and/or if excess capacity is prevalent in other countries and if the readjustment required is substantial, any competitive spurt

---

[1] Even Mrs. Robinson's treatment of this problem (ibid. p. 197) suffers from implicit neoclassical assumptions.

on the part of a given country will meet with counter-bids by its competitors nullifying its temporary advantage. There is no reason to assume that when full employment is *not* safeguarded internationally the attempt to increase exports will not be resisted by competing countries, whatever the means employed by the country undertaking the additional export.[1]

(ii) *Supply*. If the deficit in the balance of payment occurs because a country which is fully employed is confronted with depression abroad, the elasticity of supply of exports is likely to be low. Depreciation as a method of readjustment in a state of full employment is not as efficient as if it is coupled with deflation. The inducement, moreover, for an adaptation towards export trades or home substitutes of any given rate of depreciation is small. Entrepreneurs will fear adverse reactions of competitive countries and thus be afraid to embark on new investment without more specific assurance than that which the depreciation of the currency will provide. New investment will only be undertaken if the current favourable expectations can be assumed to be stable. But risks involved in foreign, as contrasted with 'sheltered' domestic trade, are notoriously higher in a system in which business cycles occur and foreign pressure groups may abruptly change the terms at which exports can be sold abroad. The unpredictable nature of these risks will certainly limit the scope of activities which traders are willing to engage in at any given rate of profit. Thus a moderate depreciation of the currency, unless more direct measures are taken, is not likely to tempt entrepreneurs to undertake these additional risks. A sharp depreciation, however, would tend to set the terms of trade *more* against the depreciating country than necessary for the *average* of export industries (i.e. would cause a profit inflation in more 'advantageous' industries) and engender, as we have already mentioned, a general tendency to an inflationary spiral through cumulative wage increases. The losses suffered in this process might be considerable.

An effective depreciation implies the adaptation of the structure of industry. Such adaptation is bound to be slow and it is even questionable, moreover, whether in violently changing conditions, which slumps and booms imply, it would be desirable. If changes in the balance of payments originating in developments abroad are due not to a trend but to cyclical fluctuations, if therefore the causes to which the change in the state of the balance of payments is due are not permanent, and if subsequent movements are not in the same direction, the accomplished readjustment—i.e. the loss of the old investment

[1] Cf. below, pp. 174 *et seq.*

undertaken as a result of the readjustment—will turn out to be un-justified and the new investment misdirected.

The theoretical advantages of the depreciation as a 'long-term policy' in that it represents an equal 'impartial' stimulus (and hindrance) and that therefore it is supposed to select the 'most productive' indus-tries for stimulation (either for export or to replace imports), render it unsuitable as a policy to deal with cyclical fluctuations, where, in the short run, it would leave the 'less' productive specific factors wholly unemployed. A more flexible policy which would enable a more gradual adjustment of available factors in the export sector would seem to accord more with the needs of a general full employment policy. In the long run, nevertheless, measures must be taken to shift those factors which have permanently lost their previous productivity on account of the change in conditions into more productive use. But the current net private returns are an insecure guide in this respect.

The same conclusion emerges if the effect of depreciation on *imports* is analysed. As long as full employment is maintained, price elasticity of home demand for imported commodities (even luxuries) may be very low. In consequence readjustments may be forced on the country to secure sufficient exports to pay for these imports at the cost of lowering the standard of life of the whole community by an adverse turn of its terms of trade. A non-selective method of repressing effective home demand for foreign products such as depreciation would in these conditions involve unnecessary sacrifice. This would be increased the greater the difficulties in the way of an increase in exports.

As Mrs. Robinson[1] pointed out, foreign assets (and income from them) and foreign debts (and their burden) can be treated as exports or imports. Their repercussion on the balance of payments will depend whether they are contracted in terms of the home or foreign currencies. Debts in terms of home currency 'may be regarded as an export of which the home supply is perfectly inelastic.' They would tend to respond favourably to depreciation. If, however, a country is the centre of a network of foreign payments—e.g. Britain—the threat of repeated devaluation will cause foreign clients to withdraw their work-ing balances (which in effect amount to a cheap credit from the point of view of the debtor) or demand a 'gold guarantee' which in effect transforms them into liabilities in terms of gold.[2] But if the debt is fixed

[1] Ibid. p. 196.
[2] The Joint Plan of Experts does not specify whether the Fund or the debtor country (the debt takes the form of a sale of the home currency to the fund) will shoulder the loss consequent on the devaluation of the debtor's currency. The U.S. proposal (White Plan) which was the basis of the new draft provided that the debtor indemnified the Fund (p. 9, para. IV, 4).

in terms of foreign currency 'they may be regarded as an import for which home demand is perfectly inelastic.' The position of the country will be aggravated by depreciation. The same is true (except if otherwise the assets would depreciate because of default) of foreign assets in terms of the home currency.

As long as fluctuations can be assumed to be small, or if any initial readjustment required on account of the break in the economic development is not considerable, general internal measures, e.g. taxation, might safeguard the interests of the community. The same applies to a completely collectivized system or to a system which reserves foreign economic transactions to government monopoly.

We conclude, therefore, that in a world economic system in which sharp economic fluctuations in important countries continue, other countries wishing to maintain full employment can ordinarily not rely on depreciation of their currency as a short-term method by which external fluctuations are made compatible with internal stability. Depreciation as a method suffers not merely from the drawback of causing a deterioration of their real income through an attempted—yet partly unsuccessful—stimulus of export and consequent 'unnecessary' worsening of their terms of trade, but also from the decisive disadvantage of not being subtle or potent enough to prevent unnecessary frictional unemployment.

The reason for the failure to realize these limitations of depreciation as a means of readjustment is threefold. First, prior to the British return to the gold standard and its reversal in 1931, devaluation was practised by weaker overseas countries where conditions for its relatively successful working obtained. Secondly, the amount of readjustment required in most of those cases was relatively small. The quantitative element through the operation of dynamic factors, e.g. the threat of secondary deflations and their effect on price elasticities of demand, causes, however, basic qualitative changes in the problem of readjustment. Thirdly, where the extent of the required readjustment was large, the depression of the domestic economy was not avoided, i.e. effective demand declined and the consequent under-employment of the domestic economy 'helped' the readjustment of the foreign balance by changing the relevant home price elasticities. The application of past experiences to problems of fully employed economies is misleading.[1]

---

[1] Lord Keynes (Hansard, House of Lords, May 23, 1944, col. 844) affirms that the liberty of changing the value of the currency and the management of the rate of interest permitted by a control of capital movements would ensure the conditions necessary to maintain full employment at home, irrespective of conditions abroad, and without further direct control of foreign trade.

We conclude, therefore, that any considerable and abrupt alteration of the effective foreign demand of a country is likely to necessitate readjustments abroad which are difficult to achieve without suffering unemployment. Even if the change is qualitative and not quantitative, serious problems arise. Full international co-operation to achieve full employment demands, therefore, that the countries participating should not merely stabilize the volume of their effective demand, but should refrain from changing it by tariffs, quotas, controls, etc., without prior consultation with the affected countries. Changes which are desirable from the point of view of the development of poorer areas should be made with due regard to their consequences elsewhere. Smooth readjustment would be facilitated if they were either spread through time and/or if international compensation schemes could be evolved.

(c) *Direct Control.* (i) *The Method and Aim of Controls.* The effectiveness of devaluation as a method of maintaining or restoring the balance of international payments has been found to be limited. The question arises how far other, more specific, methods of readjustment can be expected to be effective where devaluation fails. In solving this problem the clue must be sought in the reasons which render devaluation ineffective. These have been found to originate in the low price elasticity of foreign demand for a fully employed (industrial) country's exports when under-employment is prevalent elsewhere. Measures in two directions can therefore be expected to be helpful, directions which were not sufficiently differentiated from one another in analysis because they were in practice necessarily intermingled.

The first method takes the effective demand abroad as given and attempts to minimize the disequilibrium in the balance of payments by diverting trade from its 'normal' channels and/or by turning

Continued from p. 145.

As we shall see, legitimate doubt may be entertained whether the monetary plan accepted by the experts permits full readjustment by devaluation. In any case his hope is justified only under the implicit assumption that foreign elasticities of demand for British exports are high. In conditions such as will presumably prevail after the war, this tacit assumption is highly unrealistic. Devaluation as a method of readjustment thus will at best be ineffective, at worst it will aggravate the problem. Moreover, if the new plan is accepted it will not be possible to devalue all currencies of an interrelated area, e.g. the sterling area, together, if some of the constituent members are not suffering from a deficiency in the balance of payments (partly because of the deficiency of Britain herself). Thus Britain may suffer from a worsening of the terms of trade to these countries and the devaluation of sterling may not improve the position unless full employment policy is discontinued and the price elasticity of demand increased. The attempt to impose on economically interrelated but politically 'sovereign' economies 'rules of game' which do not apply *within* sovereign countries must lead either to political union or to economic paralysis of smaller political units.

the terms of trade by specific measures in favour of the readjusting country. To this extent it might be termed exploitative. The second method is to increase by conscious action the foreign demand for home products. We must finally analyse the technical arrangements which permit a country with a given economic system to utilize these methods.

The first method will utilize the fact that the elasticities of foreign demand for various export items and the elasticities of home demand for various import items are unequal. The effect upon the balance of payments of appropriately differentiated export premia and import controls (tariffs, bulk purchases, etc.) is more favourable than a depreciation equivalent to the *average* of these export premia or import restrictions. The direct regulation of imports permits the exclusion of those which appear to be least urgent from a social point of view. The pressure to export is thus relieved. Thus in cases where depreciation cannot succeed in improving the balance of trade easily, differential methods may still sometimes do the job.

This amounts to a direct control of the home propensity to consume foreign goods and of the supply of exports. A reduction in foreign demand in such a system would find its expression not in the unemployment of industry, but (i) in a smaller fall in the value of exports achieved by decreasing the price to the foreign buyer, and (ii) in the restriction or direct control of imports.

The utilization of the second method is somewhat limited by the fact that the country which is contemplating the policy will be suffering from an excess of outpayments and thus the *laisser-faire* method of promoting effective foreign demand by the granting of foreign loans does not come under consideration. To be successful the method must automatically ensure that an increase in the demand for foreign products will be matched by an increase in the foreign demand for home products, or rather that the maintenance of the home demand for foreign products in the teeth of a depression abroad will result in a re-expansion of the foreign demand for home products.[1] It does not represent a mere diversion of existing foreign demand from the cheapest market, but the creation of conditions in which foreign demand can be induced to increase to the mutual benefit of all participants.

(ii) *Modification of the Current Balance of Payments through Direct Action not affecting Total Effective Demand directly.* The first method of

---

[1] This method, therefore, consists in consciously re-establishing the high price elasticity of foreign demand which otherwise would *not* obtain and on which the hopes of the devaluationist *laisser-faire* school, which *implicitly* assume it, are really based. It can be, and in war was, used to extort more favourable terms of trade.

achieving readjustment is to stimulate exports and to restrict imports by measures which are not 'monetary' in character.

If the Government has full monopoly over foreign economic relations it can directly secure this aim. Economic systems based (at least mainly) on private enterprise, which wish to maintain full employment, will have to achieve similar results by tariffs, quotas, exchange restrictions and export subsidies. *Unilateral* bulk purchase or sale agreements which use the monopoly or monopsony position of the initiating country to secure better terms than would result from the 'free interplay' of market forces and thus redress the balance of payments come under this heading, except in so far as they are not supplemented by (or do not give rise to) arrangements in the partner country which permit an increase in that country of effective demand and real income. Unilateral bulk purchase agreements can be discriminating or non-discriminating.

(*a*) *Export Stimuli*. The selective stimulus of exports can be financed, and thus the real burden of the worsening of the terms of trade can be borne, in different ways. It will in all circumstances be less than that caused by devaluation. One of the methods is to finance exports by a levy on home trade. This is both inefficient and inequitable.[1]

A second and more efficient method of finance would be to employ direct grants to private firms from the Treasury to stimulate exports.

---

[1] The establishment of a fighting fund by individual industries which form autonomous cartels in order to be able to bargain collectively with foreign competitors and to be able to secure discriminating prices is the method adopted by preference in this country. It is an uneconomic, ineffective and pernicious method. The bargaining power of the cartel, even if backed by the Government, would depend primarily on import surpluses in the commodity in question (e.g. the success of the steel negotiations after 1932). The capacity to accumulate a fighting fund sufficient to be effective depends on the relative size of the internal market and on the elasticity of home demand. This expedient could only be used with some force in the case of products which have a large internal market and which are relatively important from the point of view of home consumers—i.e. with respect to which home demand is relatively inelastic. This method means, therefore, the stimulation of exports by an indirect tax on the consumer—i.e. by regressive taxation. The levy on home sales would moreover be camouflaged by a rise in the price of the home product or a worsening of its quality. The door is thereby open to an infinite variety of abuses and its result would be to stimulate inefficiency.

A variant of this method is the sale of goods at less than full cost. If the rate of exchange is not kept at optimum level as far as the average of transactions are concerned this procedure would amount to an unselective subsidy on exports and not merely to an offsetting of the export tax levied by keeping the exchange 'over-valued.' If the difference between full and prime costs are different in different industries the principle of comparative costs is moreover infringed. The productivity of labour is thereby lowered by a misdirection of effort and by setting the terms of trade against the country. A better result can be achieved by home full employment policy, coupled by protective devices, if the balance of trade demands such interference (cf. Mrs. J. Robinson, op. cit., p. 222). Even worse effects are produced if the wage level in the export industries is kept low by general unemployment (cf. above), especially if the degree of monopoly in the export industries is less than in home trades (both of which are extremely likely in the case of deflation, to the vicious effects of which these secondary repercussions contribute in no mean measure).

This policy is not without its internal and external dangers.[1] It is, however, not more dangerous than devaluation of equal effect. Any increase in exports in the teeth of declining foreign demand represents a pressure on foreign countries and will be resisted. By trying to concentrate the increase in exports to industries the price elasticity of demand for whose products is relatively high, the full employment country might at least hope to avoid running foul of the most depressed of its foreign competitors, who are likely to put up the bitterest fight. The relatively high price elasticity of demand for any one country's products is *a priori* an indication that competitive foreign excess capacity in that industry is not too large.

The stimulation of exports—whatever the means employed, apart from measures which increase effective demand abroad—will tend to depress prices abroad. The change of relative prices will change the differences in opportunity costs which render the international exchange of goods profitable. If then exports are maintained by 'intervention,' productive factors will be diverted from their 'optimum' current use. As a weapon of employment policy, a stimulus to exports must be condemned because of the unnecessary loss in real income. Whether in any given situation it should nevertheless be used to permit the continuance of a certain level of imports, depends on the *ex-post* opportunity cost differences which will be determined also by the possibilities of re-employing the non-specific factors engaged in the export industries elsewhere, or for other purposes.

(*b*) *Control of imports*. The control of imports must accompany the stimulus to exports. Failing this it is possible that exports will have to be undertaken beyond the optimum.

The control of imports can be indirect, through the price system (tariffs), or direct through the fixing of quantities either by way of quotas and exchange licences or by centralized buying.[2] All protective

---

[1] The most efficient alternative would be to establish Government wholesaling organizations under a Government Department which would combine the advantages of a competitive system internally with those of a foreign trade monopoly internationally. Transactions which need not be subsidized should not be subsidized or controlled. Apart from stimulating exports in which the country has a relative and absolute advantage, these agencies and their controlling Department might act as a central co-ordinating and supervisory agency for all those export or potential export industries which could not be employed for export at the prevailing prices, costs and exchange rates, and which cannot take the risk of producing for stocking pending a subsequent sale. The machinery could also be used to bridge the gap by producing for stock between the current demand of export and the productive capacity at full employment. At the same time, the existence of such foreign trade organization would represent an effective check on monopolistic tendencies, as they may, in case of need, divert part of their stocks to the home market, thus preventing the charging of exploitative prices. The problem, as in all these cases, is that of the selection of personnel.

[2] The latter can be discriminatory or non-discriminatory.

measures[1] tend to improve the terms of trade and thereby—at least temporarily and partially—to offset the fall in real income of the community (which finds its expression in the increase of the price). In principle[2] a level of tariff can be found exactly equivalent to any given direct restriction of imports. On closer analysis it appears that this equivalence is severely limited to the effect on the balance of payments. Unless the tariffs are wholly prohibitive (in which case there is, of course, no difference between indirect and direct 'restriction', as it is absolute) their influence both on employment and on the distribution of the national income differ from that of the 'equivalent' direct restriction. A direct control will give a far greater security to home producers than tariffs (and *a fortiori* than depreciation) because the entrepreneur will know in advance the effect of the quota on the home market while the effect of the duty—unless prohibitive—will depend also on the readjustment of foreign competitors to the new duty. If, therefore, the establishment of new or the extension of existing production is aimed at in a slump abroad, indirect restriction will hardly suffice to encourage it. It is only the fuller use of existing excess capacities which can be effectively brought about by Government intervention working through the 'price' mechanism. One of the main difficulties in isolating a fully employed economy from fluctuations abroad will be encountered because the loss of confidence will tend to spread into the full employment country (i.e. the consequent rise in the risk premium and a fall in investment). Some control of imports will probably have to be an integral part of full employment policy in an unstable world system. The difference between long and short run cost might be so substantial as to render stability at home, in the face of fluctuations abroad, difficult short of State investment or guarantee against losses on new investment.

(c) *Unilateral Bulk Purchase.* Unilateral bulk purchase agreements use the monopsonistic bargaining power of a country with respect to its imports to secure better terms and thus reduce an adverse balance of trade. American writers, e.g. Professor Viner,[3] hold that all direct transactions involving a monopolistic influence on markets are discriminating and exploitative. A differentiation between exploitative and non-exploitative readjustment on the basis of static concepts is

---

[1] Except for the system of granting quotas or licences practised, e.g., by the British Agricultural Administration before (and the Exchange Control in the first few months of) the war by which the increase in home prices could accrue to the foreign seller.

[2] Cf. League of Nations: *Quantitative Controls of Foreign Trade*, p. 20.

[3] *Trade Relations between Free Market and Controlled Economics*, League of Nations 1943. A general deflation, which would have identical results on the terms of trade and would depress foreign national income very much more sharply, is not condemned as exploitative.

ıt legitimate. Whether such bulk purchases will be exploitative or
ıt will depend on whether or not the national real income of the part-
ır country will rise or not.¹ This cannot, as we shall presently see,
determined by price relations alone. Long-term purchase agree-
ents eliminate the risk inherent in producing for an uncertain market.
is clear, therefore, that the purchasing country performs a service
the selling country which might be, and mostly is, of considerable
ıportance. The producers in the selling country, especially if they are
ıall and weak producers, as a result of the purchase agreement will
enabled to tap cheap sources of credit and modernize their produc-
ın. The possibility of such reorganization of their production was,
ithout the agreement, completely closed to them.²

An industrial country which undertakes to purchase a considerable part
the output of another at a fixed price, will be unwilling to commit
rself if she is not assured, more directly than any general monetary
rangement might succeed in doing, not only that she will be able to
y for the supplies, and on terms which will not subsequently be
ndered too onerous by events over which she has no control (e.g.
flation in the supplying country), but also that other countries will
ıt be able to obtain the same goods at better terms elsewhere at a
bsequent date. The supplier of the (primary) products, on his part,
ıst have the assurance that once the sale is concluded the purchaser
ıll not insist on unreasonable prices for his exports.³

Whether the method adopted will in fact be exploitative or not will thus depend not on the
chanism adopted as e.g. Mr. Kaldor suggested (*The Banker*, 1943), who implicitly assumes that
monetary discrimination is exploitative and all non-monetary discrimination non-exploitative,
: on the volume of exchange and its terms. The renunciation to conclude *monetary* agree-
nts would, however, represent a worsening of the position of industrial countries (such as
tain) because they import standard foodstuffs and raw materials and export varied manu-
tured products. It would be more difficult to conclude bulk purchase agreements with
pect to the latter than to the former.

The importance of the consequent improvement of their credit for their production costs is
siderably greater than has as yet been admitted. Small producers in primary countries, because
the risk of crop failures and of market changes, are subject to considerable exploitation. A
e of interest above 20 per cent per annum or more is the rule rather than the exception. The
rganization of agricultural credit in the Balkans played on important role in securing for
rmany favourable commercial agreements at a time when she had no political power to force
h agreements on the Balkan countries. It is by no means true that, in the first period of her
ıth Eastern commercial expansion, Germany exploited the agricultural producer. In some of
countries her purchases saved them from complete economic annihilation. Even where
rmany subsequently imposed an obligation to buy her own produce at higher prices,
charge of exploitation, which was levelled for propaganda purposes, cannot scientifically be
ıgether maintained; though Germany forced these countries to buy products which could at
ruling rates of exchange be obtained more cheaply elsewhere, these prices were completely
oretical as far as the Balkan countries were concerned, because without German purchases
se countries would not have been in a position to buy anything abroad. Their money and
l income would have had to fall in order to balance their trade by 'liberal' methods.

The reciprocal agreements might be restricted to certain main products on both sides, leaving
general trade to be conducted by multilateral clearing or free exchange machinery. It has

In the absence of an international monetary agreement which saf‹
guards the interest of the purchasing country, a wide extension of un‹
lateral bulk purchase is not very likely.

(ii) *Methods influencing Foreign Effective Demand.* Both monetary ar‹
non-monetary means are at the disposal of a full employment count‹
to influence effective demand abroad for its products. The nor‹
monetary method consists of reciprocal bulk purchase; monetary e‹
pedients are clearing agreements and payment agreements. The need f‹
such auxiliary methods in helping the readjustment of the balance of pa‹
ments arises because the maintenance of full employment in a count‹
results in a maintenance—or rather increase—of the purchases of th‹
country relatively to the purchases of the depressed countries abroad.
more orthodox methods were followed to readjust the resulti‹
disequilibrium, a fall in national real income could hardly be avoide‹
As long as employment (and/or investment) policies are not co-ordinat‹
in such a way as to balance international payments, the purchase or sa‹
internationally of commodities without the assurance of a reciproc‹
transaction cannot be taken as the equivalent of the same transacti‹
undertaken with the certainty that a reciprocal transaction will in d‹
course automatically follow. The neglect of the reciprocal transaction
a factor determining the advantage of the first transaction implicitly re‹
on the assumption that the system as a whole is fully employed, i.e. th‹
'Say's celebrated Law of Markets' operates internationally,[1] and th‹

been argued that such an attempt to secure favourable terms of trade by way of clearing agreeme‹
or long-term purchase agreements would not merely anger competitive exporting nations, ‹
also result in defensive action on the part of the countries which could conclude sales only ‹
condition that they used their export proceeds in a pre-arranged manner. It is contended t‹
these countries will try to escape this restraint. If primary producing countries can be assured‹
a stable and growing market, it is unlikely that they will want to forego this advantage, even ‹
the cost of foregoing the chance of top prices in exceptionally favourable periods. At the sa‹
time, it is also obvious that Britain and other European countries will need all help in restor‹
their balance of payments, whatever the position elsewhere. The attempt to proscribe mor‹
polistic price agreements on industrial products which Europe exports, while at the same ti‹
organizing, through buffer stock agreements or other ways, a conscious control of raw mate‹
prices, would further turn the terms of trade against Europe and thereby increase her proble‹
The technique of combined multi- and bi-lateral clearing was elaborated by the present aut‹
for the French Economic Mission, mainly in order to evolve a method of solving the finan‹
problems caused by the 'cash and carry' provisions of the United States Neutrality Act, wh‹
had not then been replaced by the Lend-Lease machinery. (The main principles were publisl‹
in *Economica*, August 1940.)

[1] Lord Keynes (ibid.), in extolling the advantages of the restoration of 'full convertibility‹
currencies by a multilateral scheme, contrasted the position of being able to export and to use ‹
results of the exports to buy anywhere (general convertibility) with the contingency of being a‹
to export and having to purchase in the country to which the export was directed. The advant‹
between these two alternatives implicitly lies with the former. But Lord Keynes' example‹
persuasive, was misleading. In a system which is liable to economic fluctuations the true alter‹
tives lie between being able to export at all (though having to purchase in the country to wh‹
the export is directed), and not being able to export at all. If these are the alternatives, i‹
probable that it is better to be able to export even if the range of subsequent purchase is limit‹

...erefore the reverse transactions take place, automatically and without any further adjustments, on the basis of the existing comparative costs, which are taken to remain unchanged by the original transaction. This assumption could only be accepted if some comprehensive international agreement were to be arrived at, which would allow for the maintenance of full employment in all member countries. The success of multilateralism depends on full employment, and not *vice versa*. If such agreement is not arrived at, then the gains from foreign trade can no longer be judged by *current* comparative cost differences. All secondary effects of every transaction, including its effects on total demand in the member countries (exerted via the necessity of global readjustment), must be taken into account.

In the absence of the application of special measures no, or much less, trade would take place as the emergence or increase of induced balances towards countries which failed in or had no full employment policies would force all countries to cut down their imports because these balances might be spent anywhere, i.e. also in areas which by their deflationary pressure absorb liquidity without increasing their demand for foreign goods and services.

All reciprocal agreements eliminate the necessity of having sufficient internationally acceptable liquid reserves prior to the purchase of goods and services. Unless the counter party to the transaction does not utilize the credits standing to his name for an immediate contrary transaction an automatic credit is provided. In the case of countries, therefore, which suffer from a lack of liquidity and whose economic systems tend to produce a bias towards deficiencies in their balances of international payments, this arrangement permits the maintenance of full employment and the maintenance of supplies from abroad. A country which has a bias to export its unemployment through export surpluses, i.e. a country which has a tendency to absorb international liquidity, has no need to fall back on this device. It is the means at the disposal of countries which do not wish to submit to deflationary pressure from abroad.

The prevention of reciprocal agreements on the basis that they imply discrimination amounts to a unilateral acceptance of the bargaining power of unstable export surplus countries, which can lend.

(a) *Non-monetary Reciprocity*. The non-monetary form of such agreements are reciprocal bulk supply contracts. Whether they will in fact modify foreign total demand depends on the internal policy of the partner country. They provide a possibility for expansionist policy which without them would possibly result in a worsening of the balance of payments. The practical limitations of reciprocal bulk purchases lie in the character of the economic system of the countrie concerned. Reciprocal bulk purchase can be practised easily by tw entirely collectivized countries. It is difficult to arrange it betwee countries whose economic system is based on individual enterprise. is then not the State, but the individual traders who export and impor and those traders who export are not also necessarily in charge of im ports. It might, therefore, be difficult and clumsy to force trade to conclude direct barter agreements.[1] Nor must it be forgotten th 'voluntary' barter arrangements, in so far as monopoly and monopson powers are brought to bear in arranging them, can be exploitativ In fact, as the exchange of definite commodities will have to arranged, which is a clumsy method and restricts the choice of th weaker partner, both in the range of commodities and in time purchase, it is liable to more abuse than arrangements by which th proceeds of exports are earmarked for purchases in the same countr but without such restriction of choice.

(b) *Monetary Reciprocity*. Monetary reciprocity takes the form eith of payment or of clearing agreements. Under payment agreements country undertakes to use a certain proportion of the proceeds of h exports for certain predetermined purposes. Under clearing agre ments all payments are credited or debited to her on a central accoun payments from that account can only be made with the permission the authority controlling the account. Both can be voluntary character. Forced blocking presupposes that the country undertakir it is a debtor country, otherwise no country need to continue deliverie No one needs to sell to the country which earmarks (blocks) the pr needs of the sale and permits their use only for internal payments. Su reciprocal payment or clearing agreements should be rather *less* e ploitative than direct reciprocal bulk purchases, as they interfere l

[1] This will be the case especially with respect to manufacturing countries trading with prim producing countries. Bulk purchases of raw materials and food stuffs are easily arranged, but it v be much more difficult to force importers in a primary producing country to buy from the co try to which the primary country exported, an equivalent amount of manufactures, if purchasing country is not as cheap a market as a third country to which sales are practicable. Yet, without forcing them to do so the primary producers may not be able export at all, and both that country and the manufacturing country would be forced into necessary autarky. Given the restricted initiative on the part of most government departme at any rate in Britain, it is almost impossible to visualize that extended use will be made of di 'voluntary' bulk barter. Lord Keynes' interpretation (Hansard, May 23, col. 870) that the p hibition of discriminating monetary arrangements exempted 'voluntary' barter agreeme from its operation, while in severe conflict with the official American thesis, as expounded Professor Viner (op. cit.), does not in fact offer any scope for maintaining international change of commodities between full employment areas irrespective of the state of trade where.

with the choice of the trading partner. Provided only that one of the partners maintains full employment (and therefore imports) such agreements automatically provide, or rather create, international liquidity to finance imports and thereby impart an expansionist bias to the economy of the selling country. It is true that by restricting the choice of the selling country they also create market imperfections in favour of the industries of the purchasing country. Without the purchases of that country, however, the seller would not be able to buy at all. To talk of exploitation in *every* case is therefore unjustified. Whether exploitation takes place depends not only on the *prices* ruling in the purchasing and selling country and elsewhere and the rates of exchange, but also on the ratio of the *volume* of the transactions passing as compared with the volume which would be possible if the agreement had not been concluded.

The main purpose of these agreements is to prevent the leakage of liquidity reserves into depressed areas, i.e. to maintain the liquidity of the full employment areas. The alternative to such agreements, if unemployment prevails in important countries, may well be national autarky. Full employment countries would then lose liquidity to under-employed countries because their full employment policy makes them good countries to sell to, but unfavourable markets to buy in. This process could obviously not continue indefinitely.

It is often suggested that the exploitative character of *clearing* agreements is due to the fact that the 'clearing' countries 'over-value' their currencies in terms of the currencies of 'free' countries. If only they devalued, it is said, their problem would be solved. But by their policy of 'over-valuation' they 'exploit' their partners as they turn the terms of trade in their favour. As we have seen, the actual elasticities of demand and supply and thus the balance of payments as well as the rate of exchange are a function of the degree of employment. There is no *a priori* reason to suppose that an equilibrium rate of exchange need exist without direct controls (including tariffs) between a full employment country and areas which suffer from under-employment and where effective demand is still falling. We understand under equilibrium rate of exchange in this sense a level which would balance international payments without a change in the short-term (liquid) capital account. This merely means that if a country wishes to retain its international equilibrium in an under-employed world it might, in the absence of direct controls or increasing autarky, have to give up full employment policies.

Thus, if a country refused to follow the rest of the world into depression and maintained effective demand unchanged (i.e. increased home demand to offset the fall in international demand) this would *ipso facto* 'over-value' the currency. The discriminating subsidies and tariffs which in this case would enable the stabilization of the trade balance towards the outside area would indeed lessen the relative worsening of the terms of trade in comparison with devaluation of an identical effectiveness (if such a rate of devaluation existed). But it would be rather fanciful to speak of exploitation in this case as it was the loss of the internal equilibrium in the outside world which caused the initial change in the terms of trade and the discriminating policy is necessary merely to safeguard full employment and minimize the unavoidable losses which this entails.

If, then, the country concludes clearing agreements and continues its full employment policy, the very reflation will now render all clearing countries 'over-valued' with respect to depressed 'free exchange' countries. Thus relations between the countries are likely to become *ceteris paribus* more intimate than before the slump as they will constitute an oasis of full employment in a desert of under-employment and thus their currencies will be 'over-valued.' To charge the full employment country that it has exploited its clearing partner would surely be a complete *non-sequitur*. The depression abroad is the *fons et origo* of the whole process. If the depression lifted quickly, no 'block' would be formed. Multiple exchange rates need not be employed.

What might constitute an objectionable discrimination are not such agreements but the exclusion, for political reasons, of countries willing to enter into *similar* agreements *on the same terms*.

Thus reciprocal arrangements, if properly managed, represent nothing less than an exchange of products of countries which could not otherwise be sold and probably would never have been produced at all in the absence of such agreements. They can be utilized not merely to secure an approximation to a state of affairs which would rule if 'free' trade is obtained. They can be a basis for the development of the production and exchange of goods which could not have been produced and exchanged even under conditions of free trade because the existence of risk would have narrowed the scope of profitable trade and neither the knowledge nor the capital for the purpose would have been available, though *ex post* the production and exchange is perfectly justifiable and profitable according to all canons of classical theory. There is no reason why both partners should not share the benefits of such agreements. The producing country by being able to sell more, and the purchasing country to buy more (by obtaining supplies at cheaper prices) than she would otherwise have been able to do.

Clearing arrangements thus permit the planning of full employment at home, which offers stable and expanding markets at favourable prices to countries having complementary economic systems. They provide in an unstable world the assurance that exports will be practicable to pay for imports without deflationary adjustment. In such a world imports might otherwise not be permitted and the exchange of goods would be further restricted.[1]

III. MULTILATERALISM AND FULL EMPLOYMENT

A full solution of the problem of re-establishing a full international division of labour and an international monetary system, without perpetuating business cycles spread over the whole world economy, is conditional upon full agreement between the autonomous units of the system on domestic economic policy. If each of the countries would pledge itself to maintain not only full employment but an agreed policy with respect to their current balances of payments—in conjunction with an international investment policy—there would be no reasons for any single country to pursue autonomous policies and institute for its protection specific measures of a uni- or bi-lateral character. The possible gains which even in these circumstances could be derived from turning the terms of trade in its favour by tariffs, etc., or exploitative bulk purchases would be small. Retaliatory action would have to be expected. Moreover, as full employment would in any case be maintained, it could not count on that extra—though temporary—gain which in a world beset by business cycles accrues to the protectionist power through a (relative) increase in its degree of employment. Indeed, so long as employment is maintained all round, real wages would automatically be adversely affected by any diminution of the scope of the international division of labour, apart from planned development. Hence to the resistance against international trading—which now represents a source of disequilibrium —a resistance in which both labour and entrepreneurs combine,

[1] If the primary producing countries give protection to their secondary industries, the maintenance of an optimum distribution of productive resources between various industries could only be achieved if subsidies were given by the same country to export industries. This could be achieved by a clearing arrangement which under-values the currency, i.e. values it below the full-employment equilibrium level. It may be asked why this complicated solution should be adopted, as it is immaterial to the purchasing country whether the exporters get high prices in their currency so long as the import is arranged at favourable prices to the purchaser. This objection overlooks the fact that it is in the interest of the importers that the products of the commodities should receive high prices in their own currency. Cf. my article, 'The drift towards a rational foreign exchange policy,' *Economica*, August 1940, pp. 254-5.

would be much weakened. But if such full agreement were possible, far greater attention than in past periods must be paid to the potentialities of industrialization in backward areas and the acquisition of new skill by the population and increase in investment capacity by planned investment financed by the State out of taxes or loans. It must not prevent the common long-term planning of the production and exchange of commodities between countries which, because of regional connections, desire to evolve such planning. It should not trespass on the terrain of internal economic organization and by the implications of its terms prevent reform or reorganization. Specifically it must not rule out the evolution of a compromise between complete collectivism and full foreign trade monopoly on the one hand and complete *laisser-faire* and full license for individuals to choose where to spend or invest their purchasing power which they have acquired in a country, irrespective of the consequences of their action to that country. This condition is important because moderate control—falling short of full foreign trade monopoly—is more difficult to institute and work successfully than an extreme solution, and can more easily be thwarted by arbitrary rules and limitations.

However natural it may seem for every country to elaborate a full employment policy and come to such international agreement which which would make it work multilaterally, we must envisage the possibility that full agreement cannot be obtained on these lines. The question arises, whether a more limited method could not be elaborated, which would at least secure that all those countries which adopt full employment policies, should be able to continue their policy, irrespective of any depression abroad, thus irrespective of the consequent worsening of their balances of trade. This means that in all cases in which a deficiency in the balance of payments of a country arises solely on account of a depression abroad, that country must be enabled to maintain its total effective demand, and deal with the resultant deficit in its balance of payments without having to reverse its internal employment policy.

Theoretically the problem of maintaining full employment in any single country, or a group of countries, can be solved in two ways by international agreement:

(*a*) Schemes can be elaborated which enable single countries to maintain full employment irrespective of the consequences of this policy on their balance of payments, by creating internationally acceptable means of payment, and restoring the liquidity of member countries. We might call this the liquidity approach.

(*b*) Alternatively schemes could be elaborated which maintain the external balance of full employment countries by offsetting the induced surplus of under-employed countries, either by creating additional demand and diverting it away from the surplus countries, or by imposing obligations on the depressed surplus countries to eliminate the induced surplus.

As all these schemes regulate international liquidity and/or effective demand in such a way as to permit the maintenance of full employment conditions in any single participating country they render unnecessary the adoption of bilateral or partially multilateral monetary schemes, such as payments or clearing agreements, aiming at the same end. They will not render the quantitative regulation of imports undertaken for the purpose of social, rather than employment, policy unnecessary. Such controls, bulk purchase and long-term development planning will, however, be possible by commercial policy rather than monetary manipulation. A satisfactory multilateral scheme has obvious advantages over less comprehensive agreements as it does not limit the freedom of choice. Once the restrictive consequences of this freedom on employment are overcome, all rational considerations favour a broader solution.

The Liquidity Approach

Schemes of this type—i.e. which permit single countries to maintain full employment irrespective of the consequences of this policy on the balance of their international payments by creating and placing at their disposal internationally acceptable means of payment—represent the introduction into the international plane of modern Central Banking. They do not create or direct *demand* so as to maintain or help to maintain full employment where it is threatened by shortsighted policy. They enable a country which wishes to maintain its international demand (i.e. deficit) to do so by putting at its disposal the necessary means.[1]

If a country suffers from the consequences of a depression abroad

[1] Lord Keynes' high hopes for his multilateral clearing scheme (cf. House of Lords, May 12, 1943, column 531) seem to be based on a similar misapprehension for which he took Professor Cassel severely to task (*Treatise on Money*, Vol. 1, pp. 188-9). This misapprehension amounts to equating the volume of money with demand. Lord Keynes in the relevant passage of his speech explains that the principle of multilateral clearing means a generalization of domestic banking to the international field, *thus converting hoarding into lending and preventing deflation.* But the failure of the clients of the banking system to use their deposits, i.e. the fall in their effective demand, does not increase the cash reserves of the banking system; hoarding of bank deposits can only be 'offset' if there exists an outside body, i.e. the central bank, which creates new cash and either induces entrepreneurs (in some of the ways mentioned in earlier contributions) to increase their outlay, or if the Government increases its outlay. Correspondingly on the international plane there must exist an 'outside' (supernational) body which creates new international cash whenever international effective demand flags, and this body must induce a country or a group of countries to use this newly created cash and thus convert it into effective demand. The automatism pos-

such schemes enable it to offset the decline in total (home and foreign) demand for its output by increasing home demand. Such offsetting internal measures, if not accompanied by increased protection, must, as we have seen, lead to a continued accumulation of adverse balances. If, however, sufficient liquid reserves acceptable to all countries in discharge of international debts can be created for and drawn upon by member countries in need of them, these countries would be able to maintain their total effective demand (by increasing home demand) until the emergence of a sufficiently large surplus in the balance of payments of, or internal cyclical factors in, the originally depressed country would restart expansion.

If this type of scheme is adopted it can be successful only if the amount of reserves available to member countries in case of need is in all circumstances large enough to permit the continuation of the full employment policy by all countries who so desire, during any depression that is likely to develop in the countries not adhering to a full employment policy.[1] The size of the reserve is the determining factor, as such schemes do not provide a mechanism for the continuous redistribution of the reserves, if disequilibria sterilize them in any one country. They are not 'public works' schemes but 'central banking' schemes. The required volume of liquid reserves will depend:

(*a*) on the importance of the potential areas of depression in the world economic system;

(*b*) on the possible maximum severity of their depression;

(*c*) on the effects of the depression (and their economic policies followed in a depression) on their balance of payments.

The larger the share of the area of potential depression in the money income of the world at current prices and exchange rates, the greater their potential instability, and the stronger their bias to develop export surpluses the wider must be the limits for the creation of additional reserves.[2] The size of the total means required for the successful working

tulated by Lord Keynes is non-existent. It could be created only by a scheme similar to that outlined by Messrs. Schumacher and Kalecki in the Supplement to the Bulletin of the Institute of Statistics, *New Plans for International Trade*, 1943. Cf. below.

[1] The internal stability of the system (e.g. the flexibility of wage rates, political conditions, etc.) will be the decisive factor in this respect.

[2] This condemns the successive plans elaborated by British and American experts first independently and jointly on post-war monetary reconstruction. The text of these plans has been published under the title, *Proposals for International Clearing Union* (Cmd. 6437, April 1943), *U.S. Proposal for the United and Associated Nations' Stabilization Fund* (reprinted by H. M. Stationery Office, 1943, and the Joint Statement of Experts already quoted). For a closer analysis see *New Plans for International Trade* (op. cit.) and an article by the present writer in the *Political Quarterly* (1943). The joint plan has been discussed by Mr. E. F. Schumacher and the present author (Bulletin of the Institute of Statistics, Oxford, Vol. 6, p. 8). All these plans fix a maximum limit for the fund without a close analysis of the likely size of balances which would arise if member countries continued their full employment policy while others were depressed.

of a scheme of this type is therefore a function of the future home employment, of the commercial and of the international lending policy of the countries which are parties of the agreement. A currency agreement of this character cannot safely be negotiated in isolation, irrespective of agreement or otherwise on policies which affect the size of the possible balances with which the scheme is to be called upon to deal.

The working of the scheme will, it must be remembered, mitigate the depression in the unstable area as the export surpluses, which it permits, have the same effect as home investment. It will, therefore, depend on the quantitative relationship between foreign trade[1] and that level of home investment which is necessary to obtain full employment in the potentially depressed area, whether an export surplus due to depression is likely to reverse or merely to mitigate the fall in effective demand in the unstable area. But even if export surpluses are insufficient to restart expansion, they will speed recovery.

To allow depressed countries to run up export surpluses which would permit the maintenance of full employment policies everywhere, has the drawback that the cumulative debt balances would be distributed haphazardly. Unless they are periodically forgiven they would tend to force mature deficit countries to adopt deflationary policies, as such countries will not in the long run tolerate a growing indebtedness, however vague the obligation to 'repay' these 'cyclical liquidity' debts.

Steps against deliberate attempts by single countries to indulge in inflating effective demand beyond their productive power, without voluntary agreement to obtain foreign loans, must be taken as soon as the whole system is in itself fully employed, for the continuation of true inflation in any one country then would tend to result in inflation of the whole system. As long as a large number of member countries are unemployed, however, the expansionist policy of a member country will merely help to re-employ idle capacity in the depressed countries. It would, therefore, not force them to forego any productive opportunity.[2] In the absence of full employment and in the absence of full employment policies, the countries with excess capacity have little reason to complain of an expansionist, or even 'inflationary,' policy in other countries.

---

[1] This, again, will depend on the relevant income and price elasticities of demand and supply in the depressed area and the full employment countries, respectively, and the initial position of the balance. Cf. Mrs. Robinson, *Essays*, pp. 193-5, and above p. 142 *et seq.*

[2] Foreign investment leads to 'inflation' in the borrowing country but this 'inflation,' if the foreign loan was well conceived, is matched by an increased productive capacity.

The Equilibrium Approach

The drawbacks of the 'liquidity' schemes which leave balances to accumulate, have led to the elaboration of schemes which consciously try to deal with these balances without forcing any of the member countries to discontinue its full employment policy. They attempt to achieve consciously what the 'classical' gold standard theoretically was supposed to—but never did in fact—achieve.

(i) The most logical and effective of such possible schemes—elaborated by Messrs. Schumacher and Kalecki[1]—creates not only *liquidity* but *demand*. It creates it in that area of the world where it is most needed—in the immature countries—by granting them loans and placing at their disposal liquid funds created for the purpose by an International Investment Board. This demand is canalized towards those countries which have a deficiency in their balance of payments which they wish to readjust because, being 'mature' countries, they must not rely on foreign loans for capital development.

In this way, additional world demand is created which permits the restoration of the equilibrium in the balance of payments of fully employed mature deficit countries. Without this help these countries would have to cut their purchases abroad, thus causing a depression elsewhere. This solution is far more complete than the 'liquidity' approach in so far as the cumulative 'induced' deficits due to the depression of a large 'mature' country would be canalized to under-developed countries. These countries would use the supplies so obtained to increase their productive capacity. The mechanism of long-term lending would be restored in an improved form. Deficits in the balance of payments of fully employed countries induced by the 'depression' in other countries not maintaining full employment, would be wiped out if they were not needed for accelerating capital equipment. Full employment would be maintained by diverting products towards those countries most needing them: products which, without this intervention, would not have been produced.[2]

[1] *New Plans for International Trade*, op. cit.
[2] The International Board will therefore only utilize or develop resources which would otherwise not be utilized. It should be noted that, in view of the vast discrepancy in the standard of life between different countries, especially after the war, this method is not a sufficient answer to the problem of international investment. International lending beyond these limits, however, would necessitate restriction in the immediate consumption of the rich countries and must therefore be undertaken (with or without the intermediary of an International Investment Board) by a conscious policy of collaboration of the rich and poor countries.

Cf., however, above on the treatment of 'autonomous' disequilibria. The existence of an International Investment Board would even in this case prevent the partial readjustment from deteriorating into a general deflation. The 'mature' deficit countries must co-operate in providing exports at competitive prices. (Cf. *New Plans*, op. cit., pp. 35-6.)

(ii) An alternative approach—which seems to have been envisaged by Lord Keynes in the original form of his scheme—would be to insulate the world economic system compulsorily from the consequences of a slump in any one country by forcing that country to undertake readjustments. This approach would demand that the surplus country should automatically appreciate its currency, and/or that it should increase the foreign import multiplier either by way of reducing tariffs and other impediments against imports, or by increasing the level of its money wages.[1] Alternatively, it might be suggested that foreign claims, if these have come about as a result of the internal deflation in the creditor country and not the conscious granting of long-term loans, should be periodically wiped out.[2]

Either scheme could, in fact, work. They could largely neutralize the effects of a slump in one country on the world, or would at least reduce or wipe out the surplus resulting from the reduction of effective home demand on the balance of payments.[3] But the first alternative would automatically aggravate the depression in the surplus countries, as it would eliminate the improvement in the balance of payments, which had arisen as a result of the slump and which tended to offset the fall in the effective demand in that country. If the depressed country does not increase home demand, by deficit spending or otherwise, the vicious deflationary spiral might continue and thus necessitate further doses of the same external readjustment, each of which would give further impetus to internal deflation. The second method of forgiving surpluses would be opposed not merely because it could be claimed— unjustifiably[4]—that goods would be 'given away' but also because it increases the internal national debt of the surplus country.[5]

(iii) The international problem of full employment could conceivably be solved on the basis of the gold standard. A favourable balance of trade represents, from the point of view of the surplus

---

[1] Cmd. 6437, pp. 8-9, Sec. 11/9, and pp. 10-11, Sec. III/7-9. These suggestions were dropped in the Joint Proposals.

[2] Cf. H. Feis, *Foreign Affairs*, 1942.

[3] If fixed foreign claims on other countries in terms of its own currency—e.g. interest— represent a large fraction of the total balance of payments, then an appreciation of the currency may aggravate the problem rather than help it, if the countervailing measures increasing the foreign trade multiplier do not more than offset this effect.

[4] Unjustifiably if the alternative to the export surplus is unemployment. Indeed, in so far as the export-surplus will, because of its multiplier effect, increase home demand its social cost would be negative.

[5] The British Scheme tried to meet this last objection by limiting the size of additional liquidity quotas to be granted to would-be debtors. If quotas are limited to such an extent as to appease the would-be surplus countries, the danger arises that their volume will be fixed so low as to lead to their exhaustion at the first severe depression. The scheme would fail in the sense that it will no longer enable the maintenance of full employment. For a discussion of the actual scheme, cf. my article and Supplement No. 5, op. cit.

country, investment. Equilibrium could still be maintained if the value of newly produced gold in deficit countries were exactly equal to the favourable trade balance which the surplus countries wish to maintain for internal reasons (i.e. because they wish to maintain employment by an excess of exports over imports). Gold production and export by the rest of the world would represent an export of a commodity the elasticity of demand for which is infinite in the surplus countries. Theoretically, therefore, a general revaluation of gold might provide the United States or other export surplus countries with the necessary quantum of liquid assets they wish to obtain against exports. There will always be a price of gold at which equilibrium must be reached. Such an increase in the price of gold might represent a mal-direction of the productive effort of the world, but it would obviously be preferable to misdirect marginal effort than to have a general unemployment problem which would represent a far greater loss. In practice the difficulties in the way of this, what one may call truly *laisser-faire* solution, are at least as great than in the way of a planned equilibrium solution. The banking structure of the would-be creditor countries is based on gold, hence the influx of gold would result in a multiple increase in the potential liquid funds. It is probable that the government of the surplus country would try to sterilize the gold influx. This would necessitate an increase in the internal debt of the surplus country which might be felt to be intolerable in the longer run. An attempt to appreciate gold and enforce equilibrium on the would-be creditor countries by way of an appreciation of their currencies and an increase in the value of gold production would hardly be acceptable. An attempt to do so would probably lead to a demonetization of gold and consequently to a break-up of the international currency system and the establishment of complete bilateralism.

This brief review of the possible methods of solving the problem of maintaining full employment in the framework of multilateral and nondiscriminating foreign trade without full agreement on the part of all countries to maintain full employment and to tackle the problems of international economic relations in a spirit of continuous collaboration shows that these various economic methods will allow countries to pursue a full employment policy while at the same time maintaining multilateral trade. The plan proposed by Messrs. Schumacher and Kalecki would also ensure the maximum economic progress, within the limits set by the fact that full agreement on internal policies is not practicable, and that therefore cyclical fluctuations must be expected to continue in some countries. That scheme would canalize supplies

where they are most needed and for the purpose they are most needed.
It would at the same time maintain international liquidity and thus
enable all participating countries to pursue a full employment policy.

IV. FULL EMPLOYMENT WITHIN A REGION

It is possible that in spite of its patent advantages, no agreement safeguarding full employment policy in the world economic system as a
whole or in single countries, can be concluded. Single countries, it is said,
will then be faced with a clear alternative of either taking by themselves protective measures lest the worsening of their foreign balance
should prevent the continuance of their full employment policy, or
resigning themselves to the repercussions of business cycles originating
in the most unstable parts of the world economic system. It is often
argued that the losses imposed upon a country by autarky would be
far more severe than the gains which could be derived from following
a unilateral full employment policy which would necessarily interfere
with the free exchange of goods. This contrast between freedom of
trade with high international productivity and *full division of labour*
and complete national exclusiveness, if countries refuse to accept an
international scheme, however incomplete, is far too crude to be convincing. Moreover, it begs the question in some important respects.
Firstly, it is likely that the same influences which drove the world
towards economic self-sufficiency will inevitably reassert themselves
in a free multilateral system as soon as any one major country experiences an internal depression, and thus endangers the full employment
policy in other countries. Each new dose of protectionism, as such,
will be justified at the moment when it is introduced, on the grounds
that it wards off otherwise threatening unemployment. As part of the
increase in effective demand would come about as a result of the
establishment of industries which could not survive without protection,
the protective measures will never be fully dropped in the subsequent
recovery. Protectionism will be extended further and further as each
depression forces new defensive measures on all countries. It will
therefore be increasingly difficult to evolve a new international system
which might combine the international division of labour with stability.
Thus the fruits of a general programme of multilateralism entered upon
without safeguards for countries aiming at stable full employment are
not likely to be considerable; the disadvantages might be serious.

Secondly, the argument implicitly assumes that a country unwilling
to enter into a world-wide multilateral system would necessarily have

to fall back upon itself and follow a completely autarkic policy. In fact, as we argued above, this may happen if a multilateral scheme breaks down, and under the stress of the crisis, short period measures are taken preventing the evolution of stable regional systems. All like-minded countries who believe that it is within their powers to maintain full employment and steady progress by appropriate policies—or at least are willing to enter into other arrangements which safeguard the stability and internal freedom of action of other members of a non-world-wide multilateral system—have much to gain, and little to lose, if they promote intensive international exchange of products and services between each other. So long as each member country does not foster exports as a means of its employment policy, or at least does so under safeguards (i.e. planned foreign lending) which prevent it from absorbing a quantitatively limited supply of international liquid reserves, there is no rational reason for national exclusiveness and for limited bilateral agreements between member countries. Moreover, the political situation within each country changes in favour of international exchange. At full employment, the deleterious effects of a protection become clear; in an unstable system they are veiled by the fact that the only possible alternative to efficient production may be unemployment.

If, then, a country capable of providing large markets offered to enter a multilateral agreement on the basis of agreed full employment policies or of an equilibrium scheme of the type discussed above, it might find willing partners. The same aim could be achieved by a regional grouping of smaller and less naturally self-sufficient national economies. The dialectical device of contrasting extreme alternatives is, therefore, misleading.

We shall in the following discuss (*a*) the policy to be followed by such regional full employment blocks and its internal and international implications, especially the advantages to be derived from adhering to such blocks as contrasted with an imperfect multilateral agreement unable to eliminate business cycles, (*b*) the question of their relations to unstable areas.

(a) *The policy of discriminating multilateralism*

A regional block devoted to the maintenance of full employment could be organized in two ways which (in analogy to political terminology) could be called the federal and confederative solution.

A federal scheme would presuppose a far-reaching agreement between its constituent units, not merely on maintaining full employment in the sense of avoiding the social evil of mass unemployment, but also on the purpose to which the full productive effort of the population is to be devoted and the means which would have to be employed. Accordingly, supernational executive organs and representative—parliamentary—organs, controlling and supervising the executive, would have to be evolved to decide on the internal policy of the federal block. Agreement would have to be reached in particular about the principles according to which intra-federal consumption and investment is to be managed with respect to the constituent units of the block. Such intimate collaboration may be successful between countries which are on the whole complementary rather than competitive and which have similar political and social backgrounds. If such a federal solution is arrived at, the regional block can be regarded as a single country.

The confederative solution entails less intimate collaboration. It restricts supernational regulation to the minimum. So long as constituent units are willing to subscribe to a full employment policy, or alternatively to participation in a substitute scheme discussed above, maintaining intra-confederate economic equilibrium, they can retain full liberty in deciding internal economic and social policy. Its members could, if they so desired, evolve over limited fields common planning of the production and reciprocal exchange of goods and services. But they would not even be forced to do that.

In both cases, however, their economic relations with an unstable outside world, unwilling to enter into satisfactory multilateral agreements, would have to come under direct control, if the immunity of the area from sudden slumps is to be safeguarded. It would have to negotiate with outside countries as a unit. The proceeds of agreed imports into the area from the world outside could be spent anywhere *within* the area. The proceeds of agreed exports by any member of the block could be sold to any other member of the block for its use. A principle of controlled multilateralism would thus be introduced which would reduce restrictions on the use of the proceeds of foreign trade to the minimum while safeguarding the liquidity and thus the full employment policy of the area as a whole.

The relative scarcity of foreign commodities within the block will depend on the ease with which they can be procured. If the 'full employment' area is large and consists of territories with varied natural resources the dependence on products outside this area may be small, the cost of replacement of such commodities by substitutes available or potentially available within the territory may in many cases not be great. The relative independence will, in this case, put the full employment area in a strong position in obtaining supplies from countries outside the area. If, within the area, considerations of stability have induced the authorities concerned to retain some of the war-time controls over the production and distribution of primary products (whose prices are subject to violent fluctuations because of the relative price inelasticity, both of their supply and of the demand for them) or replaced these controls by the establishment of buffer stocks, these control organs will have to be charged with the control of the imports of these commodities and their substitutes. These controls or pools can be charged with more positive tasks not merely in promoting the balancing of international accounts but also in securing supplies at favourable terms for both producers and consumers by bulk production schemes within the block.[1]

We must, however, especially in the shorter run, envisage a more unfavourable possibility. If the area of full employment is less naturally self-sufficient than that of a wide union, its Government or Governments will find themselves confronted with a more serious bottleneck of imports. This bottleneck will be tighter in slumps abroad than in booms. Unless there is direct control over not merely the import but also over the distribution of foreign (primary) products, the relative shortage of material might, and probably would, lead to speculative withholding and with it to cumulative price-movements. It will depend on historical, quantitative, conditions whether mere internal quota regulations of supplies, together with appropriate price-policies, will suffice to avoid speculation, or whether further measures such as rationing of the ultimate consumer will become necessary. If the scarcity of foreign supplies makes itself abruptly felt (e.g. because of the boom outside the area) and if it was an important raw material it may be necessary to control not merely the foreign supplies but also the home substitutes. A sharp depression in an extended area with which the full employment area is in intensive exchange relations may well, in the short run, before readjustments have been made, demand far-reaching controls if employment is to be maintained and the terms of trade are not to deteriorate.

In the longer run, the full employment area will be able to take steps which render irksomely strict controls unnecessary. Two escape routes are feasible, which can be used in suitable proportions according to the special circumstances of the case. The first is the accumulation of stocks by the Government, or under Government control, in times

---

[1] Cf. above, pp. 148 and 150-7.

when the balance of payments permits it without strain.' The second is to replace foreign products by home produced substitutes. The investment necessary for this purpose can be provided by using the unemployed thrown out of work by the slumps in the outside world. If this is an alternative to unemployment or to a serious worsening of the terms of trade it will represent a relative gain. These considerations also show that the membership of a regional full employment block presupposes specific obligation on the part of its members not to change abruptly their economic relations with each other. Whether these are controlled directly or indirectly does not make any difference. Abrupt changes would force other countries to further sudden alterations and the disturbance so created might cumulatively destroy stability. The fact that the members of the block will be able to maintain full employment eliminates the need for such 'beggar-my-neighbour policies.'

The degree of instability abroad and its consequences on the terms of trade and employment in the block on the one hand, the difference in comparative cost in the block and abroad, which determines the gain from international exchange, will indicate whether the second, and more drastic, and permanent method is to be utilized and to what extent. General statements about the advantage derived from foreign trade usually do not specify the assumptions which are implicitly made when it is claimed that the optimum employment of factors can always be achieved by 'free' trade.

Even more important are the differences between the direct and indirect methods of influencing foreign trade in relation to the possibility of controlling the distribution and use of imported supplies. Tariff protection does not permit an alteration of the price mechanism as the basis of production or distribution. Direct regulation of imports can, if necessary, be used for the direct regulation of prices and consumption. The potential control over a strategic point of the economic system might be essential if imports constitute the ultimate bottleneck in the expansion of production.

A word of caution, however, is necessary at this point. The direct control of imports and a conscious stimulus to exports involves not merely legislative regulation but administrative discretion in matters which affect the economic position of the citizens of the State. It was the disbelief in the competence and honesty of the Executive and its capacity to withstand the selfish designs of pressure groups which led the more sophisticated of the older generation of economists to declare themselves for Free Trade for an advanced country like Great Britain, though they saw the possible advantages of protection. The subtler, more flexible, and hence the less bound by internal legislation or international treaty, protectionist measures are, the graver the possibilities for frank abuse. Apart from political pressure to obtain unnecessary subsidies or protection (in the sense that production could continue at the existing level of prices if the industry were reorganized) and so sustain inefficiency, there is an acute danger that the suggested mechanism will be used not so much to smooth transition as to resist change, however advantageous it would be for the community as a whole. It is also probable that, unless monopolistic practices are curbed by an effective direct control, protection will result in an increase in the degree of monopoly and the stimulus to employment will amount to no more than the creation or increase of excess capacity.

If monopolistic interests dominate the State, both tariff-protected multilateralism and controlled foreign trade will lead to undesirable ends. But while 'free' trade in its novel sense, i.e. tariff-restricted trade, does not permit effective action to prevent abuse, controlled trade might provide the weapons—if there is the will to use them.

We have seen that the dilemma between full multilateralism subject to economic fluctuations and extreme national autarky is misleading. In the absence of a satisfactory world-wide multilateral scheme, the full division of labour (which is always implicitly assumed in the argumentation of the protagonists of *laisser faire*) will not be restored. Indeed, a greater exclusiveness might be enforced. The case for 'discriminatory multilateralism' is strengthened if we consider that it is by no means true that a world-wide 'non-discriminatory' multilateralism would be equivalent to a full international division of labour with an adequate international scheme to maintain or at least permit full employment. There is, for example, no question of abolishing existing tariffs. And without a home full employment policy the same reasons, for which additional protection in times of crisis is justifiable economically, will prevent a relaxation of these protective measures. *Regional* agreements will prevent the recurrence of competitive *national* isolationism, i.e. autarky in areas far more restricted geographically and economically than regions. The 'extra' loss between regionalism and 'world-wide' multilateralism, is therefore further diminished. Indeed *if* tariffs are high, *if* the newly created regions are wide, and *if* intra-regional restrictions are relaxed, as can happen if full employment is maintained, the loss will certainly turn into a net gain. A system of 'indiscriminately restricted' trade will render impossible any conscious and continuous planning of economic development by any country or a group of countries, and will prevent them from maintaining anything approaching full employment in the face of fluctuations abroad. It is nevertheless obvious that a less than full world-wide division of labour does infringe the principles of comparative costs. It is also true that the establishment of small exclusive areas of planning, especially if planning means protection for existing vested interests to establish monopolies, might certainly result in a fall or the prevention of a rise in the standard of life which cannot be offset by however full employment. We shall therefore have to consider how the policy advocated in this paper is affected by these arguments.

The problem of the probable gains derived by the world economic system as a whole and each of its constituent units from international trade has not received adequate attention since the application of the general theory of effective demand and the theory of imperfect competition rendered earlier contributions to the question obsolete. Intensity of international as contrasted to national exchange of goods cannot be regarded as a desirable end in itself by a country which pursues full employment policy. Contemporary references to the desirability of maximizing international trade are, at least sub-consciously, too often based not on the wish to achieve a balanced exchange of goods but creating employment through export surpluses. A balanced exchange of goods and service, as such, does not create employment. It increases productivity. 'The case for a large volume of international trade rests on the different endowment of nations in respect of national resource, human skill and equipment.'[1] It enables a country to obtain goods by offering for them other products and services which cost in terms of effort less to produce than commodities which are obtained in exchange. The greater the area of internal trade, the more varied its resources, the less can be gained from such 'indirect' acquisition of supplies.

Preferential or total customs unions or blocks, therefore, must be studied from the point of view of how far they increase efficiency within the block and in the world as a whole. Nor must it be forgotten that what might be desirable from the point of view of the world as a whole is not necessarily desirable from the point of view of any one of its constituent units. The original theory of foreign trade was an application of the conditions of pure competition to the relations between countries, i.e. it was assumed that a country could not affect the international terms of exchange by its policy. This *a priori* excludes the problem. If, however, tariffs are enforced or other protective

[1] 'The Future of International Trade,' Professor D. H. Robertson, *Economic Journal*, 1938, p. 1.

measures taken, the exchange of goods between countries can obviously
no longer be assumed to yield results which would originate from
perfect competition between countries, even if perfect competition continued within each of the separate units. The demand and supply of a
sizeable number, if not most, individuals within these countries is then
affected, thus the demand and supply of the country as a whole changes.
It can no longer be assumed that those countries are in the same
relationship in respect of all commodities which they export or import
as individuals in a state of perfect competition, i.e. that they cannot
affect relative price levels of the world system outside. They will be
in a position of a monopolist, and will be confronted with falling
demand curves. The exchange ratios at which it can obtain foreign
products for its own goods and services are no longer independent of
its own trade policy. The simple formulation of the principle of
comparative costs will accordingly have to be modified. Any attempt
to exploit this position, however, will result *ceteris paribus* in an increase
in its real costs, the gains are subject to retaliatory action.

Apart, however, from the possible gains of a transient nature
resulting from exploitation, there are other more fundamental factors
which suggest that the probable gains from a 'free' international
exchange of good are likely to decrease while its disadvantages (unless
international agreements of the far-reaching character discussed above
are arrived at) are likely to increase.

It is not possible in this context to analyse those structural and
dynamic changes and trends. They can be classified under several
heads: (*a*) the trends narrowing the differences in comparative cost due
primarily to technical progress and the increasing importance of the
secondary and tertiary industries; (*b*) the growing discrepancy between
optimum output and the structure of production resulting from the
'interplay of market forces,' (i) due to unemployment, (ii) due to the
increase of risk associated with foreign trade, (iii) due to potentialities
of planned development of poorer areas stifled by 'free' trade (imperfections due to size), (iv) due to monopolistic competition and its
consequences on location and methods of production, (v) due to the
quantitative aspects of post-war readjustment.

These reasons favour (in the absence of full international agreement
on a satisfactory basis) the formation of regional blocks adhering to
full employment and planned development policy.

A special problem is posed by *international capital* movements. In
this respect the character of the organization of the area will be of
considerable importance. If a federal type of organization is adopted

o intra-block problem of capital movement will arise. The whole investment programme of the area being controlled all intra-area transfers will be *eo ipso* controlled. If, however, a confederative organization is established, the problem of intra-block liquidity will have to be dealt with on the basis of an equilibrium scheme of the type discussed above.[1]

Capital movements within a confederative block, other than those agreed upon on the basis of planned inter-block liquidity, as well as all capital movements between a full employment block and the outside unstable areas, must come under direct control by licence.

The economic defence of the freedom of capital movement is based on the argument that capitalists will choose to invest in areas and outlets where returns are the highest. It is taken for granted that if this condition is fulfilled the real productivity of capital will also be at its maximum. Any interference with the free flow of capital, it is argued, would not only hinder economic progress in backward areas and thus constitute a discrimination against the poorer countries, but richer countries would also be acting against their own interests since they would receive a smaller return on their investment.

This argument completely neglects the existence of the business cycle and the causal connection between it and capital investment. The process of foreign investment was not, as the underlying assumptions of this theory would have it, a transfer between high and low return countries, but an almost simultaneous wave spreading over the world and resulting in cumulative movements everywhere, which having seemingly justified themselves, lead to a cumulative instability.[2]

The classical theory, furthermore, assumes that pure net returns are more or less equal or at least proportionate to gross overall returns irrespective of national areas, and that they depend entirely on the

[1] Cf. page 162. The intermediate international equilibrium would have to be safeguarded by enabling mature deficit countries to balance their current account. The development of the poorer areas within the block with the aid of long-term foreign loans from the richer areas at favourable rates would be in harmony with this concept. Further collaboration would, however, be needed, especially in periods when the unstable countries within the block experience booms, to ensure that the foreign capital supply should not be suddenly cut off. A steady basic flow of foreign investment must be assured. An alternative to such schemes would be a stricter co-operation between the members of the block in order to create over-full employment in potential surplus countries, i.e. to increase their effective demand beyond the level which can be fulfilled by the productive capacity of those countries. It is probable that a reform of the economic system will render poorer areas less dependent on foreign capital than in a system where industrialization is exclusively based on voluntary capital accumulation. Total capital autarky within the block or of the block itself is not necessary or desirable in a system where capital movements are regulated.

[2] A more comprehensive treatment is to be found in an article on 'Some Theoretical Problems of Foreign Investment,' *Oxford Economic Papers*, 1944.

relative capital intensity of production and tend to be equalized by competition. These assumptions, however, give an incorrect picture of the present position. The internal rigidity of the economic system has increased substantially; competition, moreover, is imperfect. In consequence, returns from investment can hardly be regarded as an index of the scarcity and productivity of capital. They are influenced much more by the degree of monopoly in industry. Economic and social policy which prevents monopoly exploitation and/or attempts to redistribute the national income consciously in order to stabilize effective demand, will reduce net private returns on capital. Progressive economic and taxation policy would therefore be defeated by creating an adverse yield difference (or anticipated difference) between the areas in which it will be pursued and the outside world.

If the Government then maintained both the rate of interest and the rate of exchange, the country would be denuded of its liquid reserves, while at the same time an easy and possibly profitable escape would be opened to the entrepreneur refusing to maintain real investment. Without strict control of capital exports supported by an effective control of all foreign payments, whatever their origin, a policy of full employment must fail in a world where all countries are not resolved to subscribe to similar internal programmes. The control of capital movements is not possible without control of all transactions with foreign countries. The aim of the control could easily be frustrated by manipulating import and export prices as well as conditions of credit at which sales and purchases take place. If devaluation is regarded (falsely) as a main weapon of currency management, even the timing of exports and imports will have to be controlled to prevent speculative attacks on the currency.

(b) Relations with the Outside Areas

It has been argued above that, in the absence of general monetary agreement, countries wishing to maintain unilateral full employment will find it necessary to apply direct control over their foreign trade in order to achieve a given readjustment of their balance of foreign payments. From the point of view of the competing foreign exporter the cause of any reduction of the price of the competing products by the deficit country is a matter of indifference. Given the extent of readjustment which is necessary, the method of readjustment differ merely in that the burden of the consequent losses fall on different shoulders, but it is by no means certain that if most of the burdens are thrust on the country which is under the necessity of effecting the readjustment—i.e. through unemployment or through the worsening of its terms of trade—the unfavourable repercussion of the other countries will be minimized. In fact, as long as there is monetary instability, it may be argued that the greater the extent of readjustment, the greater the fall in price, the greater is the likelihood of starting in the surplus countries a secondary deflationary spiral which eventually will have a more unfavourable effect on the real income of the surplus countries than the readjustment by the deficit countries.

The problem of discrimination and retaliation evoked by it becomes important if the increase of exports of one country tends to cause unemployment in another country. Thus the argument against export subsidies and even depreciation rests on the fact that they are far more potent weapons in this respect than the increased efficiency in the export industries or a decrease in wages which is necessarily piecemeal.[1] Depreciation and export subsidies differ from increased efficiency only from the point of view of the readjusting country in that they involve a loss of real income because the worsening of the terms of trade is not offset by higher output per head at home. If a readjustment of the balance of payments is inevitable, export subsidies financed by the Budget combined with some import duties or prohibitions, represent the fairest method of distributing over the whole community, whilst at the same time minimizing the extent of, the decline in real income originating from causes abroad.

In spite of this fact, a sharp differentiation has been made between 'legitimate' and 'illegitimate' methods of readjustment. On the demand side direct control of imports or payments agreements are outlawed as 'discriminatory,' whereas unemployment and wage and other income reductions enforced by a general deflationary policy are adjudged 'legitimate' (and if the tone of the comments is taken into account even laudable). On the supply side, sharp exchange depreciation and subsidy are outlawed partly as discrimination, partly as 'dumping,' while a cut of wages and the charging of less than full cost by exporters is accepted as a legitimate means. In our opinion this differentiation is fallacious. It tries to represent as a moral code a realistic attempt to secure superior bargaining power for countries whose capacity to invest abroad is high, because they suffer from a tendency to export surpluses as against countries whose bargaining power rests on their

---

[1] Even the greater risk which depreciation or subsidies create around competing industries (because no one can be sure how far the weapon will be used and who could withstand the subsidized competition) arises from the quantitative and not from any qualitative difference.

import surplus—i.e. on their capacity to absorb foreign production. Pure ethics cannot be said to be involved.

American writers and the Government define as discriminatory any practice which enables a variation of the supply price of any commodity competing with U.S. exports according to the circumstances of sale if the variation is made possible by subsidies or multiple currency practices. It is difficult to agree that this term is applicable as long as all buyers or potential buyers are treated identically. Subsidies of fixed proportion (i.e. most subsidies of primary products in contrast to subsidies on manufactured goods, which to be effective must be varied according to circumstances), e.g., are not held to be discriminatory. But even as far as the problem of dumping is concerned grave ambiguities remain. There has been no objection to, and no discouragement of, dumping in any of the countries adhering to this definition to sales of products below full cost. Nor has there been any objection to sales made possible by the fact that wages in certain export industries are being cut. Yet there seems no logical reason to differentiate between a decrease in export prices made possible either by entrepreneurs foregoing part of their profits or by labour accepting less than 'static' efficiency wages. Export subsidies financed by the State merely spread the loss of real income suffered by the worsening of the terms of trade over the whole population. It has not been held discriminatory or dumping to promote exports by the granting of long- or short-term loans, yet such loans would have the same effect as export subsidies in promoting foreign sales and would have to be considered discriminatory against suppliers who are not in a position to forego the proceeds of their exports because they need imports and are unable or unwilling to use the excess of exports merely for the purpose of stabilizing the level of their employment.[1] The creation of imperfections in favour of the lending country by granting financial facilities or by direct investment must logically be held as discriminatory against exporting nations not having these connections as the use of the bargaining power inherent in the capacity to purchase from abroad.

Foreign trade measures affecting the demand for foreign imports are scrutinized much on the same basis. Preferential tariffs and *a*

---

[1] In many cases the grant of credit, e.g. in the case of the U.S. the Export and Import Banking, is explicitly contingent upon the purchase being made in the country granting the credit. But even if such explicit discrimination in favour of the country's exports is not practised, it is probable that the borrowing country will view with favour the export industries of the lending country with an eye for further favours to come. In any case export credits will tend to turn the terms of trade of third countries against them. Is that not discrimination?

ortiori a diversion of purchases from the cheapest market measured
by current cross rates of exchange are held to be discriminatory even
if undertaken on the plea of shortage of exchange on what is normally
the cheapest market. On occasion the restriction by direct quantitative
regulation of luxury imports in order to enable the pursuit of a policy
necessitating the decrease of the propensity to consume foreign manufactures was objected to as discriminatory.

The alternative to such control would be an increase in tariffs to
prohibitive levels and/or a decrease in effective money demand by a
policy of deflation. Such measures would depress purchases in the
same way as direct control of imports. There seems to be no logical
ground to differentiate between the curtailment of purchases enforced by a slump and that enforced by government measures, i.e.
exchange control enabling the country to pursue a full employment
policy internally even if conditions of foreign markets would prevent
it from doing so if it was forced to permit the import of foreign
(luxury) products. Non-monetary general remedial action, e.g.
steeply progressive income taxes or the institution of consumer rationing with respect to imported foreign commodities, might be politically
impossible. The importing country would therefore be forced to increase its exports in order to maintain imports and might be unable
to do so, or at any rate only on very unfavourable terms tantamount to
a general decrease of the real standard of life. A definition of the term
discrimination as excluding all steps to control directly the level of
imports irrespective of the level and character of nominal national
money income would probably imply an abandonment of the policy
of full employment in the absence of an international agreement.

The fear has been expressed that an attempt to organize consciously
the production and exchange of goods and services would evoke
retaliatory action on the part of those countries which desire to maintain *laisser faire* as the basis of their economic organization.

Provided the full employment block is large enough and possessed
of diversified national resources, the risk as well as the seriousness of
the consequences of retaliatory action by individualistic unstable surplus
countries have been very much exaggerated. First of all, the possible
monopoly and monopsony power of any outside country with respect
to the exports or imports of the block would be small, as the cost of
replacing exports or imports would not be considerable. It is, moreover, not in the least likely that an outside country would undertake
the far-reaching reorganization of its internal economic system necessary to retaliate effectively. If it did, it would also be able to join the

full employment block and a rational solution of the problem would be possible.

Conclusion

We may now sum up: 1 (a) Ideally a comprehensive and multilateral agreement and the maintenance of full employment on a worldwide basis should be attempted. Such agreement would have to comprise the planned development of backward areas on a regional basis, taking into account the possibilities of promoting economic progress, provided by better technical knowledge and education.

(b) Failing such a comprehensive solution, schemes could be introduced which would permit single countries to maintain full employment in spite of fluctuations in productive activity elsewhere. Only schemes which accomplish this task without involving a growing indebtedness of mature economic areas can, from this point of view, be considered satisfactory.

(c) In all these cases the planning of the exchange of goods between countries as well as the internal policy of each of these constituent units must be safeguarded. Each of the constituent units must be enabled to exercise such control as they deem necessary over the export of capital and over their foreign trade. It would be essential, however, to arrive at binding agreements that no country should use foreign trade policy in order to provide internal employment, i.e. that they will refrain from abrupt changes in their foreign economic policy to achieve export surpluses or a mitigation of adverse balances.

2 (a) Failing a satisfactory world-wide scheme of a multilateral character the possible gains derived from unplanned multilateral exchange restricted by tariffs are unlikely, even in the long run, to yield gains commensurate with the losses arising out of a recurrence of international cyclical fluctuations and the encroachment on domestic planning and policy. This seems likely even if we disregard the likelihood that such cyclical fluctuations would, in fact, tend to give rise to increased economic isolationism much more unfavourable to a rational international division of labours than a conscious policy of regionalism.[1]

[1] It is more than doubtful that the political constellation in the more important countries would permit a fully international arrangement on the lines set out in this essay. The fact that rationally no disadvantage would accrue even to prospective surplus countries whose possible, or rather probable depression, is likely to be mitigated, is not necessarily an argument in favour of their adherence. In part the resistance will come on account of inherent ideologies which, though no longer rationally valid, retain their political strength. Partly the resistance will spring from rational motives. The collectivist members of the world economy would have no impulse to strengthen the non-collectivist part of the world economic system for fear that this renewed strength might at a subsequent date be used against them. They are likely, therefore, to give

(*b*) It is unnecessary to emphasize that the loss from foregoing the potential maximum international division of labour by the formation of regional blocks (devoted to the pursuance of a multilateral interchange of goods and services among each other, while at the same time adhering to a policy of full employment), would be the smaller, the larger is the block; with increasing size the block would have a fairly high degree of natural self-sufficiency. In analogy to a world-wide scheme the block would have to possess a common Monetary Fund and an Investment Board. Members of the full employment block must, moreover, undertake not to change without agreement of the others their intra-block economic policy (tariffs, quotas, etc.).

(*c*) Small and poor countries are likely to lose most from a restoration of the uncontrolled action of international market forces. The highly imperfect character of the international markets for manufactured goods, the high risk and the automatic acquisition of selling power in the lands of large economic areas will tend to stabilize their existent inferiority. Their internal investment, and hence their economic progress, would be restricted, and their employment policy imperilled.

(*d*) The relations of such economic blocks with the outside world will have to be based on reciprocity, either of a monetary or a nonmonetary character. Devaluation, as a method of adjustment in any full employment area confronted with unstable outside areas, does not safeguard full employment policy.

(*e*) The larger the block, moreover, the easier it would be to readjust any adverse balance which it had with other countries. Combined with its power to grant stable and expanding markets on the basis of her planned economic progress, the block could secure advantages without exploitation, which would not accrue under perfect competition for uncertain markets, and thus offset losses, if any, originating from the limitation in the international division of labour. Any retaliation against the block will be less effective, the larger the block, for any restriction of her purchases would react sharply on the export industries of any one country outside, while, at worst, retaliatory action of any one country could not considerably harm its own export industries.

strong support to the most orthodox individualist prejudices. The militantly individualistic nations, on the other hand, may be to some extent justified in rejecting any reforms, because such reforms would unquestionably weaken their influence internationally. In a rationally working system export surplus countries lose their dominance over debtors. Moreover, within these countries the adoption of a full employment policy, the working of which depends on the power of the Government (which is democratically elected), tends to weaken the influence of those classes which are economically strongest, i.e. of the economic oligarchy.

(f) The advantages which a poorer country joining such a regional block would derive, in security of employment, high productivity and rapid economic progress through planned redistribution of industrial resources and skill, should secure the adherence of most countries, even against the blandishments of foreign loans from possibly adversely affected export surplus countries.

PART VI

AN EXPERIMENT IN FULL EMPLOYMENT
CONTROLS IN THE GERMAN ECONOMY, 1933-1938

by K. Mandelbaum

The Relevance of the German Experience

THE studies in this book are mainly analytical. The principles of a full employment policy in a capitalist society have been outlined, and attempts have been made to examine the difficulties which might arise in maintaining full employment. To complete these studies it is useful to analyse the actual behaviour of a capitalist society under these conditions. But where can the material be found? No major capitalist country, with the exception of Nazi Germany, experienced a period of sustained full employment between the two wars. Attempts elsewhere to stabilize economic activity at a high level were not successful.

If then in this essay we examine certain aspects of the fully employed German economy before the war, we do so because the German experience is all that there is in this field. Clearly, certain major reservations must be made. Full employment in Germany was associated with a large increase in the compulsory powers of the State; in particular, the free organizations of labour had been destroyed at the outset of the Nazi regime. Certain economic controls were a direct reflection of this political set-up which is neither obtainable in free societies nor desirable. Secondly, full employment was only a short transitional stage in a development which in peace-time already transformed the under-employed German economy into an over-employed war economy; and in any case full employment was not achieved for its own sake (or for the sake of social welfare), but was a mere by-product of rearmament.

To reject the political ideology and methods of the Nazis need not, however, prevent us using the German experience to throw light on certain technical problems which arise in full employment. Suppose that State investment and State inspired private investment had been in projects serving civilian needs rather than in military establishments. Total welfare would have been higher, but what of the working of the system? Would the need for, say, wage and price control still have not arisen? Or were not these and other measures of control largely conditioned by the fact that Government spending in support of employment proceeded in a deficit country during a period when depression or wide trade fluctuations occurred in the outside world? Again, it must not be overlooked that the system of controls left intact in Germany such essential ingredients of our present system as titles to property, free choice of occupation, the profit motive and private initiative. Nor was totalitarian control always tantamount to the arbitrary imposition of Government terms on the economic groups concerned. Except in wage determination, decisions regarding industrial policies, price formation and similar matters were usually arrived at by way of negotiation with the interested groups or their 'leaders,' and were the result of sectional pressures and compromises. Conditions, therefore, were not in all respects so fundamentally different as to make any reference to this experience futile. They were, on the other hand, so peculiar that no useful lessons can be derived from this historical precedent, unless we can distinguish the controls which were necessitated by genuine economic requirements from those others which merely reflected the particular political driving force of the system.

The present paper will deal with this question without, however, giving a historical account or a detailed description of German economic policy during the 'thirties. The most relevant period for our investigation are the eighteen months from the late autumn of 1936 to the beginning or spring of 1938, when unemployment was small, but not yet appreciably lower than the number of unfilled vacancies. Some measures which were taken in the years preceding this stage of full or near-full employment will have to be considered. But on the whole the policies pursued in the early emergency period, which followed the familiar line of a public works programme, need not concern us here. The developments during the last fifteen or eighteen months before the outbreak of war are equally irrelevant; the German economy showed at that time all the symptoms of an overemployed war economy. The free reserves of labour had practically been exhausted by the autumn of 1937, when the number of unemployed represented no more than $2\frac{1}{2}$ per cent of the total active labour force. To set the rearmament target still higher and to accelerate public spending was bound, under these conditions, to lead to a general scarcity of labour and, in consequence, to many new restrictions on 'unnecessary' production and consumption. This experience obviously yields no lessons pertaining to peace-time full employment; it reflects a state of over-employment inherent in a war economy, and is therefore outside the scope of this study.

We shall in this essay concentrate on three fields of economic control:

foreign trade; wages and prices; and the regulation of the labour market. Hardly anything will be said about financial policy.[1] It is sufficient to note that from 1933-4 to 1937-8 rather less than half of the public outlay required to finance expansion was derived from borrowing; the rest represented increased revenues.[2] The relative smallness of the deficit is in accordance with the normal experience that part of the public expenditure comes back in the form of higher tax yields. The 'return flow' to the Treasury was the greater, because the existing high rates of taxation were gradually stepped up during the process. The consequent reduction of private spending was followed by a rise in State activity, i.e. in the ratio of Government purchases to total spending. The apparent orthodoxy of German finance was to that extent a reflection of the rearmament policy.

The Control of Foreign Trade

Full control of foreign trade and of foreign exchange transactions was established under the New Plan, in the autumn of 1934. The internal expansion which had raised the volume of industrial production by over 40 per cent since 1932 now came up against a formidable trade (import) bottleneck. Exports had continued to decline for reasons which seemed largely beyond the control of Germany herself, while imports were beginning to rise in 1934 with expanding employment. In the absence of adequate reserves of international cash Germany was unable to sustain the resulting trade deficit; nor could she continue to live on stocks. This bottleneck was not specifically connected with rearmament. Any vigorous policy of increasing internal employment and incomes above the depressed world level would have created a strain on the balance of trade. In fact, had German policy been committed to raising consumption, the (initial) difficulties might have been even greater than they actually proved, if only because the German consumer goods industries require, on the average, more foreign materials per unit of output than the constructional trades.[3] Hence, given the lack of reserves and of a buoyant foreign demand, the employment programme, whatever its nature, had to be protected

---

[1] For an analysis cf. T. Balogh, 'The National Economy of Germany,' *Economic Journal*, September, 1938.

[2] Public expenditure over and above the level of 1932 adds up for the period 1933-4 to 1937-8 to about RM 40 milliards. The increase in the Public Debt was about RM 18 milliards (including the 'secret' debt). At the beginning borrowing was almost exclusively on short term, while in the later period long-term loans gained in importance. Total public expenditure in the same period was of the order of RM 115 milliards.

[3] While the share of industrial consumer goods in total industrial output was 40 per cent in 1928, the importation of raw materials for these industries accounted for 60 per cent of Germany's total imports of industrial raw materials.

against external influences, if it was not to be surrendered for the sake of relieving foreign exchange difficulties.

Whether straightforward depreciation of the currency could have restored the balance is doubtful; the elasticities of home demand for imports and of foreign demand were certainly not great enough to permit the position to be rectified without a serious worsening of the terms of trade. Rejecting the course of (uniform) depreciation the German authorities chose to extend the existing machinery of exchange control, which so far had in practice covered capital movements only,[1] to current trade. Exchange control was not, however, a simple device; it comprised a multiplicity of measures which were co-ordinated from the centre. Imports, through licensing or through centralized trading on account of Government Controls, were restricted to goods which could neither be dispensed with nor be replaced by home production; they were thereby reduced to the minimum consistent with the Government programme.[2] A growing proportion of the smaller volume of imports was at the same time diverted to countries which did not demand payment in *Devisen* and were willing to hold Mark balances; by 1938 only about one-fifth of Germany's foreign trade required and produced free exchange. To place exports on a competitive level in spite of the continued over-valuation of the official Mark rate, Germany resorted, whenever necessary, to subsidies and to the practice of exporting at depreciated special Mark rates which were adjusted to the strength of each market ('discrimination'). Moreover, the formation of a highly organized regional block, built up from bilateral agreements, opened possibilities of fostering exports by means other than price concessions. In the years following the adoption of the New Plan Germany had a small surplus on her current visible account (except in 1938); she used these active trade balances as well as the proceeds from shipping and other services and from the sale of foreign assets for liquidating part of her outstanding foreign debt, while, at the same time, accumulating new debts on clearing accounts. The volume of her exports increased considerably, but imports, at rising prices, were further curtailed, until they expanded again in the second half of 1936.

---

[1] Exchange control dates from November 1931. The original scheme allotted to importers a certain percentage of the *Devisen* used by them during the base year 1930-31, but until the spring of 1934 allocation was more or less proportionate to the general fall in production and demand, and was carried out without discrimination against particular kinds of imports. Exchange control, therefore, does not seem to have been used as an instrument of trade policy. (Cf. Howard Ellis, 'Exchange Control in Germany,' *Quarterly Journal of Economics*, Supplement Vol. LIV, Part 2, pp. 26 and 114).

[2] The effect on the volume and composition of imports may be shown by comparing the whole period 1934-38 with 1926-30. Raw material imports declined by 3 per cent, while the imports of finished industrial goods, of foodstuffs and of semi-manufactures were reduced by 54, 27 and 17 per cent respectively. The fall in the volume of total imports was 22 per cent.

The central control of foreign trade had obvious economic advantages. Germany was able to determine by her internal arrangements both her balance of trade and the volume of employment. At least theoretically the system could be so administered as to maximize the foreign revenue and to secure the best terms of trade obtainable. The extent to which Germany actually benefited in this respect is, of course, difficult to assess. According to Howard Ellis, whose estimates may be accepted as the nearest possible approximation, the official Mark rate was over-valued after 1933 by from 45 to 75 per cent, relative to sterling. This over-valuation was incompletely offset by differential subsidies and rates, so that foreigners still paid on the average 12 to 20 per cent more for German goods than for British.[1] It is possible that the discriminating prices at which Germany sold in different markets were so much higher or lower than the optimum obtainable under conditions of monopolistic trading, that they yielded in the end less than sales at uniform prices. But unless one assumes extreme clumsiness in discrimination—an assumption which is perhaps not entirely absurd, considering that the system was developed with little insight into its principles—a monopoly gain, including the additional benefits of discriminating monopoly, should have accrued to Germany. Whether or not there was on balance a gain in foreign revenue, however, it must be regarded as an *a priori* probability that exchange control, including over-valuation, gave Germany more favourable terms of trade—that is: her exports fetched more imports —than global depreciation would have secured. A comparison of the German with the British terms of trade may give an indication of this advantage. We use again H. Ellis's figures.[2]

INDICES OF GERMAN AND BRITISH TERMS OF TRADE AND
THE OVERVALUATION OF THE REICHSMARK

	German Terms of Trade[3]	British Terms of Trade[3]	% Excess of German over British Terms	% Excess of German over British Wholesale Prices (Gold)[4]
1929	100	100	—	—
1930	108.2	106.1	2.0	—
1931	123.8	115.7	7.0	11–45
1932	144.4	115.5	25.0	38–50
1933	142.8	119.9	19.1	46–57
1934	135.9	118.8	14.4	60–77
1935	126.3	115.3	9.5	67–78
1936	122.0	112.6	8.3	59–69
1937	117.6	108.0	8.9	44–57
1938	128.8	114.7	12.3	61–86

[1] Cf. H. Ellis, op. cit., pp. 76–86.
[2] H. Ellis, op. cit., p. 120. The excess of British over German terms (column 3 of the table), given by Ellis in arithmetical form, has been calculated as a percentage.
[3] For methods of calculation, cf. H. Ellis, op. cit., p. 139.
[4] Minimum and maximum quarterly averages within each year.

After 1931, when the pound sterling depreciated, Germany's terms of trade were appreciably higher than the British, the margin being widest in 1932-3. The subsequent reduction of Germany's advantage followed partly from the extended use of subsidies and special rates, and partly from the higher cost of imports, relative to world prices, which attended the German policy of buying within the confines of bilateral clearings. In fact, in trading with her clearing partners Germany was often more interested in securing large turnover and long term contracts at fixed prices than in obtaining the best terms. After 1934 Germany's advantage was only a fraction of the estimated over-valuation of the Mark. The margin in Germany's favour may be regarded as too small—and the basis of calculation as too doubtful—to substantiate the 'terms of trade' argument for exchange control. But it must be remembered that the British terms would have deteriorated more than they actually did after the depreciation of sterling, had not the existence of the sterling block enabled Great Britain to maintain parity with countries responsible for a high proportion of her raw materials and food supplies. No such possibilities were open to Germany, and it is therefore almost certain that her terms of trade would have been reduced below the British level, had she taken the 'liberal' course of global depreciation.

The economic benefits Germany derived from her unorthodox trading practices were not wholly secured at the expense of the rest of the world. At full employment level Germany's imports were higher both in volume and in value than in 1933, and although she had an active trade balance, the surplus over the whole period was not significant. Where Germany forced her exports by selling below manufacturer's costs, as she did in most free exchange countries, the loss to the German home consumer, who in the last instance had to pay for the subsidies, and to the competing foreign producer was the gain of the foreign buyer; the discrimination operated in his favour. Apart from that, Germany mainly relied in her export drive on the clearing mechanism: as the most substantial buyer of the products of some of her clearing partners she was able to force these countries, e.g. the Balkans, to buy in the German market, even though it was often the dearer market (because of the over-valuation of the Reichsmark). But she also *bought* from these countries at higher prices. And in any case, she employed her export forcing methods for the purpose of obtaining the maximum volume of what she regarded as essential imports. Her attitude to foreign trade was in this one respect more rational than that of some other countries which tried to stimulate exports for the sake of creating employment. Germany, having overcome the failure of home demand, wanted more ('essential') imports and valued exports[1] only as a means of payment for them. Within the area which came to form a, German economic bloc, bilateralism—combined as it was with full employment in the 'leading' country—thus actually operated as an expansionary factor; it offered to Germany's suppliers the advantage of producing for and selling in an expanding and guaranteed market. They obtained this benefit partly at the expense of foreign competitors and, perhaps, at the cost of some deterioration of their terms of trade, although this is questionable. For in her regional trade German's main concern was not with current terms, but with the continuity (and political security) of supply which she tried to ensure by inducing the dependent countries to change over to the production of goods she needed most.[2]

We have pointed out before that Germany's foreign trade position would not have been easier, had expansion been in the direction of higher consumption instead of rearmament. It can also be conceded that direct planning of foreign trade was, under the given conditions, a safer way for her of assuring necessary imports than devaluation which might not have reconciled full employment at home with trade fluctuations abroad. Yet, when all this is said, it can be shown that the import bottleneck could have been broken and a new equilibrium reached at a higher level of foreign trade and—ultimately—with less interference than was inherent in German economic policy. Suppose that strictly economic (or welfare) criteria had directed the rearrangement of Germany's foreign trade and of her internal economy, an adjustment which could in existing conditions best be effected through exchange control. The central control of exports and imports, including the possibility of establishing export prices independent of individual cost, *could* have been used for fostering exports up to the point where foreign trade, conducted under deteriorating terms, became a more expensive method of supply than production at home of the nearest substitutes (i.e. substitutes with the smallest cost disadvantage). The existing capacity of the German consumer goods industries, partly un-

---

[1] I.e. goods available for export after covering military demands.

[2] The Royal Institute of International Affairs summed up the effect of German trade policy on South-Eastern Europe as follows: '. . . up till the spring of 1939, the countries of South-Eastern Europe on balance have gained, in a material sense and in the short run, by the increase in German purchases. Germany has helped to raise their export prices and to increase their national incomes, and she has not so far taken advantage of her bargaining position to turn the terms of trade in her favour, so that their 'real' incomes have been raised. On the other hand, one of Germany's objects may be to associate the economic systems of these countries so closely with her own as to make it difficult for them to sever their connections in time of war' (*South-Eastern Europe*, London 1939, pp. 198-9). See also N. Momtchiloff, *Ten Years of Controlled Trade in South-Eastern Europe*, 1944.

used throughout the whole period of rearmament, would presumably have been fully employed at a fairly early stage; while the elasticities of foreign demand would have determined to what extent the German heavy industrial and engineering capacity would be employed for either home investment, particularly in the expansion of consumption goods industries (including the industries supplying them with materials), or for exports. Through increased production of substitutes and/or improvement in exports a situation would finally have been reached where the restrictions on imports could have been relaxed and partly abandoned without disturbance. The development in Germany was, however, quite different. For the pace was set by the practically unlimited demands of the military supply services and by their insistence, for political reasons, on a high degree of autarky, irrespective of costs. The very magnitude of these demands so swamped the productive capacity of the German investment goods industries, which are the main producers of export goods,[1] that with the progress of rearmament they found it increasingly difficult to accept and execute export orders. What opportunities were lost in foreign markets, because of this failure to reserve adequate manpower and plant for exports, it is impossible to estimate. But surely the volume of Germany's foreign trade would have been higher, had welfare considerations prevailed; moreover, Germany need not have chosen to use her active service balances for re-paying part of her foreign debt.

Another closely related point emerges more clearly from the development of Germany's raw material supply. In 1928, at the peak of the pre-Nazi prosperity, German industries working at or near full capacity, consumed about RM 17.5 milliards of raw materials, equal to about 21 per cent of gross output. Net imports of materials amounted to RM 7.5 milliards, while RM 10 milliards were supplied by home producers.[2] The volume of industrial output in 1937 exceeded the level of 1928 by 17 per cent, and we may assume that raw material requirements had increased in the same proportion, i.e. to about RM 20.5 milliards. The actual supply of materials was, however, considerably higher. Net imports of materials were reduced by just under RM 1 milliard (in prices of 1928), but with an expansion in home production by RM 5.6 milliards, total current supplies were at the rate of RM 22 milliards; they therefore exceeded estimated full employment needs by

---

[1] Between two-thirds and over three quarters of Germany's industrial exports consisted in the period 1929-1937 of investment goods, if 'General Utility Goods' such as coal, coke, fertilizers and chemicals, etc., are included in the latter.

[2] Cf. Rolf Wagenfuehr, 'Die Bedeutung des Aussenhandels fuer die Deutsche Industriewirtschaft,' *Sonderheft des Instituts fuer Konjunkturforschung*, No. 41, (1936), p. 56.

over 7 per cent.[1] Official data also show that the ratio of stocks in hand (at all stages) to production was at least as high in 1937 as in 1928, when sizeable stocks, particularly of finished consumer goods, had accumulated.[2] The supply position, therefore, was so improved that many restrictions could have been abandoned, had the easing of exchange difficulties or the maintenance of employment been the dominant purpose. It would have been reasonable, even then, to keep the machinery of control in being so that it could be applied again when conditions demanded it, say, during an international depression. But once the scarcities had disappeared, no more was required for insulating the system from short-run external influences than (perhaps) a limited general licensing of selected imports, combined with arrangements with individual countries to secure on long term contracts essential quantities of materials and foods. But there was no relaxation in the German controls. They remained as restrictive as ever, not because the supply position left no other choice, but because the limitation of consumable supplies had become their primary function. This, however, is not inherent in exchange control, nor was it enforced on Germany by her foreign trade position.

Wage and Price Control

The cut in imports and its corollary, the substitution of more expensive home produced materials for foreign goods exerted a strong upward pressure on prices. Although the cost of raw materials forms a small proportion only of the total cost of most finished goods, the shift away from international trade was on a sufficiently large scale to become an important factor in the movement towards a higher price level.[3] Let us consider first how this price effect *might* have been handled.

1. Suppose that nothing had been done to keep the upward movement in check. Since it affected goods which entered heavily into the cost of living (textiles, food), wages would have followed more or less closely, in the absence of repressive controls. Leaving aside for a moment certain short-period problems, this rise could have had no harmful effects, as long as there were unused resources, although higher

[1] This is no more than a rough calculation. Exact data are not available, but the statement in the text is confirmed by the Institute für Konjunkturforschung: 'If surplus raw material imports were added to domestic production, the resulting figure for raw material supply—compared with 1928—would exceed the increase in finished goods production to a considerable degree.' Weekly Report, February 23, 1938 (Supplement).

[2] Cf. Institut f. Konjunkturforschung, Weekly Report, January 26, 1939.

[3] The rise in world prices from 1934-1937 was an additional factor making for higher domestic prices. This influence will be dealt with later.

export subsidies might have been required to maintain exports in the face of rising domestic costs.

2. An attempt could have been made to stabilize living costs so as to preclude large wage increases (relative to wage levels abroad) and to moderate the deterioration in the terms of trade. Two ways were open to achieve this purpose. Subsidies could be paid to cheapen wage goods (or to stimulate high-cost output in the autarky sector while preventing the rise in costs from being translated into a corresponding increase in prices).[1] Or manufacturers and dealers could be required to bear a share of the additional costs, consumers' prices being unchanged or raised *pro tanto* less. This control of profit margins could be expected to encourage economies through concentration and standardization; the fall in real income per unit of employment, following from a deterioration in the terms of trade, could to that extent be avoided altogether. These methods of stabilizing the cost of living played some part in German price policy,[2] but they could not avail in the bottleneck sectors.

3. Where raw materials were scarce, as was frequently the case in the early period, and where home substitutes were not yet produced in the required quantities, prices tended to rise sharply in relation to prime costs. Such shortages cannot be fought by subsidies or price control, as can cost increases, but only by a restriction of demand. Generally speaking, they may conceivably lead to a noticeable rise in the cost of living, followed by higher money wages, and thus initiate a cumulative process even in an under-employed economy; this would last until the bottlenecks were removed by increased home output. But it is more probable that substitutes can be provided before the scarcities drive up the total cost of living sufficiently to induce demands for higher wages all round; or that institutional rigidities in the cost of living will absorb the greater part of the price rise, before it reaches the consumer; or that stocks are available to bridge the gap between supply and demand during the critical period. Sectional inflations may therefore not do much harm under conditions of unemployment. If desired, they can be avoided by temporary rationing; or their influence on the cost of living can be averted by compensating price reductions in other lines.

[1] In Germany the Government frequently subsidized suppliers by underwriting risks that were regarded as too great for private enterprise.

[2] The control of prices and the organization of markets were most complete in agriculture which was the largest single 'autarky industry.' Prices payable to farmers were raised to induce higher outputs; they were at the same time fixed so as to prevent speculative movements. Import monopolies absorbed the difference between the higher domestic prices and the prices of imported foods. Margins of processors and dealers, including retailers, were controlled, so that part of the price rise was absorbed before it reached the consumer; price discrimination and subsidies were used for the same purpose.

In Germany there was a strong case for limited intervention in certain fields to fight scarcities and speculative price increases arising out of the foreign exchange shortage. The control of raw material prices actually served this purpose. By the end of 1934 this control was more or less complete, and almost all materials, imported as well as home produced, were distributed among firms by quota systems or similar methods.[1] Apart from this specific control, which helped to check the inventory boom of 1934, it would have been perfectly possible to permit both wages and prices to rise before the stage of full employment was reached. Unfavourable effects on foreign trade could have been offset by export subsidies. The actual course of German price policy was, however, different. It was conditioned by the wage stop which was the first substantial economic intervention (in 1933).

Decreed at a time when unemployment existed on a large scale and when there was no danger that public spending would lead to inflation, the freezing of basic wages may have served the political purpose of winning the confidence of the propertied classes; but the economic arguments in favour of the wage stop were certainly based on mis-conceptions. It was argued that deficit spending as such was an infla-tionary practice which must be counteracted by keeping wages and prices down. The employment effect of a given public expenditure would then be greater and the supposed dilemma that re-employment necessitated a deficit in excess of available savings would be avoided. The same misconception—the scarcity of savings—provided at that time (of unemployment) the main argument for the severe restriction of private capital issues[2] and, in general, greatly influenced German financial policy.[3]

Once the decision was taken to peg wage rates, control of prices became necessary to safeguard consumers' standards or workers' morale. This called for intervention in three directions. Price rises resulting from the use of more expensive substitutes had to be

---

[1] In some cases each individual transaction was licensed. Where licenses were granted for basis quota, different standards were used in different industries for computing the quotas. Import and purchase licenses were accompanied by inventory regulations, by regulations con-cerning the use of materials (including admixture of substitutes) and by processing licenses to cover vertical concerns processing their own materials. Cf. H. Block, 'German Methods of Allocating Raw Materials,' *Social Research*, Vol. IX (1942), p. 356.

[2] The control of the capital market became later an instrument for directing savings into the desired channels. The various bans on real investment had similar functions, but more often they were used for protecting existing cartels against outside competition or against disruptions through quota fights.

[3] Much thought and effort was devoted to fighting non-existing dangers, e.g. the supposed inflationary consequences of 'credit-creation' as distinct from what was regarded as the sound method of absorbing 'genuine savings' through long-term loans.

suppressed or minimized by profit squeezing or subsidies. Scarcity prices in the bottleneck sectors had to be prevented by rationing, or had to be offset by compensating price reductions. A policy starting with a wage stop was in addition compelled to fight price increases due to conditions abroad. This would have been quite unnecessary in a system of free wage bargaining; wages could have caught up with this price rise which, originating from abroad, could not have impaired the competitive position of German industry in foreign markets. But German price policy had to take a different line. When world prices of primary products recovered after the depression, the German authorities, intent on reducing the effect of dearer foreign materials on the domestic price level, altered 'marking up' practices by prohibiting percentage additions to the rising costs of foreign goods; only the absolute increase could in some cases be added to price. This eliminated 'pyramiding,' but could not remove the price pressure. Nor were the other methods for stabilizing the cost of living effective enough to prevent a very marked fall in real wage rates (see later). The price rise was particularly noticeable where there were temporary shortages. Materials—both foreign and *ersatz*—were allocated at fixed prices, but this in itself was not sufficient to stabilize prices in the bottleneck sectors, since the demand for the final product was not rationed. Had German policy seriously aimed at keeping real wages reasonably stable, more interventions would have been required in the early period, given the wage stop.

Some of the difficulties inherent in the German situation during the period preceding the stage of full employment were connected with the foreign trade position; many others were avoidable. Later, however, new difficulties arose. At the end of 1936 the problem of wage and price stability presented itself under conditions not too different from what a full employment model might show. The process of re-absorbing idle labour was approaching its end, with demand pressing further against the limits set by the productive capacity of the system. Many industries in the heavy and engineering sector, where plants were fully, or almost fully, utilized, were facing a rise in short period costs. This tendency was strengthened by changes in the labour market; the listed basic rates, though legally frozen, were gradually transformed into minimum rates, as labour—or certain grades of labour—became increasingly scarce, and there were frequent evasions of the wage stop in more or less subtle forms.[1] The rise in money wages, accentuated

[1] To stop these evasions the Labour Trustees were authorized in 1938 to impose wage ceilings, i.e. to fix maximum wages. But this was only done in two industries before the war.

by more overtime pay in the constructional industries, involved an increase in labour costs per unit of output, since productivity per man hour remained stable (or declined slightly) after 1936. How labour shortage can produce inflationary tendencies in a fully-employed economy, has been described on pp. 63-4; in Germany this danger resulted exclusively from competitive bidding of entrepreneurs, not from demands of labour whose bargaining power had been destroyed by the dissolution of the trade unions. To counteract the inflationary tendencies, which the further expansion of public outlay was bound to carry with it, the limited price control of the intermediate period (1933-36) was replaced by a general price ceiling.

The price stop decree of November 1936 pegged prices to the level of an arbitrarily chosen date (October 17, 1936) and prohibited all further price increases in response to rising demand. Rising costs had to be taken into account, but in order to prevent producers from using the argument of rising costs as an excuse for whatever price increases they liked, it was found necessary to define what constituted 'legitimate' cost increases. As a rule permission to increase prices was only given where higher costs originated from higher import prices or from the use of more expensive substitutes.[1] Great efforts were made to keep these cost items as stable as possible. The principle that 'scarcities are no justification for price increases' had already been applied since 1934 to imported goods which were allocated in Germany at the ruling world price plus the customary (mostly absolute) margins, irrespective of the market constellation at home. The prices of domestic materials had, of course, to be so fixed that additional supplies were forthcoming. Here price control was mainly concerned with the elimination of speculative short run price movements. Since 'legitimate' cost increases occurred over a wide field, because of rising world prices and the policy of autarky, the measures which we have already described—e.g. decreed or negotiated price reductions to balance price increases—had to be continued and extended.

The success or failure of this policy may be judged by comparing price changes in the finished goods sector with wage levels; a fairly stable relationship between them was the avowed aim of the control. If this criterion is applied, it appears that the German price policy can hardly claim to have been a complete success. For, while wage rates

---

[1] Another set of exceptions was conditioned by the rise in export prices which were of course not subject to the price ceiling. In order to secure a steady flow of supplies to the final exporters permission to raise prices had also to be granted to their suppliers.

were kept substantially stable at their 1933 level, prices of industrial finished goods rose as follows:

PRICE CHANGES OF INDUSTRIAL FINISHED GOODS
(1928=100)

	April 1933	October 1936	April 1938
Finished Goods General Index	70.2	77.2	79.4
Capital Goods . .	83.3	82.6	82.5
Consumers' Goods . .	62.4	74.0	77.6

The German cost of living index shows for the same period a rise of just under 8 per cent, but its inadequacy has been admitted by official German sources.[1] On any showing there was a marked fall in real wage rates and probably also a decline in the purchasing power of hourly wage earnings (which in money terms increased between 1933 and 1937 by 8 per cent). This stands in sharp contrast to the rise in real wage rates during the upswing of 1926-28, when, however, productivity increased substantially. No improvement in output per man hour occurred, on balance, in the period from 1932-3 to 1937-8,[2] so that a small decline in real wage rates—or, at best, stability—was to be expected as a normal corollary to prosperity.

The price increase was confined to the consumers' goods sector. These industries were, on the whole, more affected by higher costs of materials than the constructional trades and they benefited less, until 1936-7, from reduced overheads. Conditions regarding overheads were, however, reversed later, when various light industries not yet working at full capacity received Government orders under the stock-piling programme (textiles, tinned foods, etc.). The continued price stability of capital goods after 1936 is remarkable and throws light on certain administrative implications of price control. It proved easy to regulate prices in all organized (cartel) markets as well as in markets— these were often identical—where the controlling authority held a strong position as a buyer (or functioned as a distributive agency as in agriculture). Where this was not the case, price regulations were difficult to enforce and were frequently evaded in the absence of quality control. The ceiling policy was thus very effective in the almost fully cartelized 'basic' industries working largely on Government contracts.[3] Here the price freeze acted under conditions of rising unit costs as a powerful stimulus to rationalization and standardization. Where

---

[1] Cf. *Vierteljahreshefte zur Wirtschaftsforschung*, 1939-40, No. 1, p. 14.
[2] See table below.
[3] Effective price control in this sector explains the quite unusual phenomenon that German heavy industry in 1937 was able to sell at higher prices in foreign markets than at home.

profit margins were reduced more than could be compensated by standardization and similar economies—in fact, there was a reduction of net margins in almost all heavy and engineering industries after 1936[1] —firms did not abstain from increasing output, except in the case of marginal producers whose output was then taken over by more efficient firms. In most industries catering for the civilian population, prices and profit rates increased during the ceiling period, or at least until 1938; official pressure on margins was largely evaded by deterioration of quality which was limited only in the case of well-established brands.

German price control was, on the whole, successful in preventing open inflation after 1937 (although inflation reappeared on a minor scale in the form of shortages, queues and quality changes). It did not stabilize the price level or the relation between prices and wages, but served to control price increases and to preclude spiralling secondary effects. Under the ceiling policy the control mainly operated through profit squeezing. But this was only a relatively short phase. On the whole profit margins were extraordinarily high compared with conditions in other countries or with conditions prevailing in Germany in the 'twenties. The share of gross profits in the value added by industry (including mining, building and contracting, and public utilities) had risen between 1929 and 1937 from 61.8 to 69.5 per cent.[2] Prices of finished goods had declined over this period in roughly the same proportion as money wage costs, but profits per unit of industrial output increased, because the rise by about 10 per cent in productivity per man hour was not passed on to the consumer. This shift in the

PRODUCTIVITY OF LABOUR[3] AND SHARE OF PROFITS IN
INDUSTRIAL OUTPUT[4]

	1925	1929	1932	1933	1934	1936	1937
Output per man-hour in industry (1928=100) . .	90	105	114	115	110[5]	115	114
Share of gross profits in industrial net output (per cent)	—	61.8	69.9	67.5	68.0	69.4	69.5

distribution of income had occurred during the depression, when both productivity and the degree of monopoly—i.e. the ratio of prices to

[1] Cf. M. Y. Sweezy, 'German Corporate Profits 1926-1938,' *The Quarterly Journal of Economics*, Vol. 54, p. 384.

[2] Cf. L. Rostas, 'Industrial Production, Productivity and Distribution in Britain. Germany and the United States,' *The Economic Journal*, April 1943.

[3] Taken from *Vierteljahreshefte zur Wirtschaftsforschung*, 1939-40, No. 1, p. 9.

[4] Cf. L. Rostas, op. cit.

[5] This decline was due to the promotion of labour intensive employment during the 'work creation' period of 1933-4.

prime costs—had increased sharply. There was on balance no material change afterwards: the share of profits declined slightly in 1933-4, but it gradually rose again in the subsequent years, until the ceiling policy stopped this trend in 1937 and finally brought about a fractional reduction (to 69 per cent) in 1938. Thus, if over-all changes for the whole period after 1929 are considered, it appears that German policy was essentially one of keeping the share of wages in total income low and the share of profits high. This distribution of the industrial product fostered savings and thus slowed down the increase in consumers' spending, following upon the rise in investment. Moreover, consumption was restricted by heavy taxation. Both factors helped to adjust demand to the small permitted increase in consumers' goods output and served to make high investment and low consumption consistent with substantial monetary stability.[1]

A more enlightened policy in a progressive society, where welfare is the main aim, would obviously take a different line. The emphasis would be on securing a distribution of income which gives a high propensity to consume. Real wages would be allowed to rise in a fully employed economy at least with rising productivity. Control of prices might become a necessary part of this policy. It would have to cope with temporary scarcities originating, e.g., from import difficulties, or—a less specific case—with inflationary tendencies set in motion by rising money wages. But it is unlikely that prices of all goods would have to be subjected to direct regulation as was the case in Germany where the wide range of control was determined by political conditions: by the partial (voluntary) withdrawal from foreign trade, by excessive public spending and by the wage stop, which from the start was a conditioning factor. This, however, does not obliterate the merits of certain instruments of control which were used in Germany. Price discrimination, subsidies and fixing of margins which played a large part in German agricultural policy may serve to keep down prices of goods which enter into the cost of living. Undesired price rises can be prevented by price ceilings which give a stimulus to efficiency where evasions can be stopped.

Mobility of Labour

German experience is often quoted to prove that a full employment policy involves regimentation of labour. The abolition of free wage bargaining had, in fact, the consequence that more and more reliance

---

[1] The ratio of total net investment to national income was 14 per cent in 1937 and 15 per cent in 1938, as against 9 per cent in 1928. Home financed investment was even lower in 1928, if allowance is made for capital imports.

was put on methods of compulsion once a general scarcity of labour had developed. This, however, was not the case before 1938. And neither during the period of re-employment nor at the stage of full employment did direct control of labour play a significant rôle. Wage differentials and certain deliberate measures of a non-compulsory character proved on the whole quite sufficient to attract labour to industries and places where it was needed. Had expansion only posed the problem of reabsorbing unemployed workers into their old jobs and of keeping them there, there would be no need to stress this point. But there actually occurred at the same time a substantial redistribution of labour. The great shift towards the capital goods industries and the decline of many export and consumer goods trades necessitated occupational adjustments and made large demands on spatial mobility, the more so as important industries were transferred to, or promoted at, new locations. Material about migration of workers from one industry or place to another is very scanty. For Central Germany (excluding the important district of Brunswick) it has been estimated that the influx of workers was 150,000, which compares with an increase in total employment in that area of 810,000 over the same period (April 1933 to January 1938).[1] The ratio of immigrant workers to total intake appears to have been of a similar order in Lower Saxony and in South-West Germany,[2] while all frontier districts including the Rhineland and Ruhr,[3] but particularly Silesia, lost workers. These and other substantial movements of labour, which required a degree of mobility almost comparable to that of a transition from war to peace, were effected through the operation of normal economic incentives and through improvements in the methods of placement and recruitment.

The inflow of labour into the capital goods industries proceeded smoothly as long as there were large unused reserves of manpower. Both unemployed and new entrants (juveniles and entrants from outside the ranks of the normal labour force)[4] were attracted into these industries which paid best and where it was easiest to get jobs. Wage differentials were quite considerable. The fixed basic rates were on the average highest in the constructional sector, a fact which in itself helped

---

[1] Cf. 'Das Neue Mittel-Deutschland,' *Die Wirtschaftskurve* 1939, p. 61.

[2] The total number of wage and salary earners (employed and unemployed) had increased in Germany between 1933 and 1937 by 7 per cent, but the increase in Central Germany, South-West Germany and Lower Saxony was 13.8 per cent. Cf. *Wirtschaft und Statistik*, 1938, p. 49.

[3] Cf. 'Das Neue Ruhrrevier.' *Die Wirtschaftskurve*, 1939, p. 277.

[4] The increase in the number employed between April 1933 and April 1938 was 6.9 million, while unemployment was reduced by 4.9 million. A large proportion of the 'new' labour force probably consisted of disguised unemployed whose number was estimated in 1932 at almost 1 million. The net natural increase was of the order of 170,000 per annum.

the redistribution. The transition in these industries from short-time to full-time work and then to overtime and the consequent rise in effective weekly earnings greatly accentuated these differences; in the consumer goods trades short-time (measured by 1929 standards) continued throughout the whole period.[1]

Improvements in the organization of the labour market and extension of training facilities contributed to an easier flow of labour and to increased mobility, when the re-employment programme had reached a more advanced stage. Short training courses were provided for workers who had drifted during the depression into blind-alley occupations and had lost their skill to a smaller or greater extent, as well as for workers who could not be re-absorbed into their old occupations.[2] Exchange of information was speeded up. The Labour Exchanges were required to report without delay vacancies which could not be filled locally; the Provincial or National Clearing Centres receiving these reports compiled and sent out—as a rule, daily—lists of transfer possibilities classified by groups. Casual engagement (through personal application, etc.) was greatly reduced in favour of placement through the official machinery; it seems that in 1937 about half the total number of vacancies was filled by the Labour Exchanges, compared with 29 per cent in Great Britain. That the Labour Exchanges had to be notified in advance of all important constructional projects planned in their districts proved a particularly useful arrangement at the time when the German economy approached full employment.

Delays and bottlenecks occurred, however, in spite of these efforts. Where labour bottlenecks were due to low mobility—i.e. where vacancies could not be filled, although there was still more than frictional unemployment in the trades and occupations concerned—financial help to migration was granted in certain cases; no material is available to show to what extent this was done. The opposite policy of taking the job to the worker was pursued on a not insignificant scale. Dispersion of public orders (including contracts given by public enterprises, but excluding armament contracts) was organized through Order Equalization Boards. The Central Board—an advisory body which also acted as a clearing centre for information—was instructed in 1936

---

[1] The increase in weekly earnings over the level of 1934 ranged in 1937 from zero in certain industries to 32 per cent in others, with an average national increase of just under 16 per cent. Cf. *Vierteljahreshefte zur Wirtschaftsforschung*, 1939–40, Heft 1, p. 15.

[2] More than one million workers went through official training courses between April 1933 and April 1937. Attendance was compulsory for certain groups of workers receiving unemployment benefit. Cf. C. Vollweiler, 'The Mobilization of Labour Reserves in Germany,' *International Labour Review*, 1938, p. 609.

to influence the placing of public orders in favour of certain relatively 'depressed' areas (Saxony, Silesia, East Prussia and others). It was intended thereby to make greater use of plants in districts where labour was relatively abundant. In 1936 about RM 1 milliard of public orders seem to have passed through the Central Board (which compares with total Government purchases of goods and services of RM 20 to 22 milliards, of which at least half were armament orders).[1]

Low mobility never really created serious difficulties except in agriculture. The seasonal character of farm work, the lack of accommodation and comfort on the land and the fact that farm work does not hold out prospects of advancement, acted strongly against the flow of labour into agriculture. In this field compulsion—i.e. conscripted labour—was used long before 1938 on many occasions (labour service, army). In industry delays occurred as a rule only as and where the required grades of labour had become scarce throughout the country. A shortage of skilled metal, engineering and building workers appeared at a very early stage, because the supply of such labour had declined as a consequence of reduced training and apprenticeship during the depression. This shortage initiated certain restrictions, e.g. the prohibition of engagements in certain trades except with the permission of the Employment Exchanges (to prevent hoarding of skilled labour). But the main emphasis was on efforts to reduce skill requirements by standardization and simplification, and on expansionist measures: on extended training and on attempts to put more life into the apprenticeship system.[2] Great care was taken to direct juvenile entrants into the 'right' occupations; it is stated that 90 per cent of all school-leavers were advised in 1937 by vocational guidance officers attached to the employment exchanges.[3] The operation of the training schemes was unquestionably greatly helped by the fact that the elimination of the Trade Unions had swept away former craft regulations and demarcation lines. But it should be possible to achieve similar success with Trade Union co-operation which may be obtained if security of employment is ensured.

Compulsory shifting of labour and tying of workers to their jobs were applied in Germany on a gradually increasing scale only during the final period of scarcity, when the number of vacancies was twice or

[1] Cf. 'Der Staat als Auftraggeber,' *Die Wirtschaftskurve*, Vol. 15 (1936), p. 258. No information is available about the policy of the Regional Equalization Boards, which were intended to function mainly as Capacity Clearing Centres.

[2] The relevant decree of November 7, 1936, stipulated that firms in the iron, metal and building industries employing ten workers or more must train apprentices in a reasonable proportion to the number of people they employed.

[3] Cf. *Vierteljahreshefte*, etc., 1938-39, Heft 2, p. 187.

three times as high as the number of unemployed. But for over one year of virtually 'full' employment a steady expansion of the volume of work was secured without resorting to compulsion, although allowance must be made for more hidden pressures. There were three main labour reserves which could still be drained. First, the very effective organization of the labour market (which is indicated by the large part played by the Employment Exchanges in filling vacancies) made it possible to reduce still further what was formerly regarded as the absolute minimum of unemployment. This 'irreducible' margin was usually put at about 500,000, consisting of persons moving at any given time from one job to another. Later calculations, which refer to conditions in the second half of 1937, show[1] that the time lag between a person losing one job and finding another had been shortened to about a quarter its former length; the necessary reserve for movement and change was correspondingly lower. A further reduction of this 'minimum' unemployment was achieved by the control of seasonal fluctuations. With better organization (and sustained demand) it was possible to reduce the winter decline in employment to about half of what it was in the upswing of the 'twenties.[2] There was, secondly, a continuous increase, beyond the natural growth, in the supply of new labour which expanded up to a point in proportion to the ease of getting jobs. Independents and borderline unemployables entered the labour market—the former partly under direct economic pressure—and there was also a noticeable tendency towards postponing retirement; moreover, periods of training and apprenticeship were shortened and the school leaving age (in secondary schools) reduced.

The lengthening of the working day was another elasticity factor; about one-fifth of the 1937 rise in the total volume of work (+ 10 per cent) was due to longer hours which, however, still exceeded only fractionally the average working time of 1929. All these reserves finally proved insufficient to satisfy the great demands made on the system. But the developments during the relevant period of full or near-full employment bear out (always keeping in mind the special 'atmosphere' of a totalitarian regime) what has been stated elsewhere: namely, that many obstacles to mobility melt away when demand is maintained at a high level, while others can be overcome with proper organization. Even when statistical unemployment is low—say 2-3 per

[1] Cf. Hans Volmer, 'Um die letzte halbe Million,' *Der Deutsche Volkswirt*, Vol. xii, 1, p. 681.

[2] In spite of the cold wave the decline in employment was only 5.5 per cent in the winter of 1937-8, as compared with 10-12 per cent in the years of the previous upswing. Cf. Weekly Reports of the Institut f. Konjunkturforschung, 1938, No. 7-8.

cent of the total labour force—there are still sizeable elasticity reserves which can be tapped to remove bottlenecks.

Conclusions

We have attempted to distil from the actual economic developments in Nazi Germany those conditions which were inherent in the German situation, irrespective of the content of the employment policy and the nature of the political regime. The main results may be summed up as follows:

1. The shortage of foreign exchange, which Germany experienced in the first phase of her economic recovery, was not specifically connected with rearmament. Any policy of full employment in a country depending on imports of raw materials and foodstuffs and having little or no reserves of international cash would have come up against the foreign trade bottleneck in a world of wide-spread depression. Obviously, many countries may find themselves in a similar situation, when the special conditions of the reconstruction period pass, and the choice before them, as long as they are determined to maintain full employment as a matter of principle, may be very much the same as confronted Germany after 1933. In order to meet the rising import demand, exports must be expanded or, if the appropriate expansion of exports cannot be achieved, socially less essential imports must be curtailed. A mere depreciation of the currency may not secure equilibrium and stability at the required level. If exports largely consist of capital goods, for which the foreign demand is relatively inelastic in periods of depression abroad, and if at the same time imports are mainly made up of foods and raw materials, an indiscriminate reduction of the exchange rate would worsen the terms of trade seriously without necessarily producing balance. The existence of an external debt contracted in foreign currencies may provide an additional argument against devaluation, as was the case with Germany. The alternative techniques of stimulating exports by differential depreciation, export subsidies, reciprocal purchase or payment agreements and so forth, and the selective control of imports have been described in some detail. They need not harm the rest of the world as a whole; if all export proceeds obtained by these methods are used to buy imports, employment abroad will not be affected, and total world employment will be higher, owing to the expansion in the one country. Moreover, if clearing and similar agreements re-start some sort of foreign lending, the expansion in one country will generate an expansion abroad. On the other hand, it is clear that all differential methods spread the effect of unilateral expan-

sion unevenly over the rest of the world; clearing partners benefit most and partly at the expense of outsiders. This could only be avoided (*a*) if the unilaterally expanding country had ample liquidity reserves or (*b*) if global measures like devaluation were likely to restore the foreign balance at full employment level, or (*c*)—and this is an important point—after the industrial readjustment of the expanding country had been completed. Assuming for a moment that the depression abroad is semi-permanent, then the full employment country will after a time have built up adequate capacity for producing goods at home which were formerly imported. The strain on the foreign balance will, therefore, cease and it may become possible to revert to global (non-differential) methods for maintaining equilibrium. A country facing a world subject to more or less violent swings in business activity could theoretically relax controls when the rest of the world is becoming more prosperous, but it must be ready to re-impose them and to extend the use of home-produced goods when the world relapses into depression. Such swings in the internal and external policy of the full employment country may be practicable only within certain limits, and it cannot be excluded that once controls have been established there will be a tendency to retain them. But even then it holds true that the expanding country is not doing a disservice to foreign countries taken as a whole.

2. A restriction of imports will increase the demand for domestic goods; as a result there may be temporary bottlenecks and hoarding of scarce materials. It was under these conditions that it was decided in Germany to combine the control of imports with price control of practically all primary products. The permitted imports did not go to the highest bidder, but were allocated to firms according to certain (varying) standards of allocation. This particular policy is not a necessary part of import control, but it may help to secure a socially more desirable distribution of scarce goods and materials than is achieved through the price mechanism. Moreover, speculative price movements can then be prevented and costs be kept down for purposes of exports.

The policy of fixing raw material prices was fitted in Germany into a general policy of wage and price stabilization. The wage stop and later the price stop were the main devices (next to taxation) used to fight inflationary tendencies. Both devices, however, have very little to commend themselves. It is certainly important to keep prices reasonably stable in full employment, particularly in a democratic society where free collective bargaining for wages continues: only if stable prices or living costs are assured can the danger of spiralling wage increases be avoided. But a general price stop presents great administrative difficulties which should be a deterrent. Even in Germany, where the compulsory powers of the State had been strengthened beyond what is acceptable in a democracy, it was impossible to stop evasions; nor were the methods of price adjustment under the 'freeze' sufficiently flexible to avoid anomalies. The objective of preventing inflation demands and justifies price regulation only of those goods and services which form important items in the cost of living, and of certain basic commodities. Beyond that, global financial measures should suffice. This selective control of prices has the positive advantage that regulations can be framed more carefully. As Government purchases increase—or within a conscious programme of Government bulk buying—the scope of price control may however be extended. Where the State is in a strong position as a buyer, as it was in Germany, it can obviously exert a considerable influence on methods of production and on marketing conditions. Price fixing may then be applied as a means of efficiency control.

3. The general belief that mobility of labour is low is derived from under-employed economies and cannot be applied without qualification to a state where demand is sustained at a high level. Nor must it be assumed that full employment implies perpetual shifts from one industry or place to another. Even in expansionist conditions, or when demand is steady at a high level, however, there may still exist *some* avoidable unemployment due to low mobility on the margin or to deficient organization of the labour market. Administrative improvements and some measure of positive control of the location of industry can reduce this type of unemployment to a minimum. German experiences in this respect are quite encouraging. Naturally allowance must be made for the peculiar political conditions prevailing in Germany: re-employment was, for instance, not hampered by those qualitative restrictions on the use of man-power which are inherent in traditional trade union policy. These restrictive practices served in the past as a protection against insecurity; if the fear of unemployment and destitution is removed, a different attitude to demarcation, simplification of work and training, entry to occupations and so forth will be possible. A certain reserve of labour for movement and change will still remain. But the German experience strongly suggests that, given adequate organization, this minimum reserve is lower than is frequently assumed. Use can be made of elasticity reserves which are available, particularly in the form of temporary overtime, even when unemployment has been abolished.

THE WIDER IMPLICATIONS OF FULL
EMPLOYMENT

The Economic Principles

THE economic principles for lasting full employment which have been elaborated in this book appear to be simple and straightforward. The deficiency of demand, which lies at the root of unemployment, can always be made good, either by income redistribution, from the savers to the spenders, or by deficit spending of the Government. This is not, indeed, the full solution. Those who advocate increased spending alone as the panacea of our economic troubles ignore the consequences of such a programme. In the previous chapters we have suggested that a full employment policy must, in all probability, be accompanied by a number of controls. The first of these is the control of foreign trade. Taking the most optimistic view of the post-war world it seems likely that Britain and many other countries will have to exercise some control over their foreign trade. How strict the control will need to be depends, of course, on the success or failure of international plans for trade, currency and investment. But, as has been shown, it is possible that a country may be faced with the choice between full employment with control of foreign trade, and unemployment with free trade.

Secondly, there is the possibility of cumulative price increases, not so much due to bottlenecks in production, but to pressure for higher money wages. To prevent this it will be necessary to exercise a wide control over prices, either directly or indirectly by means of subsidies.

The third control necessitated by full employment is an overall regulation of the total volume of private investment. Its purpose is to ensure that capital equipment expands in pace with technical progress and changing population. The modern banking technique of controlling interest rates and appropriate adjustments in the method of imposing income tax are important means of regulating investment, but more direct controls, e.g. licensing, may prove necessary. Finally it seems likely that, to a greater or lesser extent, the State must exercise control over the location of industry. Such a control may well be desirable on other grounds; here we are only concerned with it as far as it facilitates a full employment policy.

Making even the most optimistic assumptions about future developments it is obvious that full employment will require a greater degree

of Government control in economic affairs than has been the rul
the past. And it is this extension of the power of the State which causes
apprehension. But the alternative to the controls which full employment brings is not some ideal state of full employment without
controls, but unemployment and trade fluctuations. The more sophisticated, and economically the more fortunate, may argue that unemployment is the price of freedom from control, and as such can be
tolerated. But it is a false argument. In the first place, sectional
controls were prevalent in unemployment. Cartels were formed,
often with the assistance of the Government, and bodies such as the
Import Duties Advisory Committee granted protection to particular
industries. These controls, being mainly introduced to deal with
particular symptoms of the general disease, tended to be restrictive
in character. The under-employed economy sought salvation through
a growing number of particular controls, internal and external, and
the failure to relate those controls to a common purpose only made
the situation worse. Secondly, the argument ignores the question of
hidden controls. In this sense unemployment is the most powerful of
all economic controls. If there is pressure on the balance of payments,
deflation and unemployment will relieve it: with unemployment there
is no danger that pressure for money wage increases will create an
inflationary spiral: instead of controlling the location of industry, unemployment forces the workers to move to wherever an employer
chooses to establish his factory. All the 'controls' directly associated
with full employment are, in fact, required to take over the tasks
previously performed by unemployment and the trade cycle. And
there is no reason why these controls should not be as democratic as
any other function of the State. The ideal is to replace the arbitrary
undemocratic 'control' of unemployment, by conscious controls,
operated democratically in the public interest.

The Machinery of Government

Even if circumstances permit the controls mentioned above to be
relatively mild and loose, a full employment policy is bound to call
for considerable reconstruction of the machinery of Government. At
the beginning of a full employment programme, the question of
'timing' public expenditure will be very important. Once the regime
is well established, subsequent variations will be random, and probably
small—but they will still call for speedy offsetting action.

The first requirement is an adequate knowledge of the economic
facts, a knowledge which we did not possess in this country before the

war. In the White Paper on Employment Policy the Government proposes to maintain permanently a Central Statistical Office which will bring together the necessary data and summarize them quickly enough for them to be a guide to practical policy. Even the collection of statistics may imply considerable changes in the machinery of Government. The various departments concerned with economic affairs, especially the Supply Ministries, the Board of Trade, the Ministry of Labour and National Service, and any Planning Ministries must act closely together, both at the top, in the matter of national policies, and also regionally. It may be, as has been suggested by the Select Committee on National Expenditure, that the Regional Boards of the Ministry of Production should have a permanent place in the British economy.

We have raised this matter of departmental co-ordination in connexion with the relatively minor question of statistical data. The problem is much deeper. A great part of 'public expenditure,' especially public investment in housing and other services, is carried out by local authorities, public utilities, or semi-public corporations. The freedom of action of the individual local authority either to 'time' its expenditure or to increase it considerably is limited by two main considerations: (1) the ruling ideas concerning the soundness of local authority finance; and (2) its direct responsibility to the local electorate. Even if the Central Government were to give the lead in encouraging 'deficit spending' this would by no means be enough. The actions of individual authorities must be co-ordinated to fit a common purpose: no one local authority can with impunity march out of step with the rest. The economics of the matter points to stronger control of local authority expenditure by the Central Government. Politics, however, tend to point in the opposite direction. Political democracy thrives upon action by elected bodies, and not upon the humble submission of advisory memoranda to Whitehall. It may be that in the shaping of a full employment economy the Central Government will be forced to take wider powers. Once the regime is established the tendency should be the other way; to hand over to local or regional authorities (should such intermediate bodies be set up) as much power as is consistent with over-all co-ordination.

Considerations of a somewhat similar kind apply to the relation between industries and Government. The control of the location of industry requires the satisfaction of manufacturers' as well as local interests and the co-ordination of local policies into a coherent national policy. New types of administrative problems will arise if an attempt is made to extend price control: to be effective price control may involve the type of control of production and distribution which is to be seen in the war-time utility schemes. The machinery to bring together the interests of consumers, producers (both employers and workers) and other groups which may be affected will have to be devised.

The Politics of Full Employment

Many attempts have been made to separate economics from politics. Such a rough separation may be of value from the point of view of exposition of ideas, but that is all. For not only does the policy of full employment which we have discussed here require the intervention of the political executive, but already before the war, in unemployment, all kinds of interventions by the State were customary and received Parliamentary support. A full employment programme does not, therefore, mean bringing politics into the sacred groves of economics. Politics has been there for some time, but has not always been very clear what it has been doing. A study of the commercial history of Britain since the last war confirms this. In the body of this book we have tried to restrict ourselves to the economic problems of full employment, not solely for the sake of academic detachment, but because this separation may help to clarify the issues involved. Politics enters into the matter in three ways.

Throughout the book we have taken for granted the desire to abolish unemployment. This desire is probably not universal. The 'control' of unemployment exerts its pressure on the unemployed: the controls we envisage require adjustments in the traditional attitude of individual employers to questions of pricing, quality control, labour management and location, and in some cases impinge directly upon sectional interests of various types. Further, the existence of full employment is likely to tilt sharply the balance of bargaining strength in favour of workers' organizations in disputes over wages, hours of work and the conditions of labour. Vaguer fears, that full employment might only be the harbinger of more profound social changes, are also likely to contribute to the resistance to policies of the type we have discussed here. The achievement of full employment, or rather, since we are at present in a state of over-employment, the taking of such steps as will prevent the recurrence of unemployment, is perhaps the greatest single political question of our time.

The second point where we make the closest contact with the political field is the question of the content of full employment. The authors, faced with the questions how much public investment against extra consumption, or how much taxation as against borrowing, have not attempted to answer these questions in detail but have simply referred to the principle of 'social priorities.' Even if the principle of the maintenance of full employment is upheld by all political parties and other organizations 'social priorities' will remain a battleground of political interests. The poor may want more bread, the rich may want faster motor roads: industrialists may prefer subsidies to private investment and to research, or export guarantees, while others would prefer a great public outlay on health services, on education and so on.

The third point where we encounter political decisions is in the choice of means. Even if we are all agreed on full employment, and upon the broad social priorities which are to determine its content, there still remains a variety of methods of fulfilling the programme. Suppose for example that it becomes necessary to cut down private investment. One way is to make the appropriate adjustment in the system of 'modified' income tax. But this is not the only way. Direct licensing of investment by the Government could be used, if it was also desired to discriminate between different industries, or between different types of investment. Or take the question of income redistribution. From the point of view of effective demand and total employment, profit squeezing and progressive taxation give much the same results. The nationalization of an industry may be regarded as the extreme case of profit squeezing. But while a reduction in net profit margins by price control, or an increase in taxation, imposed by one government can always be reversed by another, it is by no means easy to restore to its original owners an industry which has been nationalized. In short, of two types of control which produce the same immediate result one may be inherently more lasting than another. Whenever this kind of choice has arisen in this book we have always shown a bias towards the least drastic type of control, not for any dogmatic reasons, but mainly because global controls seem open to less abuse than direct controls, which may fall into the hands of sectional interests or semi-autonomous industrial associations.

We have seen that a full employment programme is likely to require adjustments and changes in the machinery of the administration. It may also be that the present local and national Parliamentary procedures are not adequate to cope with all the economic and political issues, which in the past have either not arisen, or have been settled outside the field of public affairs, but which now must be brought fully into the light of democratic discussion. Of their very nature and in the means by which they can be finally determined social priorities are essentially political. But these political questions in turn cannot be settled unless there is a full understanding of the economic problems involved, and the limitations which must be imposed upon any particular project to make it fit in with the general programme. The six studies are intended as a contribution to this understanding.

INDEX

DATE DUE

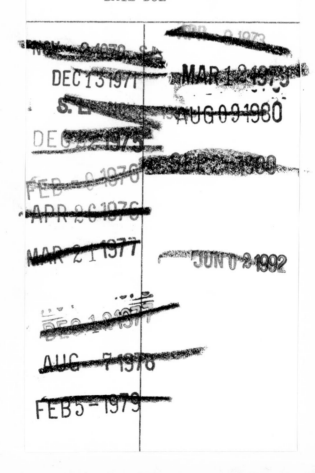